DEDICATION

To Tobias "Excel" Sjögren for charting the course through three years of night.

WHITE WOLF ENTERTAINMENT

Martin "Elricsson" Ericsson – LEAD STORYTELLER | Karim "Redemption" Muammar – EDITOR IN CHIEF
Dhaunae "Eternally Bonded" De Vir – BUSINESS DEVELOPER | Tomas "The Old One" Arfert – ARTIST AND EDITOR
Jason "By Night" Carl – COMMUNITY AND MARKETING

DESIGN

DEVELOPED by Kenneth Hite and Freja Gyldenstrøm
STORY & CREATIVE DIRECTION – Martin Ericsson

WRITTEN BY – Matthew Dawkins, Kenneth Hite, Mark Rein • Hagen, Juhana Pettersson, Martin Ericsson, and Freja Gyldenstrøm
ADDITIONAL WRITING BY – Ari Marmell, Karim Muammar
EDITING – Freja Gyldenstrøm
ADDITIONAL EDITING – Karim Muammar
LATIN TRANSLATION (MEDIEVAL LATIN) – Petra Lindve

ART

ART DIRECTION – Mary Lee, Martin Ericsson, and Tomas Arfert
BOOK DESIGN AND LAYOUT – Christian Granath and Fria Ligan AB, with Tomas Arfert
COVER – Tomas Arfert | INTERIOR ART AND ILLUSTRATIONS – Mary "TwistedLamb" Lee, the CCP Atlanta art team directed by Reynir Harðarson, consisting of Erling Ingi Sævarsson, and many more; Tomas Arfert, Mark Kelly and Mike Mignola.
CLAN SYMBOLS, CLAN FONTS, AND VAMPIRE: THE MASQUERADE LOGOS – Chris Elliott and Tomas Arfert
| CLAN FASHION DESIGN AND PHOTOSHOOTS – Mary "TwistedLamb" Lee
PHOTOGRAPHERS – Viktor Herak, Derek Hutchisson, Sequoia Emanuelle, Julius Konttinen, John-Paul Bichard, and Anders Muammar

MODELS

BRUJAH – Grace Rizzo, Jackie Penn, Jacqueline Roh, Lee Dawn, Marcus Natividad, Mario Ponce, Mila Dawn, Nate Kamm, Paul Olguin, Daphne Von Rey, Casey Driggers |
GANGREL – Zoe Jakes, Pixie Fordtears, Aram Giragos, Allesandro Giuliano, Hal Linton | MALKAVIAN – Ramsey, Custis Donner | NOSFERATU – Henrik Lillier, Hampus Ahlbom,
Camilla Palermo, Louise Björling | TOREADOR – Indhi Korth, Mariano Mavrin, Nisse "Septekh" Meseke | TREMERE – Mary Lee, Taara Tati, Karis Wilde, Cassandra |
VENTRUE – Eve Harper Close, Angelo Delacruz, Amir Khaligi, Buzz Cuccia, Lola Tatlyan, Stacy LeLand, Aram Giragos | ADDITIONAL MODELS – Viktor Herak, Vera Kochubey,
Sanuye Shoteka, Gregory Homa, Ossian Reynolds, and Martin Ericsson

SPECIAL THANKS TO

Simon Bevis, Jenna Bevis, and Andre Martinez. Arhan Ağaoğlu, Mohamad Rabah and Khaldoun Khelil, Mikko Pervilä, Anne Rice, Father Sebastiaan,
Nicole Sixx, Maven, Matthew Webb, Lorenzo Melchor and Logan South.

VAMPIRE: THE MASQUERADE CREATORS – Mark Rein•Hagen with Justin Achilli, Steven C. Brown, Tom Dowd, Andrew Greenberg, Chris McDonough, Lisa Stevens,
Josh Timbrook, and Stewart Wieck.

VISIT WHITE WOLF ENTERTAINMENT ONLINE AT WWW.WHITE-WOLF.COM AND WWW.WORLDOFDARKNESS.COM

HOW TO USE THIS BOOK

The Camarilla is part of a two-volume set of dedicated lore books for *Vampire: The Masquerade 5th Edition*. Like the classic line of Clanbooks for Vampire they are written to be enjoyed and used by storytellers, players, live-action enthusiasts and non-gaming vampire-fans alike.

Together with its companion tome *Anarch*, this book describes the polarized society of the night, entirely through the voices and viewpoints of the Damned themselves. This book consists of personal correspondence, surveillance protocols, official reports, e-mails, documents, lectures, sermons, and oaths. Their contents reveal the inner workings, hierarchies, cities, and laws of the Camarilla, the most dangerous secret society the world has never known.

Every text is intended to be useful not only as background material for your chronicle and a good horrifying read but as an in-game artifact. Are your player characters investigating or being invited to a mystery cult? Give them the Passion of Uga Dugud (p.33). Are they up against the Second Inquisition in Washington, DC? Give them the section on The Information Awareness Office (p.69) as a starting point. Do you need a rousing speech before a Conclave? Use "We Must More Than Endure" (p.44).

We also chose this format to make the book welcoming to newcomers. The Camarilla is a book about a secret society of vampires and can be enjoyed with no prior knowledge of the World of Darkness setting.

All you need to know is that vampires are real. Here and now. Some say the first of the blood-drinker was biblical Caine, who murdered Abel and was cursed with eternal life and endless hunger. Hidden from us by an elaborate masquerade, great clans of "Kindred", as they call themselves, influence every aspect of human society, waging secret wars driven by personal vendettas lost in the mists of history.

In addition to the inner workings of the Camarilla, this book contains a comprehensive section on the Banu Haqim clan - stern judges and warriors, now in service of the Ivory Tower. Finally, a set of new Loresheets allow player characters to reap the benefits of associating with many of the Camarilla luminaries that you will meet in these pages.

In the end it is vitally important to remember what the Camarilla are not: they are not the good guys. They are a society of undead predators that exists for the sole purpose of keeping themselves safe and in power. As you will come to learn from these documents, they are a conspiracy of the dead that set themselves above both mortal society and every Kindred that disagree with their right to rule, and these pages should be viewed through that lens of undead arrogance. They are the ultimate lesson in the corrupting influence of power. Glorious, sophisticated, remorseless and endlessly resourceful, these cultured immortals have a space open at their table. Take a seat and try the mantle of power on for size. We promise you will enjoy it.

TABLE OF CONTENTS

This is a work of speculative horror fiction, set in a dark reflection of our own world. Thus it contains graphic depictions of sex, blood-drinking, drugs, violence, abuse, political oppression, coercion, occultism, heresy and many other potentially upsetting themes. Recommended for mature readers and players. For advice on considerate play and how to handle sensitive themes in tabletop roleplaying games, see the section "Considerate play" in the PDF version of the "Vampire: The Masquerade" rulebook.

INTRODUCTION

My Dear Childe,

Kindred.
What a beautiful word.

When you became one of us, you may have thought of other words. "Vampire" is a favorite of mortal mythmakers. "Lick" shows the vital vulgarity of the Anarchs. Such words are no longer adequate. You are Kindred.

Your first change was physical. You tasted the Blood of the Embrace and became a vampire. What you must understand is that this is merely the first step. The first Embrace.

The second Embrace is when you truly become Kindred, when you are initiated into the Camarilla, the greatest society of immortals the world has ever known.

It was not always like this. When I became one of us, a long time ago, the Camarilla still labored under the frankly ridiculous notion it could gather all those of the Blood under its loving care.

This was never the reality and I'm glad the lie has finally been abolished. The protection of the Camarilla is now reserved for those deserving it, and thus a singular Embrace has been separated into two.

Turn or Die

The first Embrace is physical, the second social, but they share one thing in common. Neither can be refused. Once invited to join the Camarilla, you accept or die for good.

You made the wise choice, my childe. The only choice. As I knew you would.

I know you have many questions. Why did I bring you into the night? Why did I leave you to fend for yourself for a decade before coming to get you? Why did I choose this moment to induct you into the Camarilla? This letter and the documents within are meant to help you make sense of it all.

I will answer the simple questions first. I Embraced you and abandoned you to see if you could make it. The Camarilla is full of the wastrel childer of the powerful, the scions of Justicars, Princes, Inner Circle members, and other luminaries. I would never presume to question their judgement in choosing who they Embrace, but I decided to follow a different path.

There is a reason we speak of the first and the second Embrace. I am sure you have cursed me during the many confused, lonely nights of the last decade, but you will thank me when you go to your first Elysium fortified with at least some independent understanding of what it means to subsist on blood and exist outside the human herd.

Why did I come to you now, only to disappear? Well, I have a wedding to attend. You will understand in time. Consider this another test: If you survive your first week in the Camarilla with only these notes to help you, you will have proven yourself yet again.

I suppose you also want to know why I chose you specifically. The truth is, I didn't. I got permission to bring a new childe to the Camarilla, so I instructed my servants to find good candidates. They found five. I Embraced all of them. I know the Prince would probably not have accepted this, but she owes me too much to complain even if she finds out. One of the five ended himself after a week. Another joined a depressing little Anarch gang where she is still scraping by, as far as I know. Two were destroyed in Second Inquisition raids.

You were the one who succeeded in taking control of your new existence. I am sentimental in many things, but when I give my Blood to someone, I want them to be worth it.

Welcome

I have opened the door for you, but you must enter on your own. I have made you a member of the Camarilla, but you must seize upon the opportunity and make it mean something.

The Camarilla is power, connections, protection. This is one of the great lessons learned by the powerful among kine and Kindred alike: Secrecy must always trump vanity. Human billionaires live in seclusion, their estates protected by armies of security guards. They travel by plane and helicopter, invisible to humanity at large, except for a few extravagant individuals who become targets of hate.

Most of the very rich keep a low profile, preferring to stay anonymous. In this and many other ways, there is not much difference between us and them. The Camarilla merely represents another layer of power at the very top. We too live in secrecy, hidden from the general population in our havens and Elysiums. Indeed, often the land of wealth is our land, the privileges society grants to its richest members protecting us too.

The Camarilla can be many things. Different cities organize in their own ways, their Kindred shaping their existence according to necessity and desire. Yet, so often wealth and influence are the two constants.

We disappear into the human elite, so it is not only the world of the Camarilla you must adjust to. It is also the world of cocktail parties, gala openings, and fundraisers. Pretty much the only avenue blocked to us is going golfing during daytime. And anyway, golf bores me.

The Camarilla protects you from many things, but do not be naive about the environment you are about to enter. Despite its profession of peace, the Elysium can be lethal, and frankly we like it like that. Playing the political game is what makes life worth living, and it is only fitting that the price of failure is death.

After you have learned everything in these papers, destroy them. It is a good habit to learn. Every document can betray you in the wrong hands. My servants have been instructed to provide you with access to my havens, including the ones in the city, the mansion, as well as my island cabin. There are also a few apartments that have not been lightproofed. I suggest you sell them. You will also gain access to my accounts, offshore holding companies, and financial advisors. The advisors need a steady supply of vitae.

You will have most of the things I will not be taking with me, but not everything. All Kindred need a secret or two...

I have arranged an invitation to the Elysium for you. Consider the impression you want to make. These people are the ones you will share your eternity with. In time, you will love and hate each and every one of them. You will be bored of them, and happy to have someone who understands you. Keep it in mind when you feel like making enemies.

Drink Deep

You must love the Camarilla and all it can do for you, more than you have ever loved anything in your life. You must bask in its casual corruption and insincere compliments, its constant backstabbing and eternal ennui. It senses weakness, Anarch sympathies, aversion to power, and seeks to expel such failures.

Like the Embrace, real immortality comes in two parts. Many only understand the first, physical manifestation of it. Yet it also has another side: Immortality means not dying, to put it banally. Most unbound are extinguished younger than they would have died as humans. They die of an inquisitor's stake or the fangs of a Sheriff. They die in the sun and in the sewers. They die because our life is dangerous and they do not have the right protection.

In a way, immortality is a lie. When I was human, society was organized into the aristocracy, the trades, the peasants, the clergy. Everyone was supposed to be happy in their place, but many aspired to better things. This sowed the seeds of revolution, because revolution was the only way they could improve their lives. In modern nights, the mortals have become smarter. They say that everyone has a chance to become one of the elite, so people forget that most never do. The opportunity blinds them to the reality. The immortality of the blood works the same way. Young Anarchs think they will live forever, when in fact they will not even make it a few months.

You are a true Camarilla immortal. You will go on. Protected by the full might of the Ivory Tower and our ancient laws, you can reach your full potential.

Through the centuries, you will gain amazing wealth and power. You will lose it all and find yourself on your knees, only to rise again. You will serve and rule, win and lose, for this is the real secret of the Camarilla: In the long run, the only thing that matters is whether you can still play the game.

Immortality means that survival is victory.

Once I have settled into my new life, perhaps I will come back to you. You can expect me in a year, a decade, a century. I want to see my domain expanded, my business holdings grown. Most of all, I expect to find a childe who has used my legacy to make something of themselves.

The Blood is a gift. Even if you choose to hate me, put it to a good use.

Your loving sire,

Victoria Ash

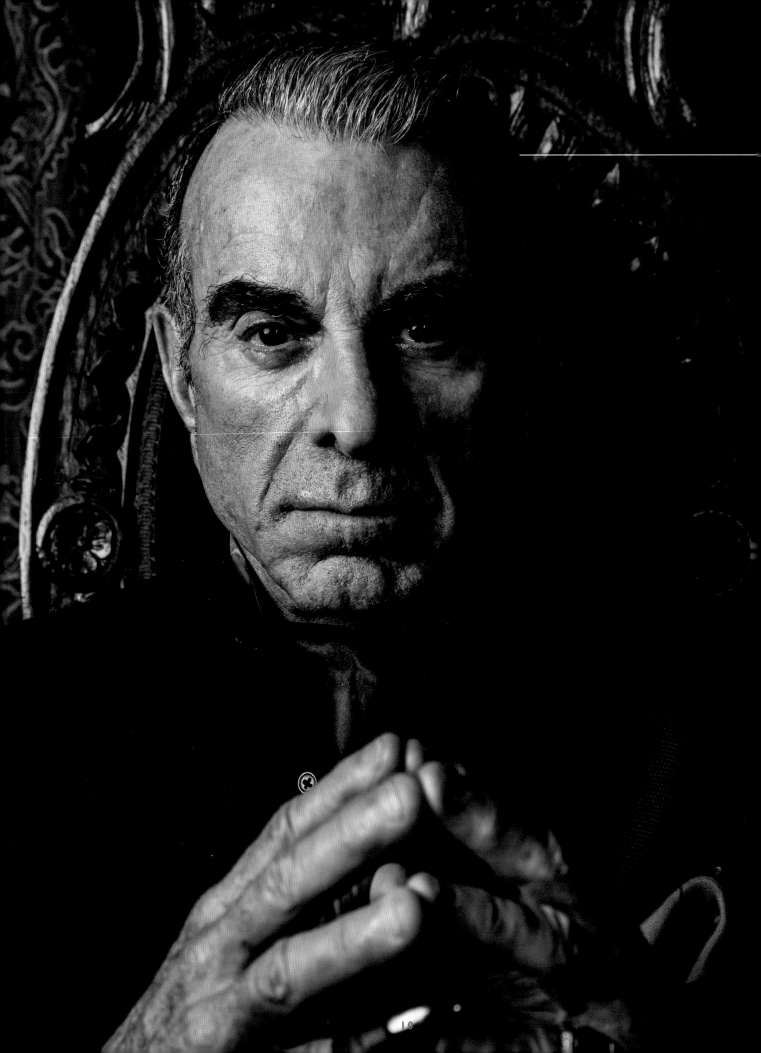

THE
view
FROM
THE
top

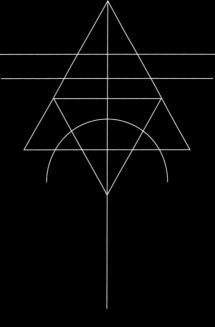

There is a difference between hiding in fear and biding our time. We wait for the perfect time to strike, like any skilled predator.

— ELEANOR ZHENG,
ARCHON OF CLAN NOSFERATU

*T*he Camarilla is a secret society. This is obvious. But what is the final initiation? When do you know all the secrets?

This experience is not unfamiliar to the mortal world. Power offers many initiations to those who would possess it. Politicians, journalists, industrialists: all get invited to social situations that turn out to conceal something more. Sometimes these secrets become formal societies: the Grand Orient, Skull and Bones, names you haven't even heard of.

When you enter such a select group, you become part of a new world. You understand how the world works from a higher level.

The second Embrace is such an initiation, but many stricter ones await you in the Camarilla. You can join the Primogen, become a Prince, rise ever higher in the hierarchy…. At last to discover that even the Inner Circle doesn't know everything. Always more secrets await.

Be careful if you are offered a title. Sometimes Princes like to test young Kindred by giving them power. Power is opportunity, and danger. You may wish to refuse.

I indulge myself in a little humor. Of course you will never refuse. Your ambition bites too hard for that.

Many in the Camarilla love the titles. They want to be a Prince, a Justicar, an Inner Circle member. You would do well to remember that while power rests in official positions, it also extends outside their limits.

Consider myself. Sometimes I have held an official Camarilla position. Often I haven't. Yet my power and influence has never been dependent on that. Title remains a matter of convenience, nothing more.

My wedding offers me a new initiation, a new phase in my existence, but no official position exists for what I shall become in the Camarilla or the Ashirra.

Do you think I will be powerless?

Every nightmare dreamed up by paranoids, every righteous fear of the persecuted, every conspiracy postulated by law and hinted at in lore: the Camarilla reaches farther and does worse. It controls lives, money, and history. They told your ancestors what to believe, they tell the media what to report. If the Camarilla want a secret kept from the kine, they bury the story … and the storyteller.

Master conspirators and manipulators do not pull together in the same harness like tame oxen. The Kindred within the Camarilla use tools of manipulation and deceit on each other just as they do on the kine and on other sects. But they agree on one truth: We are stronger inside the Camarilla than anyone outside of it.

As spoken by Fiorenza Savona, ascending kingpin of Clan Ventrue:

Understand, my little neonate, that Fortune smiles upon you. Those less blessed say our sect drinks vanity as well as blood, that it cares only for its own shadowy reflection in the mirror. Your low Anarch companions may even have told you that we are "an elitist vampire country club." Jealous lessers often mistake vanity for pride, it is true. And indeed, we protect our own and withdraw our protection from those too foolish to accept it. To descend to their argot, we are truly elitist — because we are the true elite. Our country club, meanwhile, plays for actual countries.

Membership in our club — our exclusive club — comes with fees, of course. We invite you when we deem you capable of mastering the Masquerade, and worthy of service to royalty. And you must pay your fees in the currency of the kingdom. In Athens, it may be enough to claim the acceptance of a majority of the city's Kindred, while in Cape Town only the Prince's word admits you to the Ivory Tower after tests of the strength of your Blood. Prove you know the rules, and you may be invited to help enforce them — or write them.

Not every aspirant enters the Tower. Some even fall back at the first shut gate, betrayed by their own doubts. Banish those doubts. If you believe yourself unfit for the Camarilla, be assured the Camarilla agrees with you. But cloak your death, sever ties with mere kine, and take your place as a player at the table — and then we shall deal you in, and perhaps even stake your play. Remember that while you play with us, Fortune smiles upon you — and her fangs only rarely come out.

"The rules are simple enough," Rider spoke softly amid the din of mortal voices, walking alongside her childe as the two cut through a subway station pouring with commuters. "You exercise restraint in all things. No errant feeding, no blatant displays of power, no creation of new childer without permission from the Prince, and certainly no telling the living about what we do."

Syl nodded, trying to keep up

We are a monolithic and ruthless cabal, expanding and maintaining our sphere of influence with hidden hands. We infiltrate rather than invade, subvert before we debate, intimidate without asking our lessers their opinions. Our power flies on incubus wings by night instead of marching with armies by day. Nothing can stand in our way, as none can stand athwart a shadow.

SOCIAL STATUS

Recent research implies that a blankbody forming part of the secret society called "the Tower" or "the Camarilla" is more well-regarded than one not of this clique. Within their society, higher-ranking blankbodies adopt regal titles: "Prince," "King," or, in the case of Subject #7, "Emperor." Other blankbodies defer to members of the Tower, bringing to mind an elite caste.

To date, we have discovered no physical distinction between blankbodies within the Tower and those without. However, analysis indicates (see attached Report #27AL) that the network provides ongoing support for concealing blankbody identities and activities, and likely provides its own intelligence and analysis to favored members. Those outside are therefore more likely to be exposed, or expose themselves, creating targets of opportunity for our action.

Assuming blankbodies operate along human psychological parameters, membership within the Tower likely provides a sense of worth and belonging, as with normal organizations. Although data remain fragmentary, the Tokyo and Belem studies indicate that blankbodies outside the Tower tend to self-exterminate (or act out so aggressively as to invite termination) at much higher rates than those within it.

Analysts remain unclear on the cause of this phenomenon: the Tower seems unlikely to offer psychological care to its members, but if internal surveillance characterizes its discipline perhaps divergence is tantamount to betrayal. One possibility: blankbodies within this group adopt a mindset akin to workers in a high-pressure sales force (see Endron Files), where competitors (other blankbodies) prey on any member showing weakness or a lapse of diligence. Self-destructive personalities seem unlikely to last long in such an environment, or even be accepted for membership.

R243 #68

Rusty   **ACTIVE NOW**

                    i hear bout a big prince party @inferno
QT
                                                          kay
You know it?
                                                          yea
Gonna be new mixers coming in tonight.
                                                 nu drinks???
New everything. Drinks. Dancers. DJ.
Chastity even got some kind of gallery goin on
   downstairs.
Wanna come?
                                        seems like a deal
Cool
Wait wait. Did the big hog tell you you were in
   yet?
                                          in the big C?
                                                      naw
                                                but soon
Shit. You can't come if you ain't with the c.
Privileges of the gang.
Fuck. Sorry. Looks like you'll be havin takeaway,
   flix and chill.
                                      can't u vouch 4 me?
Absolutely fucking not.
I had to work my ass off to get in
I shouldn't have told you this much.
You'd better not show.
You hear?
                                            yea i guess
                              u r such a big c cunt now
                      u keep all the best shit and leave us wit
                                                  nothin
Fuck you, you bottom feeder piece of trash. I
   can't believe I answered you. I feel dirty.
   Fuck. Delete this fucking record once we're
   done. Speak to me again when or if you're ever
   in. You got me?
Yeah?
Fuck off then

with her sire as she somehow flowed through the kine like a fish effortlessly gliding against the tide. "You said I could ask you anything, right?" She bumped into an elderly woman and apologized despite herself.

"That's correct. I would rather you ask than make a mistake that comes back to haunt me," Rider called back, her pitch barely discernible above the chatter of travelers on phones and speaking among each other as they walked from A to B.

"Well-" Syl quickened her pace, catching up with the vampire who had created her, "what's the point in living forever if we can't let it all out occasionally? I mean, we must have these powers for a reason, right?"

Rider stopped abruptly, the kine continuing to seamlessly move around her despite her almost blocking an escalator with her presence. Syl had to step back to avoid getting carried away with the wave of human traffic. "Yes, we have these powers for a reason. This thing of ours, which we will not name in such a public place, prizes, rewards, and bestows title upon those who master their gifts. Ours is a group dedicated to control, both of our world and ourselves. Control is not letting claws spring from your hands whenever you feel angry, or telling someone to jump in front of a bus whenever you feel upset. Control is having this power, letting others know you have this power, and choosing not to use it."

Syl's confusion turned into a smile as she finished her sire's thought. "So that when we do have to use it..."

"Exactly." Rider flowed onto the escalator, Syl in her wake.

The Upper Echelons

As described by Fearless Alys, King-maker of Clan Tremere, Traditionalist Faction, Bucharest

There's them and there's us. Yeah, we're Camarilla. We uphold the Traditions, play our political party games, and quaff rare vintages of bloody nectar while a string quartet plays nearby. But, and it's a big one, we aren't the policymakers. I've built up three Princes who still hold their thrones to this night, even with all the trouble we've had recently. But neither I, nor they, are anything compared to the big bosses in the shadows.

Yeah, we know shadows. We know how to hide from mortals. But these guys know to hide from us. They are shadows. You think an Archon tells you before she comes to the domain to cut off the Sheriff's head? Do you think she tells you why she just decapitated the poor bastard? Tell me, who do you think is leaking all that Church of Caine crap into our domains? It's not a few faithful neonates. If the Justicars want us to build a church, we'll find ourselves building a whole bunch of the things without even knowing why.

So yeah, we go on with our busy little non-lives and pretend we're important. Just remember there's someone who can raise you up in an instant, or destroy you with a thought, and you don't even know their name.

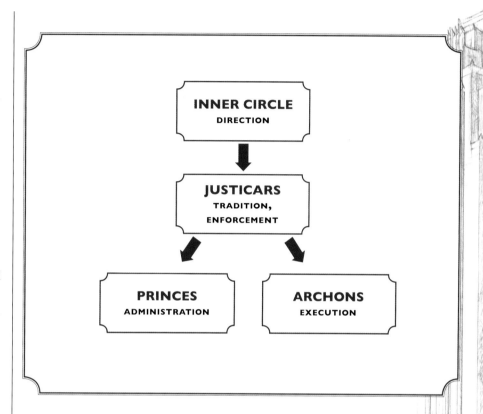

The Inner Circle

by Carmelita Neillson, Archaeologist and Archivist of Clan Toreador

It is difficult for a historian such as myself to educate others on the Camarilla's long, colourful history, when so many gaps intentionally exist. I can name a few — new Traditions passed but swiftly abandoned, a clan receiving an invitation to join our sect but burning the bridge before crossing for no apparent reason, much surrounding our past involvement with the Setites...

Appropriately, among our greatest mysteries we count our greatest masters. The Inner Seven must once have been the lords of their clans but who now dare indite their names? By concealing identity behind law, needed cruelties and exactions are enabled. Without a target, revenge cannot be aimed, resistance cannot flourish. The orders come in whispers in the Blood, sudden certainty within the Justicars, a brief feeling of talons gripping the neck.

But mystery does breed speculation, as well. My favorite? Remember this is but rumor, but... what if the Inner Circle comprises more than the Camarilla clans? Think of it. They were seven, we are now five. Do the Gangrel and Brujah elders truly wish to abandon ultimate power within the Tower for mere principle among the Anarchs? Or say the Lasombra leader never left, or that ambassadors from the Banu Haqim sit at the table. Perhaps one of the Old Clan claims a seat by some unimaginably ancient law of Enoch.

It's all just theory, of course. It would be a little disturbing were we to find our Inner Circle was comprised of four members of the Ministry, two Malkavians, and a Lasombra, wouldn't it?

The Justicars

With only five clans inside the Tower for now, the five Justicars take on even more responsibility ... and power. They must represent their clan, decide matters of war and law, and act as the voice of the Inner Circle. Above all, they enforce the Traditions. A Justicar descending on an unprepared Prince in a loosely held regnum — well, harpies still whisper about what happened "when the Veil came back down hard in San Antonio" and who wound up under it when Petrus visited in 2006.

Justicars act as monarchs of their clans, appointed by the Inner Circle to 13-year terms. Few, save the Ventrue, serve more than one. Justicars may command any of the assets and resources of the Camarilla at will, including every member of it. Whether such exactions seem more like a valuable honor from royalty or a loathsome theft by tyranny depends on the Justicar's etiquette, and on whether it was your childe and haven they confiscated.

CURRENT JUSTICARS

- **JULIET PARR**, Justicar of Clan Malkavian and former Sheriff of North London
- **MOLLY MACDONALD**, Justicar of Clan Nosferatu
- **DIANA IADANZA**, Justicar of Clan Toreador and Bane of Clan Gangrel
- **IAN CARFAX**, Justicar of Clan Tremere and former Archon of Karl Schrekt
- **LUCINDE**, Justicar of Clan Ventrue, named "Justicar for Unlife" in 2018

Clans Gangrel and Brujah were represented by Geoffrey Leigh and Manuela Cardoso Pinto, respectively, until their clans departed the Camarilla. Rumors abound of a neutral Kindred soon to be appointed as Justicar of Outsiders, representing antitribu and officially unaffiliated clans.

Archons

Archons are not simple hired killers. Archons are elite hired killers. And warriors, and scholars, and investigators. Each Justicar handselects their own Archons, even competing for exceptional servants. The candidate Archon gets one chance to decline. If they accept, they serve the Justicars, enforcing Camarilla law, seeking out secrets, or spying out the foes of the Tower.

Some Archons operate alone, others in coteries. Often, the Justicar binds these Archons to themselves, or to each other, with a Blood Bond. Even unbond, the Archons have less freedom of action than their masters — but they can order a Kindred put to final death, and expect to be obeyed. Indeed, an Archon can decimate an entire domain or regnum

AS FORETOLD BY IVY REO,

ORACLE AND COUNSEL TO THE JUSTICARS, CLAN MALKAVIAN

The number of Justicars will again number seven, for seven is an important number not only to the Usurpers but to the al-Amin, and all remain present. Yes yes yes.

Listen. Can you hear it? Gears are turning. Change is happening. The Justicars must remain seven for the Camarilla to remain strong. The Inner Circle knows this. They know without seven the pillars will collapse. The roof is too heavy with five pillars alone. Five? Who ever heard of five pillars?

Mm-hmm. Yes yes yes. If we cannot make two pillars we must import them. From where? Egypt, perhaps? I know of at least one strong pillar in the dark. I know of a pillar drenched in blood. I know of a pillar once drawn by the architect, but it snapped in two in the builder's ropes. What to do? What to do.

without explanation. Learning to avoid such punishment, or at least to avoid such Archons, remains an exercise in loyalty and survival.

Sectarian Diplomacy

Kindred of the Camarilla hold themselves above the rabble of the Anarchs, but they see some sects as possible peers and even partners. The Second Inquisition plays no favorites, and even the Justicars must perforce agree with the argument. These nights, Archons carry messages of deep respect, even arrangements for local alliance and

"Drag wants to become an Archon, become a legend
   for the Camarilla. I get it. He's tough, too. He
   can hold his hand over a fire for minutes without breaking. Primogen would be blind to turn him
   down. And he knows our city better than anyone.
   He knew just where to hide out when those Anarch
   assholes burned out the trailer park. But when
   you're an Archon you can't hide from the heat. You
   can't take your hand out of the fire.
You join up and you never retire. I heard you die in
   your first thirteen or they put you down for knowing too much. You only leave as dust.
Of course Drag knows all about dust. Those fuckers… his childe was in the trailer park… well, you
   know."

perhaps more, back and forth to the Ashirra. Diplomacy, even for the Kindred, remains the art of the possible. And much is possible for the Camarilla.

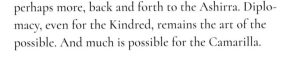

My dearest Victoria,

I am only in Baghdad for a brief period, observing the activities of Kindred caught in this "Gehenna Crusade," but as you asked I share my observations. Even a duller eye than mine could hardly miss the Ashirra's disgust at the Sabbat — not just their sectarian madness, but their sheer blatancy. Perhaps shared tastes can unify us where our diverging interests — politics on our hand and religion on theirs — have failed to do so.

Indeed, if our spheres of interest are so separate, why not bring them together? Why not replace the Brujah rabble with the Viziers of the Levant? New allies are not so thick on the ground, after all, especially as we further conceal ourselves from Kindred of other sects.

I leave it to you to take this further with Iadanza, but I believe the prospect worthy of entertainment.

With love and devotion,

Thomas St. Maur
Childe of Amber
Grandchilde of Mithras

"We must discuss the status of Berlin, Giering. The problem will not go away of its own accord." Nanette passed her Prince a glass, filled near to the brim with rich blood, harvested from the finest stock the Herz Brothers could provide. If she recalled correctly, this was a new varietal the blood-traffickers had found after moving into the Netherlands two years ago.

As the Prince sipped, he waved his hand in dismissal. The old man with his Van Dyke beard had never cared overly about city politics beyond his own domain. "Cologne remains Camarilla. What do we care if the Prussian capital falls to the Anarchs? Nanette, my sweet thing, you must know the city's fall can only lead to our rise. If Berlin collapses, our domain climbs to prominence, perhaps along with Munich or Frankfurt. Even Hamburg." He took another sip. "The Inner Circle stopped viewing Berlin as a viable domain a long time ago, I am told. It will be a domain beyond Berlin that receives assets and support from the Ivory Tower."

The young Warlock held her tongue, wanting to speak of domino effects and Anarch fervor. Ignoring other cities was one thing, but even here in Cologne he seemed oblivious to the rising Movement on the streets below. She said none of that, merely "Of course, my Prince."

Giering narrowed his eyes and downed the remaining blood in a single draught. "I am more than capable of interpreting your expressions, dear, sweet childe. I know you disapprove. What is that saying? Better to rule in hell than serve in heaven?"

She nodded.

"None of us will see heaven. We tried to work with the Anarchs. We tried for five long centuries. We tried crushing them, but that only leads to greater rebellion. It is time to drive them into their own ghettos, let them fester among themselves, and let the problem eliminate itself. If we interfere, we will be held accountable. If we allow the rot to set in and the tooth to fall out, we will be the only ones left."

Nanette watched as her sire made his way to the balcony, contemplating whether now was the time to make her arguments more forcefully. He was awfully close to the ledge ∎

The truth
is rarely
beautiful

OUR *faith*

Faith in ourselves

We are known as a sect without faith. I say this is untrue. We do not flaunt our faith, but we believe. Our ways are more courtly than sacred but when we kneel in worship, we do so with personal conviction. We pray alone, for our own souls, when we have erred, we commune with our ancestors for guidance in secret gatherings of sworn siblings. We have faith in our war against our lower impulses, in our role as the enlightened shepherds of mankind, and in the wisdom of the ancients. We pray to the God of our breathing days. Some of us do so for the same reasons we did then. Others twist scripture to find a role for themselves in God's plan, and sadly, more and more of us find faith in blood-soaked heresy, designed to make us feel better about being monsters.

A history of faith, or, how we killed God to survive

By Eberlin Albertzen, childe of Albertus Magnus

Our founders were, with some notable exceptions, of the same Catholic faith as I was born into. In 1494, even the truly ancient would admit that God was as real as any temple in Constantinople. Even the Cainite heretics of Languedoc were born from an inversion of Christian doctrine. So why did the Camarilla Kindred turn from Rome, and then from God altogether? Why did we, as an organisation if not as individuals, abandon faith and hedge our bets with Lutherans and rationalists? Why did we have to kill God to survive? And what did we replace Him with? How did it happen and what ideas have guided our august institution after His demise?

It began as a necessity. To hide our existence and avoid another Inquisition, the Camarilla had to undermine human belief in hobgoblins, angels, and devils like ourselves. To neonates like you and anchilla like my childer, it is tempting to see our sect as an enlightenment project. This position ignores the fact that ideas of empiricism and natural rights were still centuries away when the ill-fated convention happened in Thorns.

Catholics

During the Burning Times the thought of a world without Christ or His Church was an impossibility. Whether we believed ourselves cursed or tested, as devils or avenging angels, we were somehow a part of God's plan, and the Church was universally seen as an embodiment of His will on earth. We had placed ourselves in relation to the doctrine of faith for centuries, and we were unable to imagine a world without Him. So as we always do, we latched onto human developments. Supported by a correspondence between the anti-clerical and

ascetic reformer Girolamo Savonarola and one of our kind, as well as the meetings between Martin Luther and Anatole, I here posit that our abandonment of faith as a sect happened gradually. Faith has always been a battleground for our Kind. Albertus Magnus and myself struggled for centuries to wrest control of the Church from the foul Arian heretic Fabrizio Ulfila, whom I hold responsible for ushering in the Burning Times. It bears remembering that initially the clergy and the papacy, not God or faith, was what we fought.

Reformation

We still needed God you see. In the mindset of us faithful we are the Damned, cursed by God. And with Damnation comes the possibility for redemption. In protestant reformation we found a way to oppose the Church and Inquisition without giving up hope for saving our souls. In Catholicism, the clergy and the sacraments we perform are the ticket to Heaven. During the Dark Ages we took Eucharist, we confessed, we repented. When the Church began to hunt us, we were cut off from Grace. This drove us into reflection and a search for a deeper truth. We found our answers in Protestantism and its precursors. In Luther's teachings the Church is worldly, human and open to corruption. What is important is a personal relationship to God. It is baptism, our confession of faith, our fiery prayers and our conduct that opens His kingdom to us. This suited us perfectly and I found my own faith transformed by the insights of the German theologian.

Wars of reformation and colonialism

For centuries the wars of reformation and counter-reformation were the outward sign of our struggle. The Schmalkaldic War, the Thirty Years' War and The English Civil War were mortal conflicts, but we did have a stake in them. Striking against the pope hurt not only the Inquisition, but also the clans that refused the call to Masquerade. War brought tragedy to the living and blood to the dead, but in the end the new Protestant faith was here to stay and the Western world finally stepped out of the shadow of Rome. I take some pride in our role in this. Our expansion into

the Americas was a continuation of this struggle. We followed the colonial expansion of Britain, the Dutch, the French. It was here, in a new world of Puritan witch hunts, genocide rationalised through religion, and nations founded on Enlightenment principles, not divine right, that we lost faith. At least I know that's what happened to me. I confess that my crisis of faith lasted almost two full centuries. You could say that as we changed America, America changed us.

The State and humanity

After the Church lost universal power, the next great object of human worship was not religion, but the concept of the nation state. This is where we discovered our true strength as a union — our feudal principles, our hierarchy, our lineage and our ideals. We became a universal brotherhood of Kindred, a global union of city states. In the tangled web of secret societies and weird religious groups that covered the early Americas, we were everywhere. Tinfoil hats and anti-semitic hate-mongers looking for the fingerprints of "the Illuminati" in early US history will find only traces of night-wars and alliances between creatures unimaginable to their limited faculties. Their efforts are invaluable to the Masquerade, however, so bless their disgusting little confirmation-biased hearts.

It's during this time of change that humanity arose as our central ideology. The sect's commitment to this radical idea — by adhering to what we believed in life, we turn away from the Beast — changed everything. We questioned ourselves and our impulses. We tempered our sense of superiority with humility, and found a way to instruct faithless neonates in proper conduct without resorting to arguments of damnation.

Cynics state that our obsession with behaving like humans is just a way to enforce the Masquerade. I say it doesn't matter at all if it is. The pretense makes us better, and it does help us hide. This is why my constant recommendation is to make humanity your guide and belief your strength. Study them, follow their fashions, understand where they are going morally, and adjust your old ideals to fit in with the state of the world right now. I ask you not to betray yourself, your faith and who you were, simply to find a moral and political niche you can inhabit with comfort and without risk of appearing archaic.

And for sure we saw in Humanism, Deism, and the rise of the Empiric method a vision of a world where mortals would be incapable of believing in us. We jumped at the chance to help bring about a world without gods and devils. It suited our recently Protestant mindset. God as morality, not as social order. No rites. No clergy. Just you and your conviction against the hunger for sin.

On worshipping the ancients and the rise of Noddism

Our union has always venerated the lineages and the past. While we have kept the most cult-like aspects to our private gatherings, we, especially the Ventrue, have openly recited our lineages in court, used rhetorics that recall the great speeches and deeds of our forebears, and we do make celebrations to mark the great moments of our past. When an elder enters court, observe the reverence and the awe as a demigod walks among us. It is the aspiration of many Princes to become the objects of such reverence, but it is a gift we reserve for the truly noble of our blood.

I personally know of a dozen methuselah cults, all of them populated by pillars of their clans and staunch defenders of our hierarchy, more than half of them worshipping ancients of lesser blood than my own. This is good and proper, and in recent years these cults to our dark saints have risen to prominence and open acceptance. So also for cults celebrating the creatures we call Antediluvians, the oldest creatures of our kind we have any indication of existing.

I believe this is partially in direct response to a less fortunate development that reached its peak at the turn of the millennium — the rise of the Noddist Gehenna cults. The less they are spoken of, the better, but I am glad to say they are on the decline, as no bloodthirsty ancients rise from their tombs and no divine judgement rains fire from above. If these were indeed the Antediluvians, they did not show the destructive appetites attributed to them. Instead their existence makes our claim to power stronger,

for we have (forgive my blasphemy) veritable gods on our side.

The Church of Caine

With the Sabbat throwing themselves headfirst into their mad crusade, the insidious Cainite Heresy has returned to our cities here at home. Are they a front for the Sabbat, preparing our childer for the return of their secret masters? Tempting our neonates into remorseless sin and base monstrosity? Or is this our chance to forge our own church of Blood, reclaim Caine as a symbol of our kind, and celebrate our role in the world without the paralysing self-criticism of ever-present humanity?

The Sabbat, hard as they are to understand, seem to proclaim Caine as the god and saviour of our kind. But they also name the Antediluvians as His enemies. Not so the Cainite Church. Their Gnostic interpretation of Christianity casts us all as angels of the True Divine, put on earth to shepherd Humankind and to oppose the false creator worshipped as God the Father.

In Cainite dogma Caine and Christ are both heaven-sent rebels against a malevolent creature they call the demiurge or Ialdabaoth, Lord of the Prison of the World. All of us, from the theoretical Antediluvians to the weakest of the thin-blooded, share the blood of the True Divine. This tempting faith, while it is obviously nothing but another Kindred distortion of Gnosticism, a human idea, does reenforce the core function of the Camarilla, especially in a time when we have stepped away from idealistic claims of universality to protect our interests against the rabble. Perhaps a new faith is exactly what we need in this time of division? One that extols our virtues as secret masters of the world. A dogma that fuels our blood with fire as we again go to war against the Church of Peter and this Second Inquisition. I fear that if we do not commit to destroying this church of Blood and refuse to accept its clergy into court, it will destroy us. What is even worse, the Heresy openly spits in the face of the Abrahamic faiths, and that will not sit well with our new allies in the East. I foresee the Ashirra will make demands that we deal with the Heresy in whatever cities we shall share. Because share them we will.

The Pillars

Just like the crusades of the past exposed the primitive warrior-kings of the West to the wonders of the Muslim world, the Gehenna War has made the Kindred world considerably smaller and brought us much closer to the Ashirra. This is the name for our union in the Middle East. Some argue that the Ashirra is another sect entirely, but I disagree. They were the Camarilla long before we were, founded on principles of hiding among their mortal kin and remaining true to the pillars of Islam, even as they are tempted by the impulses of death. Our cooperation is no less close than the bonds between Chicago and St Petersburg. Both Camarilla, but worlds apart. So while many see the impending marriage between the hidden masters of the West and those of the East as a monumental shift, I see it as the correction of a misconception. If you see in this some great idealism, some inclusive victory against divisive cultural prejudices, I ask you to think again. We are not on the side of the people, of the millions who are turned away from refuge in our cities, and nor are our friends in the Ashirra, their professed piety notwithstanding. We are in this to rule and to survive. We are diplomats, kings, businessmen, elite soldiers, cult leaders, and generals. We are the elite. We are vampires. Thinking the Ashirra is a single thing, a single culture, is a prejudiced idea that will get you killed in the courts of the future. Consider this: among our new allies we find Saudi Princes dining on the blood of women stoned to death for infidelity, a liberal IT-millionnaire from Jordan, Turkish nationalists dreaming of the Ottoman empire, Kurdish freedom fighters and Persian nobles longing for the glorious days of disco in 1970's Teheran. They are all Ashirra. They all believe in Allah's pillars. Yet none of them think and act in the same way.

We have a choice. God or Caine. Faith or Isolation. Either we, as a sect, strive to return to our moral foundation as believers in the God of Abraham, or we risk our new allies and take our chances with the Church of Caine. As I have argued in the essay above, our moral compass is our faith. Staying human is adhering to the beliefs of our breathing days. No one knows this better than the Ashirra. Instead of Traditions, they use the five pillars of Islam as their code of conduct and

as a bulwark against the Beast. To awake during day to pray to Mecca requires astounding self discipline, yet they all do it. Do we want to present ourselves as faithless atheists, or do we accept that we are still People of the Book and share a common story and a common morality with the Ashirra? These questions will be answered differently in every domain of the future. One will play host to a court ruled by a Cainite preacher and avoided like the plague by faithful Ashirra. Another will be run like a company by an Ashirra judge maintaining a strict front of impartiality while picking off the unjust one by one. A third will uphold a paranoid Prince trying to fan the rising flames of nationalism in his city to keep the future at bay.

The Gehenna Crusade and the Beckoning have brought us close to our origins, to our venerable ancestors, and to the Ashirra. Now we must choose how this will change us and what we believe in.

THE CHURCH OF BLOOD

I attach these transcripts as further proof you have a heresy problem. It's getting popular and claims to have abandoned the Noddist eschatology, yes, but the Church of Caine is never harmless. Ideas like these are the first steps towards radicalizing our neonates and softening them up for the inevitable return of our enemies. No matter how much these thoughts stroke your ego, we must stamp them out or risk everything. I know it's painful to kill a childe, but I fear I must insist you act decisively.

By the oaths of Blood we made on the September 14, 1856, in the domain ruled by my sire Lawrence Westfield, under his princely witness,

Sanguines et Animi,

Angus

To your face we will tell you our conspiracy is secular, that we reject superstition and faith. We lie. The Camarilla is a church of Blood for a licentious congregation and a venal world. Ours is a spy mission into enemy occupied territory ruled by the auguries of anarchy and lorded over by fools. We are the only salvation for our kind, all others are false prophets. We are the most death changing and revolutionary institution of power that has ever existed on Earth. We are dedicated to the proposition that total infiltration of the world is not only possible but necessary. This goal ultimately involves the destruction of the natural human way of life, their ways of thinking, and their freedom. We are just biding our time in the shadows.

Within our Traditions we contain many clans, sects, secret cabals and coteries, but in the end we are all the same: We are dead and we feed on the living. We manipulate governments and kill off whoever we cannot buy, trick or intimidate. We corrupt everything we touch and blight everything we try to love. We offer protection to those who serve us and obliteration to those who defy us. Ours is a hidden control system that seeps into the daily life of every living being on this planet. We are everywhere. We are nowhere. We are all-powerful. We are a whisper. We are like Him.

Malevolence is a point of view. No other creatures under God are so like him and his childe Caine as ourselves. We kill as freely and with as little remorse. Our true curse is that we share in his responsibility — a far more profound one than simple hunger, dementia or the other various hardships of nocturnal unlife.

We priests of death have transcended time and become immortal, and now in service to our sect we are as dark saints — beings of such grave and fearful powers that we transcend the mortal and define the corruptible. To the youngest Kindred we represent the longing for true immortality and total power.

On Believing in Something Larger Than Yourself

Excerpt from Guide to the Tower *by Addison Payne, Ventrue Primogen of New York*

At first glance, you'd swear our sect is a secular body. More of a political union, an alliance of lords, than a temple. But we are both. Think of Russia. See how the people there saw the Tsar as the living embodiment of God, infallible and pure no matter his actions. Realize how Lenin, to a degree, but ultimately Stalin took that devotion and made a nation live in fear and idolatry of him. He was the living embodiment of the people. He was the living embodiment of the state. And if he fell, Russia would fall also. The Russians never gave up religion, they just transferred their worship from one individual to another, and they do it to this day. What we do in the Camarilla is much the same.

We speak of organized religion as a cancer; the Church is the bastion of our enemies, and our faith is personal, nothing but a part of our quest to remain humane.

Believe first and foremost in the sect.

Believe first and foremost in your elders.

This isn't a criticism. All power structures built to hold must be built on a strong foundation. You need your supporters to believe in something to make them loyal. Turn your soldiers into disciples and you can claim the world.

Things have changed recently. Contrary to dogma, the ancient beings we might well name as Antediluvians, are said to be rising from their graves. Even if it should have, this revelation has not destroyed the Camarilla. The Gangrel left us, yes. The Brujah have left as well, for different reasons. But the rest of us stay, clinging to what we know, asking our elders for advice, for guidance.

And the elders have answered. The Antediluvians may well be real and mighty beings, but they want us no harm. They are on our side. Our leaders had hidden the truth from us only to protect us. And the Sabbat lied worse — they wanted, and still want, to destroy our living ancestors. They might as well be sharpening their sticks to drive through our own hearts! In response, we have hit at the Sabbat and Anarchs with unmatched venom. We follow them into war zones to dig them out of their holes, to demonstrate our unmatched might. We have erected our structure, and we will not let it go. It is built on the worship of our elders, our shared Blood, and that worship can reach all the way back to the Antediluvians if needed.

For 500 years we were told they did not exist. Now we look to them as proof of our own divinity, our potential to truly live forever if only we follow the path put before us by our elders, however ancient they may be.

STATE OF GRACE:

Introduction to the Religions of the Ivory Tower

By Carmelita Neillson

From Heretics to Great Religions

Christianity, as a religion, is an outgrowth of Judaism. Same God, same part of the world. The Messiah and his rebellion against Rome and the old ways were played out inside a Jewish cultural context, but gave birth to a new faith entirely. As Christianity is intertwined with Judaism, so are also our sanguine myths intimately connected with both the old warrior Yahweh and his later, more peaceful, incarnation.

The Cainite Heresy believes Christ was one of us, the second coming of Caine. From this point of view, essentially all of Christianity becomes a vampire-myth cult, made palpable to mortals through a centuries-long process of canonization and the veiling of sanguine ideals. A process that culminated in the First Council of Nicea, where the idea that Christ was

a supernatural entity was finally laid to rest and he became what we know today — the Son of Man.

If one looks for them, our fingerprints are all over Christianity. The miracles, Lazarus and Longinus as revenants changed by the blood of God, the resurrection, the obsession with His Blood, the thirteen at the table, the promise of eternal life. Some of the most extreme interpretation is found in the works of a now red-listed thin-blood in Los Angeles known only as "Hollis." Their pamphlets tell us that all of the Bible was written about us, for us and by us, and was only later cleaned up for human use.

Many find that this Lasombra myth of Christ Embraced only muddies the waters, but it can also be seen as a fascinating example of how blurred the lines can become between our kind and the mortals. Our myths travel across species, carried by the power of infectious ideas rather than any kind of concrete evidence to their veracity.

So it was also with Mithras, who's unlife gave birth to a cult crossing the boundaries between the living and the dead. He is worshipped by not only his descendants but other vampires who want the rewards his cult promises and a way of tracing back his activities through mortal history. If we are looking for a vampiric saviour, a verifiable paragon of our kind, there is no need to look further than Mithras.

Mithras' Mysteries is the cult comprising the greatest number of Kindred in the Camarilla, despite Mithras holding only nominal membership in our sect. The Menelaen Order is similar in their dedication to Menele's purported belief in enlightenment over violence. I could mention also the Eaters — Kindred who attempt to consume the names of others — and the Gorgons, worshippers of Gorgo. As history shows, wherever we go, new myths are created, and our kind have given birth to cults that span wide geographical and cultural distances. For the most part, these cults do not emerge because the object of veneration decides to form a religion around themselves. They are created in the telling and retelling of stories that become myths that become miracles.

Now, when it comes to the effects on culture and society, the power of a thought-up miracle is no less than that of the truly impossible come to pass. This makes every new cult potentially dangerous to that which it would replace, and doctrine reacts accordingly. Think of the Jewish and Roman persecution of the early Christians and Catholicism's careful eradication of heretics. Among our own Camarilla cults and orders, the tendency is the same. Do you know how many cults of Mithras existed before the current one, how different it was before Roger de Camden took charge of the cult? No, because such groups, once properly established, can tolerate no internal struggle against their truth.

Ancestor Worship

Kindred who can recite their lineage generations back and tell tales of the deeds of their ancestors — good or ill — are often well-regarded by their peers and elders. Respect and remembrance of the past is a comfort to many, and from this springs, no doubt, the practice of ancestor worship.

There's something Roman to the idea of building a shrine in one's haven, bedecking it with little idols of sire and grandsire, and asking them for guidance each night upon waking. I have encountered numerous Kindred who do this, as well as some warlocks who claim to quite literally commune with their ancestors in this way. Whether the prayers truly channel the power that allows one Kindred to telepathically link with another, I cannot say, but they clearly help the one praying, not least by lending them the author-ity of the will of their ancestor.

Ancestor worship is not limited to the material plane. Many ancestor cults revere the dead as well as the undead. Michael of Constantinople is among the most hallowed of the Toreador methuselahs. We know he was destroyed along with the Dream, but that does not stop his lineage leading a church in his name. Michael-ites, sometimes called Nephilim, receive tribute and service just through dint of their bloodline, many holding positions of religious authority throughout the Kindred world. Some even have figures of worship beyond Michael himself, but due to their ancestry, are taken at their words as paragons worth following.

Another example can be found within Clan Tremere. Karl Schrekt's traditionalists believe Tremere himself was the pin-nacle among magi, and they find great reassurance in attempts to replicate his successes, frequently sacrificing blood and worse in his name, mixing their belief in the power of the Blood, with the Hermeticism inherent in their clan's origin. Thus the neologism "Hemetics" was born. The occult-ists have affected the belief system of the Camarilla profoundly. Even when we turn away from miracles, we tend to believe in magic rather than scientific theory to explain both our condition and abilities.

Perhaps this is the true core of our beliefs. We may not believe in God or Caine, but we sense there is a hidden order to the universe. Prophecy, curses, fate, poetic justice, synchronicity, wages of sin, good and evil. These are real to most of us. "The Emerald Tab-let," a second century text from Alexandria, states, in modern lan-guage, "As above — so below." The meaning of this is that all things are connected and can affect each other through unseen connections. Many Kindred, especially the Hemetics, follow the recent break-throughs in quantum physics with great interest. Perhaps the science of our breathing days will finally unify with the bloody miracles of our long deaths.

Antediluvian Worship

To the unworldly, worship of a clan founder is just another form of ancestor worship. However, the likely — current or previous — existence of the Antediluvians not been confirmed for very long, and the worship of these beings is traditionally more akin to that of a concept rather than an individual. You do not light a candle and tell your sorrows to beauty and art as you would your great-grandsire. For these reasons, it is rare to find a formal faith built up around an Antediluvian, with that of Set be-ing the exception due to the clan's former hierarchy of hierophants speaking for the founder.

Antediluvian cults often run synonymous with Gehenna cults, but have taken on greater perma-nence in the decade since the idea of global catastrophe first hit our society with full force. A Kindred who wishes to revive their founder, be their chief slave, and usher in a period where Haqim (for instance) rules all Kindred, can be said to be nihilistic at best. Deranged and homicidal at worst. All we really know of our founders are rumours and speculation. But if what happened in Bangladesh at the end of the 20th century had anything to do with them, it does not bode well.

Yet, they are our most promising link to the genesis of all vampires, and the Book of Nod, the Erciyes Fragments, or other fabled texts may go a long way to explain what our true origins might have been. Did any of them meet Caine? Was he real? With all these questions, and their godlike stature, it is no surprise many fall to this kind of faith. Some claim religion was humankind's first faltering attempt at philosophy. "The world is at it is because the gods will it." It is tempting to think, how much nearer the truth would we get, if the gods could answer us. Still, it would be wise to remember that our myths have cast them in our image — they may not be what we imagined or even have our answers, not assuming they would want to merely enlighten us when they might as well set us on fire.

Mortal Religion

Am I cynical because I am an archaeologist, a scientist, and a woman Embraced in the 20th century, or because I still identify as a (lapsed) Catholic? It is difficult to escape one's mortal faith, and is it really wise to try? Without even considering it, I will find myself

praying, wanting to attend mass, or wishing I could cast off my sins in confession to a priest. Blame an ingrained belief or a hard upbringing, but this cross is mine to bear until I become ash.

The Camarilla neither encourage nor discourage mortal faith, but it does have many believers amongst its members. Death can shake belief or it can reinforce it. In my case, it stayed as natural as putting on clothes when I rise. It is a core part of our ideology that we retain habits, customs, and perspectives from our mortal lives in order to remain virtuous. So why do we often frown at mortal religion? Because the church has hunted us almost to extinction once, and now are doing it again. With this in mind, it is not strange that our sect is critical of organized religion.

The Ashirra are our opposite in this regard. Their sect spans much of what we regard as the Middle East and holds Islam as its fundamental core. There is certainly a hypocrisy there, given what Islam disallows and what the Ashirra definitely do, but they do not punish Kindred for remaining Muslims. Quite the contrary: if you want influence in the Ashirra, you need to appeal to, or at least be tolerant of, Islam. The great eastern sect respects and includes many Kindred of Jewish and Christian faith, all the people of the book are seen as brethren and are given freedom to practice their own religious code. To the Ashirra, faith holds many of the answers behind their existence.

Judaism, Christianity, and Islam are doubtless the most influential of the mortal religions represented in our sect and among of our close allies. I have met but a handful of Orthodox Jewish Kindred, to these most faithful, final death is often preferable to a long unlife outside the laws of God and Israel. Reform Jews and many of the other schools of Judaic faith often see themselves as a part of God's plan, humbly accepting their sentence. Many of these act as protectors of the Jewish communities in their cities, bringing just death to anti-Semitic groups and Kindred. But there are as many faiths and more among the undead as among the living. Buddhism, for instance, shares many principles with the fabled path of Golconda and I know many Kindred practitioners who find states of spiritual balance with their Beast through following its message, despite frequent gross misdeeds.

Hinduism's polytheistic faces to the singular Brahman, the espousal of quests for purity, and belief in the immortal soul, likewise has Kindred members. Many find the faith hard to reconcile with their condition, but some elders of the Hindu faith twist it to place themselves as the Brahman's deities, creating an intriguing heresy within its vampiric adherents.

I have encountered few Kindred Sikhs, Jainists, Shintoists, or Taoists, but that is not to say they do not exist. I have heard there are at least four Princes of Sikh religion in the Punjab Region of India, so any vampire can cling to their mortal faith.

Conversely, many Kindred exist who still hold to Zoroastrianism and the old pagan religions of Greece, Egypt, and Scandinavia, but I suspect many times that is due to the age of the vampire and extended periods of torpor. Here, though, I must add another, altogether more frightening perspective on the rise of religion. According to celebrants of the Gangrel Cult of Odin, the Aesir were just like our latter-day religious charlatans. They were Kindred who gathered a mortal following. It follows, they say, that so were the gods of Greece, of Indochina, of Persia. Of Jerusalem. One might well shudder at the idea of a world where the only gods are dead and faith is a trick to milk the last blood from the veins of the living. I wish the idea would not be so logical, so well aligned with all I have seen and learnt in my communion with the past.

Cults, Heresies, and Orders
by Lord Roger de Camden, Pater of the Cult of Mithras

You must forgive the old weak hand at work here. It does so shake when I put pen to paper, so I find myself typing in the modern style, but alas, I do so slowly.

In my long, long life, I have encountered more cults than I can count. Many flare up like the pox, and are eliminated before the decade is out by a rival or internal disharmony. Such is the way of our kind that we never encourage growth. We see something new, and desire to stamp upon it. Alas, I barely shuffle, let alone stamp. I would need to ask my Heliodromus to do so for me.

But you wish for a sampling of the cults extant tonight? I can provide you with a few, certainly. You need to wash out the bad taste of the word "cult," however. It is not what the modern presses would have you think, where all cults are led by megalomaniacs looking to indoctrinate herds of ignorant followers. Far from it. Those cults exist, but rarely outlast a century. Consider it more akin to how Romans, including my master Mithras, referred to the "Cult of Christianity." To creatures as old as we, few religions outgrow the word "cult." I am older than Islam, after all.

I will not mention the Cult of Mithras. Extant for two millennia despite attacks from all sides, it speaks for itself. Instead, I will mention some lesser known and more recently formed cults and orders. You will find among the examples cults of pure Kindred origin as well as ways faithful Kindred find a role in the faiths of the breathers. For no matter what the Inner Circle tells us, we are as prone to self-delusion and the comfort of divine purpose as any of the living.

The Meneleans
Menele or Menelaus is of course a prominent figure in the Iliad. He was the King of Sparta, and generally

regarded as one of the Brujahs most powerful generals during the Punic conflicts with Ventrue-supported Rome. Despite his war prowess, the cultists of the vanished Menele believe their icon was a seeker of enlightenment and peace, quite the opposite to his clan's stereotype. Some pray to him for wisdom when their Beast calls.

As with many cults, the Meneleans require some target for their rage. You do not form a cult on peace alone, for all need to divest hatred somewhere. The Meneleans blame the Toreador for betraying Carthage, and routinely indulge in the sacrifice of captive Degenerates, or so I'm told.

Eyes of Malakai

This cult is recently emerged. It is led by Malkavians, but joined, for some reason, by many who seek to share in the mad visions of that clan. The eyes believe madness incarnate is the only way to absolute truth. By losing their minds, they hope to gain insight. I myself have encountered one who was remarkably lucid. It was she who gave warning about London's fall.

The sacrifice cultists make to this cult is one of sound mind. I cannot claim to know all their rites, but I hear tell they quite literally stare into the abyss, the underworld, or some nebulous hell, waiting until all mortal thoughts leave their minds. What replaces them, I cannot say.

The Aspirants of Yima

Is it so unusual that the Nosferatu fall prey to vanity? When one must live with hideousness for an eternity, it is easy to succumb to dreams of beauty. This odd cult has existed for at least two millennia, comprising Kindred in worship of the supposedly flawless Yima. Tale tells, he was Embraced before his founder was cursed with ugliness by Caine, but who can say?

Either way, this decadent, but ultimately vapid cult has gone to great lengths to stage great pageants and carve their own bodies to resemble something a little less offensive. Many members were beautiful in life. Known as Cleopatras, they spend their years trying to regain what they have lost.

The Amaranthans

A dangerously-named cult, who has fallen afoul of persecution many times over the centuries despite their frequent protestations. Yet, the tenets of their belief will not allow them to change their order's name, for they love their idol so dearly. Amarantha was the first victim of diablerie, and Amaranth is the archaic name of the crime, you see. It is an easy leap, therefore, to see Amaranthans as diablerists.

They are quite the contrary, however. The Amaranthans pursue diablerists with a violent fervor, acting outside the usual limits of Camarilla Tradition. They revere their idol for her martyrdom and innocence, striking down the guilty in her name.

The Ur-Shulgi Cult

This cult is evidence that with enough time, dedication, and wherewithal any group can ascend to become the orthodoxy. Prior to the waking of the methuselah Ur-Shulgi, I would have described the Banu Haqim as a predominantly Islamic clan. But with his return, the vampire claimed Islam a sham, and demanded that all Children of Haqim must revere their namesake rather than Allah and the prophet, or be punished by the loss of their Blood and soul through diablerie.

In the name of Haqim, his maybe-sire, Ur-Shulgi has become an active, powerful leader of his own cult. Claims of his skillful use of sorcery and purge of a thousand Banu Haqim have reached even my ears. Many call this methuselah "the Great Destroyer," with good reason.

It is worth noting that the awakening of the Skinless One parallels the growth of extremist interpretations of the Qur'an on both sides of the Sunni-Shia divide. His thirst for destruction is shared by many mortals, and in his wake violence rises, tainting the image of Islam (and the Banu Haqim to those who know) in the minds of the West.

The Patmostine Order

Named for the isle of Patmos, where St. John received his Revelations, the Patmostine Kindred combine several unusual doctrines into a Christian sect with a truly peculiar view of the world: Rapture has come and gone. The seven years that are supposed to pass between the Rapture and the Day of Judgment are symbolic, much as some people interpret the six days of creation. Thus, no way exists of knowing when these seven "ages" will have passed, but the sect points to the Gehenna War, and the Patmostines are certain that the Four Horsemen ride closely behind it.

The Patmostines also believe that Caine was blessed, not cursed, by God. In fact, they believe that the Kindred received their undying status so they could survive all the years from the Rapture to the final judgment, that they might usher the worthy through the Gates of Heaven. They believe the Kindred themselves, not any of the remaining mortals, are those who will be saved on Judgment Day. Only someone worthy of Heaven — even if no mortal or Kindred can comprehend why they are worthy — will survive the Embrace.

The Patmostines have taken it as their mission to track down and Embrace the most worthy mortals they can find, thus securing them a place in Heaven come Judgment Day. The sect believes no more than 50.000 Kindred exist in the world tonight. If Judgment Day arrives before 144.000 have been Embraced, many who could have been saved will instead be damned.

The Shepherds of Islam

The Shepherds are a group of Muslim Kindred who believe that Allah himself have chosen them to be the deathless caretakers of the words of the last prophet, Muhammad. It is their goal that Islam live on through those who personally witnessed the Word.

To the Shepherds of Islam, all arguments that have arisen since the lifetime of Muhammad, from the growing morass of interpretations of the ḥadīths to the discrepancies among so many bickering caliphs, should be answered simply by asking those who were there. For this reason, the Shepherds maintain a comprehensive list of all those Kindred who endured through that special time in history. They call these Kindred "witnesses" and strive to keep them undead at all costs, even risking their own unlives to ensure that Allah's plan for them is carried out. Whenever a new witness is found, they are typically invited to join the group to become one of the "inner circle" of Shepherds. A great many mortal believers are employed in the endeavor of seeking out witnesses, forming a fairly extensive network worldwide.

Consumptionism

God, as Nietzsche so succinctly put it, is dead. It is not, however, a recent passing; Consumptionist Kindred believe that the almighty has been dead for thousands and thousands of years, ever since Caine diablerized him. According to their doctrine, God was, if not an actual physical entity, at least a spiritual being who could be reached with the proper magical ritual. And the killing of Abel was not a sacrifice but the culmination of a ritual intended to summon God made manifest. When it succeeded, Caine drew from God all his power, consuming his essence.

As the Consumptionists tell it, Caine walked among mortals for many years. After a time, however, he grew lonely. He could never know the presence of an equal — was he not God, after all? Thus he Embraced the Second Generation and in so doing spread out and diluted the power of God. Over time, other Kindred repeated Caine's act, passing portions of their own share of God's might onto their childer, and their childer after that, until the modern era, when the Kindred have grown so numerous and so distant from Caine that the latest generations carry hardly any power of God at all. The world, Consumptionists believe, will come to an end only when the last Kindred, having reabsorbed all God's power into a single form once more, recreates Caine's feat and becomes God, allowing Him to sweep away the ruins of the old world and give birth to a new one ∎

The Passion of Uga Dugud

(The Great Gathering of Ravens)

*5th Generation Brujah Methuselah.
In Torpo. Circa 2600 BC
Translation by Converyx (1861).
Revered of the Revered. Book: 41,
Chapter: 28*

**IN NOMINE NOSTRI CAINE.
INTRABO IN ALTARIA GLORIAE.**

1. During the reign of the profane Sargon of Assyria there was a persecution of Kindred in the rebellious exanimate princedoms of oriental (East) Anatolia. At that time a vainglorious Kindred by the name of Prince Azu ruled over Trebizond, and he was unduly hostile towards worshippers of Caine [written "Kagn" in the original text] because of his own self-idolatry. Of the Fangs given to his command the uttermost had joined his cult and worshipped him as a god and forgot the name of their common forebear.

2. Yet among his adjutants, like a rose among thorns, there arose secret a faithful servant of Caine known only as Uga Dugud. Because of his zealous ardour, boldness in battle, and conquest of many citadels he had become renowned among his kind. He was sought out by those who deemed him worthy of homage and wished to be taught his methods.

3. Azu become jealous of Uga Dugud and banished him and his small group of followers—who like Uga Dugud had refused to pay homage to Azu as a god—and sent them to live on Mount Ararat. There they stayed for seven score years and it was here Uga Dugud began developing and teaching an unknown style of warfare, known as the Path of Fury, that employed schismatic fits of frenzy to turn both he and his Sphinx Riders into ghastly warriors of retribution.

4. Many years later it happened that the main force of the Assyrian army crossed north into the borderlands and engaged in war against Azu. The haste of the assault and the number of mortal attackers greatly disturbed Azu, he remembered the military skills and daring of Uga Dugud and summoned him to return to his inner-council.

5. Calling upon Uga Dugud's heedless courage, and out of his own fear, Azu addressed him as an equal. "Your fierce powers," he said, "and the victories you have won against larger forces are well known to all who hold the sceptre. I entrust to your valour this grandiose invasion of mortals in order that your reputation will grow even more."

6. When Caine's best warrior heard these words—trusting not in numbers, nor in weapons or in armour, but only in his Path of Fury—he arranged for his few followers, still small in number, to follow him and go into battle formation, and led them against the vast enemy who was arrayed against them.

7. It was the darkest night and Sargon's far-flung camp was spread across a plain like red locusts. Just before they were about to enter close combat, he presented to his men as a matter for discussion his superior knowledge of the Kindred as vengeful lords of retribution. He said the following thing to them: "Within your fitful spleen is the rage of hell, the vehemence of Caine, the convulsion of possession by the Beast within. Tonight you are the demons all mortals fear. Spring upon them like the eruption of Hyksos. Caine will catch you if you fall."

8. This is what he said to them and they believed in him, and charging forward with wild boldness they went from fire-to-fire and tent-to-tent and slew every man who wore sandals, and put flight to all the chattel warriors. By dawn they had gained a huge victory against Sargon, who had fled naked in dishonor. By making his chosen men witnesses of their own Blood power and by giving them knowledge of their own rage and fury in this way, the

holy prophet of the Path of Fury instilled in them a supernatural confidence and purpose.

9. All of this much disturbed Azu who had been hoping for defeat and planning on the victory for himself, and he deemed what had happened a personal affront. By freeing from the mortal coil so many who were possessed by unclean spirits, Uga Dugud inflicted a vital blow upon the mortal claim to sovereignty for all Kindred and this very greatly humiliated that proud and evil Azu.

10. Uga Dugud heard of this and so returned to Azu and slew him and became the new ruler of the regnum, and all who knelt before him honored him as the Wrath of Caine and as his true witness and prophet. Yet never did he claim he was a god or anointed by the one; he humbly taught the ways of savage umbrage and took nothing for himself except the obligations of command.

11. Over three mortal generations of chattel all continued to go as the prophet planned, and he joined together many Fangs under his command and triumphed over many princedoms and greatly expanded his regnum. At last he became so famed that he was invited to the High Court of the Thirds, and so he travelled north and was adorned with a great welcome and his due rewards at their mountain citadel, which still existed then, as was fitting.

12. However, certain wary Kindred there, pursuing a project of envy and spite, yet accomplishing a good though they did not mean it, assailed Uga Dugud and his loyal Fangs in a courtyard with 166 of their own finest Fangs. Uga Dugud and his followers at once went into a cyclonic dance of fury and dispatched them all. All who witnessed the event were unsettled and made afraid by what they had seen; it was later said to be the greatest exhibition of martial valour and skill in the history of the undead.

13. The Thirds took the matter angrily and sent Fangs to learn the truth of the matter and report it back. When they had determined, by means of those whom he had sent, that these things were so, they again summoned Uga Dugud and using flattery and threats, reminded him of his hatred for and bitterness towards the Apostates.

14. Veddartha said to him "You have devoured many of our greatest Fangs. Since you know how and why I cast out Malakai, the greatest Apostate, with what object or hope do you now make your case on behalf of yourself and your followers?"

15. In reply Uga Dugud shouted: "You only strengthen my resistance by what you have said. For if all those you named had done me no harm, they would be standing here yet. Still you mock me by accusing me of waging war on you here in your own home, when I have arrayed against me a vast army of ancient beings. I cannot hope to win against you, yet

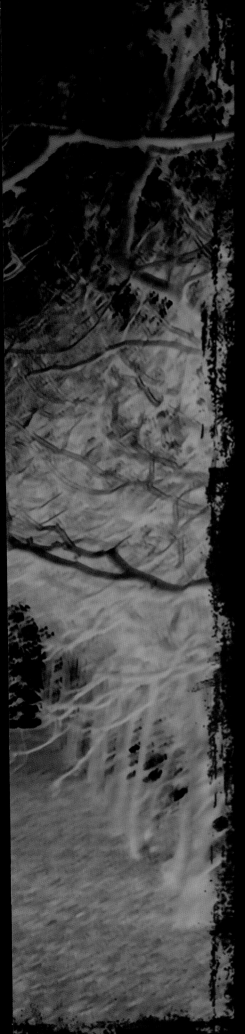

I promise many will perish in the attempt. Perhaps even you will fall."

16. Veddartha then ordered a bronze chariot to be readied, and when this had been made very hot by a great fire, and saying he would spare Uga Dugud's followers if he did as he was asked, he commanded the prophet to step upon it. Uga Dugud, protected by his cold fury, leapt onto the chariot, as if onto a soft carpet, and sat on its floor. He immediately felt great pain as his whole body was burned and shaken, but he resisted with cold anger and the rubicund metal yielded to his fervour. An hour later he stepped off unburned and unharmed. All were amazed.

17. Therefore he was allowed to leave after a promise to not conquer more princedoms or war against mortal kingdoms. He and his followers turned havenward and continued to develop his techniques and theory of violent wrathful frenzied war. None dared to stand up against him and for many long years he was left in peace to rule over his regnum.

18. Then a messenger came to him who gave him the sceptre of Troile, his long lost grandsire, saying he had summoned him to a place called Tarsus. This was a strait where two warring mountain peaks clashed together with between them a twisting narrows produced as a result of a river flowing downwards along many falls that are nearly impassable. They form a precipi-

tous chasm between them which is fearful even to even gaze upon.

19. Uga Dugud made the journey to Tarsus but there was no Troile; instead an army of vengeful iniquitous Fangs laid in wait. As Uga Dugud and his most trusted followers rose up the fourth cataract fell upon them and slew many within the first ten score heartbeats. Uga Dugud, undaunted, led a sortie up the waterfall but was struck down by a golden javelin thrown by a Fourth and fell onto the rocks below. He was carried off on his own shield by his force of ever loyal bodyguards, The Sphinx Riders, as the rest of his followers bravely held off the enemy host and were slaughtered to a Fang.

20. The bodyguards eventually found a cave and wandered ever deep into the earth over many nights until they found a place so close to Hades that it could never be found, and there they laid him to rest in a deep and abiding torpor.

21. They then travelled back to Anatolia and beyond to the west, praising and lauding their prophet and spreading the word of the Path of Fury. Never since has the legend of Uga Dugud been forgotten: he who befits all glory, honour, and exaltation, together with the founders and forebears, now and forever and unto the ages of ages.

Sicut erat in principio, et nunc, et in morte, et in saecula saeculorum ∎

The Reformed Congregation of the Veneration of the Methuselah

CHANCEL OF THE PROFANE APOSTLES

This is the formal service of the restored Black Mass of the Reformed Venerate Church which was refounded in 1999 in Venice at The Conclave of the Volto.

The High Priest enters to stand before the altar and chants the dire dirge, while raising arms to the relics of the methuselah. Then rings the gong nine times.

HIGH PRIEST: (CHANTS)

"In nomine nostri Caine, in excelsis Methuselahum!"

"In the name of Caine, to the Methuselah in the highest!"

COVEN: (CHANTS)

"Ortus ascendero in altaria Methuselahum."

"I will rise up to altar of the Methuselah."

HIGH PRIEST: (CHANTS)

"In the name of the Venerates, rulers of Death, the scabs of the world, the lords of the undead, I beseech the forces of darkness to bestow their terrible blessing upon us. Save us, of Venerates, from the treacherous and the soft. Sleeping spirits, lords of retributions, awake now and come forth from the abyss to strike down the unworthy!"

HIGH PRIEST: (CHANTS)

"Gloria Veneratorum, et Caine et hospiti spiritus malevolentiae."

"Glory be to the Venerates, and Caine, and the host of malevolent spirits."

COVEN: (CHANTS)

"Sicut erat in principio, et nunc, et semper, et in saeculo saeculorum."

"As it was in the beginning, is now and ever shall be, unto the age of ages."

HIGH PRIEST AND COVEN:

"Hail Menele, Altamira, and Uga Dugud, spawn of Troile!

Hail Mithras, Hardestadt, and Orthinia, spawn of Ventru!

Hail Mancheaka, Tegyrius, and Ur-Shulgi, spawn of Haqim!

Hail Mictlantecuhtli, Enkidu, and Matasuntha, spawn of Ennoia!

Hail Montano, Boukephos, and Sybil, spawn of Lasombra!

Hail the Eater, Malakai, and Nissiku, spawn of Malkav!

Hail Yima, Gorgo, and Azazel, spawn of Absimiliard!

Hail Beshter, Helena, and Amarantha, spawn of Arikel!

Hail Tremere, Goratrix, and Meerlinda, spawn of Tremere!"

HIGH PRIEST:

"Vester Methuselah vobiscum."

"Your Methuselah be with you."

COVEN:

"Et cum spiritu tuo."

"And with thy spirit."

HIGH PRIEST:

"Let us pray . . . Urged by the bidding of our Venerates and schooled by his infernal ordinance, we make bold to say:"

HIGH PRIEST AND COVEN TOGETHER:

"Death is the source of life!" {gong}

"Death is the engine of creation!" {gong}

"Death is the engine of destruction!" {gong}

"Death destroys the weak!" {gong}

"Death exalts the strong!" {gong}

"Death is eternal!" {gong}

HIGH PRIEST

"I raise up this chalice, symbol of the Blood of Caine, to exalt the torment and glory of eternal Death. We drink of the elixir of ecstasy to inflame within us the forces of Death."

HIGH PRIEST:

"Children of my office. By the favor of our Lord Venerates, I have the power to pass on your wishes, should it please me to do so. Now, lift up your heads, and tell me your prayerful desires."

COVEN:

"One who repents all heresy and craves to be accepted into your grace of the Venerates, hear my plea oh _____ spawn of _____."

HIGH PRIEST:

"May your will be done."

{Celebrant drinks from the chalice.}

COVEN:

"May their will be done."

HIGH PRIEST

"Let us be exalted by our lust for Death! In the names of the great Venerates our Death shall be fulfilled. While they still sleep, we shall awaken them. As their torpor wanes, we shall prepare the world for them."

"The restoration of the Venerate shall renew all Death after the long dark winter of life. Let fools and weaklings deny and disparage the power of Death. We know that he who denies Death, denies Truth!" {gong is struck}

COVEN:

"Hail Masters! Have mercy on us!"

"Mercy in Death! Mercy in Death! Mercy in Death!"

HIGH PRIEST

"Aptus et iustus est, ut semper tibi gratias agamus: Domini, Reges infernales, Imperatores mortis. Jubilantes, omnes immortales te laudant et nobis voces cum eis iungimus, dicentes:"

"It is only fitting and right that we shall at all times give Thee thanks: Lords, Infernal Kings, Emperors of Death. Jubilantly all the immortals praise thee, and with them we join our own voices, saying:"

COVEN:

"Ave, Ave, Ave."

"Hail, Hail, Hail."

{Gong is struck three times}

HIGH PRIEST:

"Domine Caine, torrentim voluptatis Tuae bibant. Quia tecum fons vitae est, et in lumine Tuo lumen videbimus."

"Lord Caine, they shall drink of the torrent of Thy pleasure. For with Thee is the well of life, and in Thy light shall we see light."

HIGH PRIEST:

"Nostra corda infusione a Domine Caine lustrent, et eos fertilibus faciat, spargens eos cum rore Gratiae sui."

"May our hearts be cleansed by the inpouring of our Lord Caine; and may he make them fruitful by sprinkling them with the dew of His grace."

COVEN:

"Ave, Ave, Ave."

"Hail, Hail, Hail."

{The High Priest hands the Blood chalice to the acolyte, who holds it out for him to dip the aspergillus into the Blood.}

COVEN:

"Ave, Ave, Ave."

"Hail, Hail, Hail."

HIGH PRIEST:

"Qui sitiunt, veniant, at aliqui qui volunt, aquam Mortis bibant."

"Those who thirsteth, let them come; and those that will, them take of the water of Death."

COVEN:

"Purga mihi, purga mihi, purga mihi."

"Purify me, purify me, purify me."

HIGH PRIEST:

"Ego radices et genus Methuselahorum sum, siderum malignorum. Transite mihi, omnes quos me cupiunt, et progeniebus meis replentur. Tenebrae me teget, et noctem lumen meum in delectante erit."

"I am the root and stock of the Methuselahs, the evil stars. Come over to me all ye that desire me and be filled with my fruits. Darkness shall cover me, and night shall be my light in the pleasure."

{The High Priest takes the knife and plunges it into the hearts of the living mortal sacrifice. As the victim dies the coven chants:}

COVEN:

"Sanguis agni, sanguis agni, sanguis agni."

"Blood of the lamb, blood of the lamb, blood of the lamb."

{The High Priest removes the beating heart and presents it to the congregation.}

COVEN:

"Ave, Ave, Ave."

"Hail, Hail, Hail."

HIGH PRIEST

"Domini Venerati, prophetae Vis, Terra et profundis Infernalis Maligni Tui repleti sunt."

"Lord Venerates, prophets of Power, Earth, and Infernal depths are full of Thy Evil." ■

OUR. *mission* STATEMENT

Caine grants us unlife,
The Blood grants us power,
The clans grant us our role,
The Camarilla grants us order,
And humanity grants us purpose.

Leading Humankind

"The truth is, mortals do not want freedom."

Why do we exist? Above mere survival and mutual protection, what justifies our improbable and selfishly prolonged unlives? The answer is something bigger than ourselves: the Camarilla.

Some see our sect as merely the system that protects us from becoming fire and ashes on the streets. But the truth is that everything that lives (or makes a decent imitation) needs a dream. Everything that thinks needs a purpose. Are the Kindred not the best evidence of this? When creatures that merely go through the motions of survival encounter those of us who carry in our veins the dreams of our ancestors, who wins? We do. Dream and purpose drive us, or they should. Without them, we may as well embrace the Beast and cease our pretence of control.

And that, in a nutshell, is the Camarilla's mission: control. By directing the most powerful and effective Kindred with a single will — that of the Inner Circle — we amplify their power and effect. By extending our reach into mortal governments, corporations, crime syndicates, churches, and everything else that tries in their own feeble way to corral humanity, we extend our control to the four corners of the earth. From penthouses to nuclear blast shelters dug out under mountains, we are influencing and guiding humanity, using our extraordinary talents to improve our common world.

For centuries humanity has worked diligently on molding an individualistic identity for itself, which makes mortals believe they have the capacity to understand for themselves the truth, all the while we can manipulate what they think by means of media control and through their passions. Even without our influence, they live out their lives in a self-made prison of the mind, editing historical documents to feed their entertainment sickness, until they can no longer tell fact from fiction. They have chosen to see reality through the prism of storytelling. All we need to do to lead them is tell the right stories.

Address of Sir Everard Keightley, at a meeting in Westhampton, Long Island, of the "Sons of Magog," influential Ventrue who escaped London in time, and their honoured American guests:

I've heard much loose talk about the "New Dark Ages" coming around again. Inquisitors burn us from our homes, our elders leave on mysterious crusades, each regnum shrinks in upon itself, medieval customs like Blood Weddings and Coterie Labours return to Elysium halls. Even some of the cannier Magisters seem interested in reviving the old partnership of mitre and sceptre these nights.

I say, if a new Dark Age approaches ... embrace it. In the Dark Ages, we kept art and culture alive. Our scribes translated ancient texts, and copied the ones they could not yet understand. Our poets inspired the tradition of courtly love and the tales of the Grail. And we ourselves — I presume I can speak freely in this august company — we ruled all Christendom as kings.

I do not pretend to any great age or distinction, although my Blood runs as royally purple as in any of your veins. I saw the same sunlight that Reynolds and Gainsborough painted, and one or two of you may recall seeing the Poussin that I bought just afterward for a song. You will be happy to know that it was in Antwerp being restored during the raids, and I have it safe now. How many of us have paid to keep mortal artists alive, or even given a drop or two to keep them alive more directly? Our Sensate friends love beauty, or at least they love talking

"As you feel the blood leaving their body, one last gasp of air, and they stare back into your eyes... in that moment you are God."

about it, but they love best the new, the fashionable. We love power because we know power, and the power of permanence, of greatness in art, can match its tradition with even our Traditions.

When I was a lad, I was taught that monasteries kept all the art and knowledge of Rome alive as the rivers froze and the barbarians burned the cities. Of course, that was a profound simplification but... what a dream! To once more keep all that is truly worthy and moving and important — made by our hands, or by living ones — alive and intact and shining. Dark Ages may be coming for us, but mortal society has already been barbaric on every definition for a human lifetime. Now, for their final vandalism, they prepare to boil the skies rather than freeze the rivers. Or perhaps they will yet manage to fry each other with atomic bombs, or unleash plagues by sheer accident.

A wise herdsman keeps a cave to shelter his flock when the storm comes. A wise kingdom builds a refuge to store up its treasures and its provisions. Even human governments dig out mountains against the disasters they cannot help but plan for themselves. Can we do less? Do we not owe it to ourselves, and to civilization, and yes even to the kine, to fortify our walls against change and foes without ... and build thick, vaulted ceilings against the storms and blazing sun above?

Ah, I see the refreshments are here, a sure sign I have talked too long. I apologize for my enthusiasm, my friends. As I said, I am still youthful.

Maintaining the Balance Between Humanity and the Beast

When we next meet, we must have a frank discussion about humanity. It's possible you have learned everything I would have to say by then, of course, but this is a subject which engenders a lot of rhetoric and little honesty in our society.

The idea that we must cling to our humanity is beautiful, and I believe in it as much as any monster who's sucked the blood of mortals for centuries can. We must hold on to human emotions, allow ourselves to be moved and touched by the life around us like humans do. Otherwise, we degenerate into rank animals. To hunt and hunger, nothing more, is pointless existence.

Humanity is our common religion. Whatever else we believe in, we recognize the necessity of holding onto our civilized selves. You'll hear similar ideas espoused by many in the Camarilla.

I remember once in the 1860's, I think, when I was visiting the court of Gustav Breidenstein, who was the Prince of Berlin at that time. He had a game he liked to play whenever he found a sufficient amount of illegally Embraced young childer in his domain. He brought them to his court and told them that if they managed to survive the night, he'd allow them to live in the city.

His whole court treated it like a festival, cruelly hounding and hunting the poor neonates. Most times, none survived. I participated in it myself, of course. I'm not ashamed. That's Camarilla life behind all the beautiful words about humanity.

One night, I was at a small salon at Breidenstein's haven. He waxed eloquent about the need for humanity to soothe the roar of the Blood in our ears. We all murmured in agreement. Who would point out the hypocrisy of a Prince like that?

Nisha Kapoor, Toreador Ambassador, Musing Aloud:

Perhaps because they remain so very beautiful. Obviously not all of them, and not for long. But together, as a crowd, gathered at the Gateway or here, in the parts of Mumbai where you could almost think you were in Kolkata. But I will say — although I shall cut you if you quote me — that even in Kolkata, beauty blooms in the eyes and bosoms and limbs of the humans. Excuse me, "mortals." For we, too, are humans: we laugh, and play, think, and even love, or convince ourselves we did.

We in the Tower have the resources and safety to practice humanity more easily than many outside it. So we should value it.

I know some Western Kindred call the humans kine or "cattle"... They mean that they are a flock, animals to be herded. But animals can be holy too, besides useful, and we should practice seeing that spark, in people, in the crowds, and within ourselves.

Remember those who prayed with you, fought with you, played with you. Especially remember those who loved you, and who you loved. Even if you believe you cannot love — and my heart breaks at either your honesty or your folly — please remember that once, once you did, and stay human with us a little longer.

AUTHOR UNKNOWN; INSERTED INTO A PRIVATELY PRINTED EDITION (GHENT, 1790) OF PERRAULT'S *HISTOIRES OU CONTES DU TEMPS PASSÉ*

Once upon a time there was a Beast that roamed the land and killed children and maidens and old men and everyone it saw. It was wild and free and obeyed no lord, for it was a Beast. And it lived in dens and caves and slept on leaves and dirt. And the young men of that land hunted it, for the Beast had fanned their anger and driven their strength to become equal to its own.

The young men hunted everywhere and stopped up all the dens and caves where the Beast might sleep. Then they drove the Beast into an open place in the forest, where they speared it through and pinned it to the ground. They chopped off its head and displayed it in their hall and boasted of their skill.

But seven of the hunters sent to explore the caves where the Beast might sleep had discovered a cub of the Beast. They hid it away in a Tower where none could see it and swore to keep secrecy should any of their fellows ask. They fed the growing Beast only that prey that none would miss, and they fed themselves on its blood. And they grew stronger than any of the other hunters, and took much land and gold. Children and maidens and old men willingly entered the Tower, and some of them left.

The seven hunters built their Tower ever higher and stronger and passed their treasures down to their heirs until all the land belonged to them.

And they kept it all, for as long as they kept the Beast hidden within their Tower.

From The Diary of Bartolomeu Casson, Nosferatu of São Paulo:

He died, of course. He died tonight, and I will see him die again for a century in flashes of dream just before sunset.

Should I have changed him? Him, who was so beautiful, even in the dull glow of the sodium lamps in the subway? I never could. It would have saved him, but torn him from me all the same.

I remember the first time it happened; João was… Funny, I don't remember if João was the more beautiful. He simply grew old and less golden. More silver, but still beautiful. And then he died, and I discovered I could still weep and I killed the doctors for not being able to cure old age.

I just looked it up in the older diaries — it was only two months after that I met, well, discovered Matheus. I saw him in the Ibirapuera, and just somehow knew that he loved it as I had. No, as I still did. Still do. Green, growing things. Only they deserve sunlight, the world's true nobility. Trees, and their beautiful dryads like João and Matheus and the one who didn't work out and Sebastião and…

And Marco, who died tonight.

I need to see the trees, and know they still shine for me, even through the bloody film of my tears.

If I see those badalhocos cutting their initials into the trees, however, I won't be the only one crying. And Marco won't be the only one who dies tonight.

Upholding the traditions

Addison Payne continued…

If the court structure is the backbone of the Camarilla, the Traditions make the heart. These sacred laws, established at the Convention of Thorns in 1439, provide our sect with the moral compass that makes us, ultimately, better than all other Kindred. But let me explain it to you in a language you will understand. You can compare the Camarilla with the UN. The Traditions are a bit like the Universal Declaration of

Human Rights, in that they are rules which all the members of the Camarilla have agreed to honor. But like the members of the UN, the Kindred interpret the rules differently from domain to domain. For instance, Article 3 of the Universal Declaration is the right to life, so most countries in the UN have agreed to get rid of capital punishment, but the US still uses that in 31 states, with the pro-life movements arguing that the rule is really all about carrying pregnancies to term. However, besides fulfilling the role of moral guidelines, the Traditions also exist to protect our continued survival as a species. We are too different without some common agreements, and we would push ourselves toward extinction were it not for our ability to work together under one leadership and with one goal: secrecy and control.

Each domain under the Camarilla keeps the Traditions in their own way. Some Traditions leave little room for interpretation, others differ vastly in execution all over the empire. So, before you enter a domain, be sure you have educated yourself on their laws. You can expect to be punished for any transgressions you commit even when you were not aware of the rules you were breaking.

For your convenience I have ordered the six Traditions by general importance, from least to most, but you should consider them all with great seriousness.

THE TRADITION OF HOSPITALITY. In one city you must present yourself personally to the Prince, in another you leave a note or call at a specific time. In most Ventrue domains, you are expected to present yourself at court, citing your lineage back as many generations as you can. In a Tremere domain, the Regent or Pontifex might demand a portion of your Blood in price for your entrance.

THE TRADITION OF DOMAIN. Domain comes with responsibility as well as authority. Whether your domain is an entire city or a few blocks around your haven, you are the one responsible for enforcing the Traditions and any other laws of your city within it. Whether you add any rules of your own, is up to you and your ability to enforce them.

After I kill I feel all the pressures and tension and rage just dissipate and vanish into the dark. For a brief time I feel not only alive again, but clean.

I am frozen, I cannot change. Over time I only become more of what I already am. You are the only way that I can change myself and become something new. My only hope. My only escape.

THE TRADITION OF ACCOUNTING. In some cities you are held responsible for your childe up until they are presented at court and are recognized as neonates. In other cities, the Prince holds you responsible for the entirety of their existence. This is one of the many reasons you should be careful who you Embrace. In recent years, it has become a common tactic to disavow estranged or treacherous childer in cities where that is allowed. If your city is about to fall to the Anarch horde, the last thing you want is to see your progeny among the enemies - better to disown them early and hope your allies forget you ever had anything to do with them to begin with.

THE TRADITION OF PROGENY. The above should make clear the need for this Tradition, but after the Second Inquisition began, a lot of cities have extended it to include ghouls as well. These years, anyone who knows about our true nature are a liability to the Camarilla.

THE TRADITION OF DESTRUCTION. This Tradition springs from the the old vampiric custom of filicide. Even if it is no longer formally included in our laws, the right of a sire to kill their own childer is still as much a part of our culture as the rule of Princes. Sires can almost always get away with destroying their childer before they have been formally presented at court. The Prince has the right of destruction as they are considered the sire of all their domain, and they can bestow it on others as they please.

It is worth noting that, as human governments get away with violating almost every article of their declaration of human rights and the Geneva convention by declaring certain groups "unlawful enemy combatants," any Cainite who has declared for the Anarchs, or in other ways against our sect, are not protected by the Traditions. If they are not prepared to follow them, they should not get to enjoy them.

THE TRADITION OF THE MASQUERADE. Although often broken, this is the most important Tradition of them all. As long as the Masquerade is intact, we are safe, but shatter it, and it will be the end of us all, not just in the Camarilla, but as a species.

We Must More than Endure

My fellow elders of the Camarilla,

I believe that this conclave is not for glory or profit, and not for war or retribution, but to create out of the materials that our forebears left us—The Camarilla— something which has never existed before. I believe we all use this moment as a pinnacle from we might say to both the old and young of our kind that there is ANOTHER WAY. That we can dedicate ourselves to something other than anguish and travail and eternal suffering of the Damned.

The tragedy today within our sect is a general and universal malaise so long suffered in silence that few of us even realize that we have succumbed. Ours is a problem of the spirit, of the will to find purpose and to fight. For many of us there is only the question: When will they find me? When will they hunt me down. When will I be extinguished?

Because of this terror of our enemies most of us have forgotten the ordinary problems of our immortal condition. We must learn to be alive again. For beyond the fear, many, if not most of us, did have meaning once, and until we find such again, we shall struggle under a curse. We now strive not for glory but from instinct, driven by this fear of defeat in which nothing is lost or gained, of victories without hope and, worst of all, of final death without meaning. We exist as though we stand among our fallen, watching the end of all our kind. As if annihilation had already happened. I decline to accept such an end.

It is far too easy to say that we are immortal simply because we endure: for when the last gong of doom has clanged and the echo faded from the windless red dust of the last mountain crag, even then there will still be one more sound: that of our puny palavering voices, still arguing here in this chamber or one very like it.

I refuse to accept this. I believe that we will not merely endure but that we shall prevail. We are immortal, not because we alone among all creatures have an inexhaustible voice, but because we have an immortal soul, a spirit capable of ferocity, vitality, and mad passion. Our duty is to accept this and to use it. Ours is the race that refuses to die, so let us not now in the eleventh hour embrace the end.

Indeed it is our privilege here now to stand up and remind all the others of our sect of the courage and honor and hope and pride and dedication and sacrifice which have been the glory of our past, and of the Traditions which will guide us from here ■

The Masquerade

The Masquerade is often seen as a law, a principle, the only thing keeping us safe. Yet for me, it has always been a great joy. Maintaining the Masquerade is a beautiful game and I never get tired of playing it. It requires me to think in terms of the mortals, to see the world as they do. I must create a story, a narrative they believe in, something to explain the inexplicable.

I like to enjoy being. It's no secret. Sometimes I have found myself in compromising situations, perhaps splattered with blood, lying next to passed-out celebrities on the floor of a hotel suite as the police break in the doors. What can I say? I have a desire to exist and experience everything.

Here's a little challenge I posed to myself recently: I am at the police station, in a holding cell. I have nothing but a torn cocktail dress. It is two hours to sunrise. Can I make it out alive without using the powers of my Blood, without revealing my true nature?

I spent that day in the arms of a beautiful young policeman who risked everything to save me and take me to his home. What might you have accomplished?

The last two decades have witnessed a revolution in the recording and transfer of information and the monitoring and policing of people. Mortals struggle with fresh paranoia and anxiety over what they can say and do. A sex tape shared with the wrong person, an ill-judged status update from ten years ago, or worse, the messages between you and your married colleague or drug dealer or kinky ex-girlfriend who was really into bestiality can suddenly float to the surface like bloated cadavers. Nothing ever disappears on the internet, they say. But have you noticed how commercials on social media will conform to fit the conversations you have face to face with friends, as long as one of you have a smart phone in their pocket? Have you noticed that people are covering their webcams with duct tape and that you'll get push notifications asking you to share your location when you go somewhere new? Your phone knows where you are, what makes you horny, and who you kinda have a crush on these days. So does your computer — Facebook, Twitter, Amazon, your email service, your browser, that website you went to by mistake for 3,5 seconds a few minutes ago — these nights, even your bloody fridge knows what you're up to. As long as no one's looking for you, you can be who you want to. Who you present to the world. But make one mistake when the search light is on and you'll be revealed as something different. Something you don't want to be or they were never supposed to find out about.

For most Kindred, this world is disconcerting and more dangerous than ever. Time was, all they needed was a fake identity, to avoid locations with CCTV, and to prey on only those who were compliant, discreet, or who would not be missed. These nights, every mortal walks around with at least one camera on their person, and if anything even slightly interesting happens, they'll be sure to share it with the world. Most everyone has a presence online. Even the poorest outsiders in society have a network of friends or associates that notice when the status updates stop. If no humans are watching, the pattern-matching expert systems of the

REPORT #45

BLENDING WITH HUMANITY

Our investigations show that while many post-mortals avoid humans, others make great efforts to blend in with society. This latter type is pernicious, and has proven hard to detect and neutralize. Of note, there are three classifications for the type of blankbody determined to blend in with uninfected humans:

1. Chameleons are the most difficult blankbodies to detect, not only upholding jobs and maintaining families, friends, and professional connections, but keeping all feeding behind closed doors. We believe their weakness will come through their relatives or close associates showing signs of abuse, but differentiating these from those of domestic abuse is an onerous task.

2. Outfits are blankbodies that construct an elaborate disguise and multiple misdirections designed to throw off our investigators. Crucially, they often do not embed themselves within units of mortals, as much as they do their institutions. A blankbody such as this will be difficult to track with a paper trail, but likely possesses few human allies.

3. Paper Masks are among the easiest blankbodies to detect. Often newly created and unsure of how to conceal their natures from close scrutiny, these infected easily falter and make ideal subjects for quick neutralization, as they offer less possible information than their peers.

R243 #45

Second Inquisition will still notice the signature of a drinking gone too far: the silence in the stream.

As diligent as the humans must be to keep up their facades, their carefully cultured online personalities with interesting hobbies and no more than a sufficiently relatable amount of personal problems, we Kindred must remain more so. Be thorough, take advice from those who have succeeded in hiding their nature. It is increasingly imperative to blend in with the kine if you do not want to be revealed for the monster you are.

The Inner Circle has forbidden us from any online presence. But often, being gone is even more conspicuous than being as everyone else. My personal advice: aim to be boring rather than silent. Invent a mask so grey that no one will want to shine that light in your direction, and you'll be able to commit your indiscretions without fear. They'd have to look to see the blood, wouldn't they?

Kindred as Kine

As explained by Roderick Lord, Hellene Courtier of Edinburgh:

We kindred must, in a way, be devoted to mortality. If we lose sight of the temporal nature of life, if we forget about the vagaries of accident, disease, the fragility of the bodies and minds of those we drink from, we risk growing cold and ungentle, leaving bloody wakes behind us on our path toward eternity.

Disappearances draw the eyes of the law and of others who would hurt us, but even if you are the perfect murderer, you should ration your crimes. If we forget that life is sacred, we will lose touch with what it was to be human. And for this reason, we keep close to the kine. We live among them in order to truly live at all.

"I just wish I could meet you during the day for once, yeah? It would be cool to actually take advantage of this weather we've been having, maybe go to the coast..." Nicky's voice trailed off as he noticed Ernesto sitting with his face in his hands. *"Hey, it's okay. I was just saying. Are you okay, baby?"*

Ernesto looked up at his troubled, beautiful boyfriend, the perfect vessel for the past six months. It has been so easy until now, and so much fun. The two of them had lived it up in Porto, but now the inevitable questioning about daylight hours, missed opportunities... Ernesto was genuinely distraught, his eyes rimmed red with blood just desperate to leak free as tears. *"I think I love you, Nicky."* Ernesto smiled sadly. *"But I can't do the daytime. It's not just the work commitments, it's..."* He theatrically looked away, *"I can't risk my family seeing me with a guy. None of them come out where we go at night, but I'm just not ready to out myself to them or anyone else. Just you."*

In a sense, it wasn't a lie. Ernesto didn't want anyone seeing him with Nicky, but more because one night soon, with all this pestering about daytime, he knew he'd lose control and Nicky would be forced into enslavement as a ghoul or childe, or meet a violent end. Until this point, it had been as real a relationship as anything between two mortals. But now, as Ernesto felt it coming to an end, it was time to cash in this long-term investment. He could let Nicky go, but then he'd be throwing away a food source. Despite everything, he couldn't throw away a good meal.

"I love you too, baby." Nicky wrapped his arms around Ernesto, and lifting his chin with forefinger and thumb, went to kiss the vampire on his lips.

A subfaction of the Camarilla call themselves the Kindred-Kine Collective, but anyone not of the group refers to them as parasites, or cleavers if we want to

be polite. These Kindred burrow into mortal families and ingratiate themselves as lovers, long-lost relatives, or lodgers who just won't move. The Parasites believe the best source of food and security is the family unit, or perhaps they get some perverse emotional nourishment from pretending to be human. In either case, they tend to be fanatically protective of their close-knit herd.

As our communities thin and the risks associated with feeding increase, these Kindred are becoming more common. Below follows an account by "the Salamander," a 10th Generation ancilla parasite from Marseille. He rarely attends Elysium or any other gatherings of the court, and when he appears he is shunned. There is something disgusting about his feeding habits. What does he mean to do with this "family" when the children grow up and realize something isn't right?

It's not easy being dead, my friend. A man such as I must go to extreme measures to find company, keep it, and avoid the scrutiny of... well, you know.

We of the Kindred-Kine Collective believe the old ways of stalking the alleys and preying in nightclubs to be... savage, frankly. The Kindred who act like that may consider themselves kin to the wolf or lion, hunting down their meal and darting off into the brush, but we can see them for what they are: Beasts. We emulate the shepherd. It is a better way.

I met my family through a dating website. Not one of those casual hookup sites, but one where a desperate person goes to meet the love of their life. It's all a little sad, my friend, it truly is.

I met my darling Yvette at a bar, we went to see a movie, we did all the things dating couples do. I did not feed from her for months. I wanted her to trust me, to get to know me — to a degree — and to welcome me into her home.

It's an old rumor that some Kindred cannot enter a house without invitation. Someone wise once said "Only enter a prey's home when they invite you in, for then feeding will be child's play." It merely lost the finer details with time.

I was invited to meet her family after four months of dating. Naturally, when I sought out a profile on this site, I looked for a homely middle aged single mother.

I wanted many sources from which to feed, understand? I was soon the kids' favorite "uncle." I made it clear my job had me working until late, but every night I would bring them a gift or tell them a story. They loved me. They still do, though it's mixed with a healthy fear. Children should fear discipline.

Once her children fell for me, Yvette soon invited me to stay with them. Just like that, a new family was born.

Sometimes I use my gifts on them, to make them forget what I'm about to do, or want it more than they otherwise would. Most of the time though, I remind them that it's just the cost of having a father figure. If they want my money, my protection, my love, even, then they owe me a kiss now and then.

At least I give them love. Most mortal fathers are absent, neglectful, and indulge in affairs. I have eyes only for my lovely Yvette, and her beautiful kids.

Paying the Bills

Contribution by Mayumi Shibasaki, corporate powerhouse of the Old Clan:

The one thing they often forget to tell you is how you're expected to pay your rent. There are a few pieces of advice I can give you, and I'll provide them for free:

- Avoid engagement in obvious illegal activity. You're only slightly more capable of deterring the police than a mortal. But if you gotta, petty crime tends to be pretty low-priority in districts that are otherwise busy.
- Do not adopt some all-night job such as shelf-stacker in a supermarket. It may pay your bills (barely) but other Kindred will look down their noses at you, and rightfully so.
- If you have the skills, consider a role in the creative arts. Something where you can produce a piece from your haven and never have to associate with colleagues.
- Invest your money. Investments provide an income, and fund providers don't care who you are or whether you can only come out at night.
- Use your gifts to manipulate one or two of the

kine to sell their companies to you. You may feel a pang of guilt, but you should think about retaining them as high-up employees. They already know how to run the company. You just need the capital to flow up to you.
- Become indebted. This is a last resort, of sorts, but we all have to start somewhere, and thankfully we have an eternity to pay debt back. I don't mean take a loan from a bank, though you could convince a ghoul or blood doll to do so. I mean ask one of your elders for the money you require. You may feel like a slave, but without money you will be cut off from the kine, making feeding more difficult, and of course, you will end up homeless.

A homeless Kindred may be as good as invisible to the kine, but unless close with the Lepers or Ferals they will always struggle for shelter, be vulnerable to inhuman enemies, and also, is that really how you'd want to spend your unlife?

Police Close in on Handbag Gang
By Clément Duval

Haitian National Police report a closing net around the Port-au-Prince Handbag Gang, known for their rife pickpocketing and bag-snatching during the last six months. While initially assumed to be an organized criminal gang or group of coordinated youths, a source within the National Police confirms suspicions that a single perpetrator may be responsible.

According to our source, police Monday morning raided an undisclosed house in Cité Militaire, recording a total of 126 empty items including handbags, wallets, and purses all stacked in one room. The house showed signs of having been recently inhabited by what appears to be a mentally unstable individual, who had been collecting not only bags, but also food items of various kinds, which had been left to decompose all over the house.

As the National Police close in on the perpetrator(s), they warn men and women to avoid Cité Soleil and the surrounding areas, especially at

Metropolitan Police Department

Incident/Investigation Report

Case No: #9009126
Reporting Officer: Heffron, Rachel R. (207)
Approved By: Somers, Alfred (193)
Location: 3715 Macomb St NW, Washington, DC 20016
Persons: WITNESS Pocklington, Andrea
        WITNESS Carluccio, James
Offenders: Unidentified black woman, 25 to 30 years of age, wearing a Washington Wizards vest top, nose piercing.
Property: 2 Amys Italian Restaurant
Narrative:

3715 Macomb St NW is a popular Italian pizzeria, with no reported disturbances prior to this. I was approximately two hours into my shift, patrolling Woodley Park when the radio called in an armed robbery taking place at the 2 Amys Italian Restaurant. I responded and used my sirens.

When I arrived at the location I requested backup immediately, as no other cars had responded.

I exited my vehicle and approached the restaurant. I could see that it was full of standing people, but no one was moving. Suspecting a hostage situation, I radioed again for backup, and called the restaurant's phone number to see if anyone was capable of responding.

As the phone rang, the people broke from their poses, some sitting down, others running for the door, while a waiter answered the phone.

Ascertaining it wasn't a hostage situation, I entered the restaurant to be told by 12 patrons that they had no memory of the last 30 minutes to an hour. Only two witnesses, Andrea Pocklington and proprietor James Carluccio, spoke about the suspect who reportedly held the restaurant patrons at gunpoint while they emptied their possessions into a bag, and then commanded them to forget what had just taken place.

Witness Andrea Pocklington professes fear of meeting this "hypnotist" again while James Carluccio has volunteered with a detailed witness account. Recommend detectives call upon him tomorrow to get more information.

"You are what you eat", or, you are what you rub yourself against in the early morning hours, lick on in a darkened corner, and seek to forget.

night. The police have not yet confirmed whether the murder of Adele Baptiste in Cité Soleil is connected to the Handbag Gang, but eyewitness accounts describe a mugging gone wrong, leading to the stabbing of the 32-year-old.

Victims of the Handbag Gang describe the perpetrator(s) as being unusually fast on their feet, some describing a "disappearing act" where the thief steals the bag in a crowded place and promptly vanishes. These reports have received no comment from the police.

Keeping up with Culture

Look Alive, Sweetness

by Jeanette Voerman, Malkavian Nightclub Proprietor, Los Angeles

I see you're new here, it's written all over your skin in cold, blue letters. They wriggle deliciously, like maggots. You might wanna deal with that, darling. Sooner or later someone will notice that you just don't look the part. But don't you worry. I'll give you a few tips and tricks. If you're good, I might even follow up with a personal demonstration...

Blending in with the kine isn't just about pushing blood to the right parts of the body... though that can be very fun... You've also gotta know how to act like them.

Something a lot of licks fail to get is they can't just hover around kine and take in trends and culture through their skin. To get ahead of the curve, you gotta diversify your social crowds. You can't keep preying on the same body, no matter how good it tastes. Once a doll starts to get boring, you move on! You move to the next scene and ingratiate yourself. That means new rules, new look, new opinions! Basically, you get to reinvent yourself every time you switch to a new scene, like a paper doll with clip-on suits and dresses.

Perhaps don't want to change for your surroundings. But if you don't, you run a real risk of growing old. Not in body, but when you hang with kids 80 years younger than yourself, and you're just sitting there smiling and nodding while they talk about their passions, you've stopped being relevant. No one wants to hear about how you met John Lennon before he died.

No, if you want to blend in and make new buddies, you're going to have to do a little research. It used to be as simple as watching MTV all night. Next night you'd go to a club and recite your favorite singers and bands, and woo! You'd be off to the races. Now there's more nuance and greater breadth of material. Anyone can look up what's trending online. Do that! Don't restrict yourself to one channel or one mortal source.

And you know something? It's better if you're genuine. Actually find something you appreciate. There's so much music out there and so many cool movies and video games. Just because nightclubs are a good place to hunt, you don't have to be a clubber. If you're a geek, play a few games and go to a LAN party, if those things still run. We used to have a room for them in Asylum, until trade dried up. If you're a cinema buff, hang out at movie theatres. If you love

PHILIPPE PARRENO – À L'INTÉRIEUR
01.03-14.04.18

Exhibition opening at MAMCO

I N V I T A T I O N   O N L Y

Monsieur/Madame,
At the request of the artist himself, you are hereby invited to attend the vernissage of our spring exhibition Philippe Parreno – à l'intérieur. The event will begin on Wednesday 28 February, precisely at the stroke of sunset at 18h20.

You have been invited due to your appreciation of the arts. We hope very much you will please us with your company.
As with the art of M. Parreno, the dress code is open and interpretive. Wine and coffee will be served to all guests.

Warmest regards,

MAMCO,
Genève

HAVE YOU SEEN THIS? THIS IS A GOLDEN TICKET TO MEET WITH THE MOST INFLUENTIAL OF THE ROSES OF EUROPE! MAKE SURE THE OTHERS GET ONE. IT'S TIME WE GO SOAK UP A LITTLE MODERN CULTURE.

reading, join one of those wino book clubs and chit chat about Paul Auster in between sips!

It's not rocket science, dummy. If you can't manage this, you'll end up like another dusty Blue Blood. Robotic, stiff, and cold. Only one of those is a good thing.

The Masquerade as a Weapon

The Masquerade is not just about hiding. It's about dancing. Specifically, about leading your partner. It's control. It's influence. It's guidance.

As revealed by Stephen Thunderhorse, Ventrue Senator of Providence:

It's never as simple as enslaving people as ghouls. Our vitae only stretches so far, and you'll never be able to dose every officer in a police precinct, every investigative journalist, and everyone who looks at you like you're a monster. Subtlety is required. That and patience. Our gifts help a great deal, but are unreliable, and excessive use of them is a guaranteed way to break the Masquerade.

Instead of working against the Masquerade you must use it to your advantage. First, it is imperative you find a mortal useful and trustworthy enough to risk showing them a little of your hand. You cannot use your circumstances to openly manipulate an entire organization, but you can pull the strings of select individuals. To make the Masquerade work in your favor, you'll need to divulge a little of your nature.

Here are my suggestions:

- Find out what your prospective target wants and needs. Come to them as a friend and benefactor.
- Confess a little of your power. Focus on the aspects that are only a little beyond what is normal: improved mental and physical capacities, a longer life, a resistance to illness. Whatever their need, underline the aspect that would solve it. Do not mention the downsides.
- They'll want to know more. Tell them you can get them the same abilities. Ask for nothing in return at this point.

- You dose them in the form of vitae secreted into some other medium: capsules, drink, a rare but questionable delicacy. You tell them they'll probably require a few more doses before they feel any difference.
- Be their friend. Talk through the changes with them.
- Once they've imbibed a few doses, they'll not only inherit some of your abilities, they'll be wanting more. The trust you've built will have more effect than simply hypnotizing someone or feeding them the Blood with none of the social massage. You'll have them considering you a friend, not a drug supplier. This is important. It's important the trust goes both ways.
- Now you ask for a favor, not too outlandish in nature. They'll rush to appease you. It's that simple. They're your friend, remember? They'll want to please you, and they won't connect it to the craving, at least not at first.
- Now you can tease them with a dose whenever they do as you ask, but lace the feeding with other benefits, such as social status, untraceable cash bonuses, and protection for their family.

I hope you can see how this tactic is so beneficial. Whether you control the chief cashier in a casino, the capo of a mafia crew, or a doctor at the blood bank,

you'll now have a servant who believes they're in on the secret. They'll want to maintain the Masquerade too, if it means they'll continue to benefit from your companionship and wonder drug.

⬩⬩⬩◈⬩⬩⬩

OCTOBER 2017, THE CALLEVA ARMS, SILCHESTER, BRITISH ISLES

I've found recently that if you use the Masquerade effectively, it can be a weapon against those bastards in the Second Inquisition. They're undoubtedly wise to our age-old tricks of using kine as cover, staying away from cameras, and so on. They must now be looking for signs also in the absence of the supernatural, as I suspect they've taken out the most flagrant abusers of the Masquerade.

This is where as a society we can use this Tradition to our advantage. We must be prepared to layer our subterfuge in code languages, introduce urban legends to popular folklore, and plan deliberate Masquerade breaches in select locations. The key in all of the above are falsehoods. The code languages we let slip are all nonsense. The urban legends are just that, but hold sufficient grains of truth to send the Inquisition in a tizzy. The Masquerade breaches we intentionally cause will be to lure the Inquisition into traps, as Sarrasine did in Sydney, or simply be red herrings, drawing them away from our real locations..

Every piece of misdirection we plant ties up Inquisition resources and time. We have both of these things in abundance. They will disappear with changing governments and the toll of age, but we will not.

We should not view the Masquerade as just some shield to hide behind while we wait to be destroyed, but as a weapon of innuendo, rumours, and lies.

⬩⬩⬩◈⬩⬩⬩

Singh eyed the men and women sat around him in the auditorium. A professor of some kind stood on stage, flicking between slides discussing "blankbodies" and "haemovores." Despite the obvious connotations, none of the presentation material referred to vampires, and the Inquisition clearly disparaged the term "Kindred."

As a thin-blood in a room of hunters, Singh felt more nervous than he had the first night he discovered he was now a blood-sucking monster.

"As you can see from this footage, the stake-to-the-heart technique is only sufficient for paralyzing a blankbody." The professor gestured with a long stick to the victim on-screen. "Their body clearly treats the heart like an operating system of some kind. The upcoming minute or so will show what happens when the heart is removed."

Singh raised a hand, as he had been instructed to do. "Excuse me. Is this demonstration being carried out at the Baltimore facility?"

The professor peered into the crowd, spotting the thin-blood. "No, this footage is from our laboratory in Naples. Some of you will have attended lessons there in recent months."

Singh nodded, and stayed silent for the remainder of the demonstration. Somehow, the Inquisition never picked up on his undead state during the entire briefing. Was it their arrogance, the thinness of his blood, or were they deliberately feeding him this intelligence?

He departed the theatre with a few quiet nods and handshakes before grabbing a taxi and getting the hell out of there. As the taxi drove him to the airport, he sent a message to all the contacts in his phone. FACILITY CONFIRMED IN NAPLES. WE ARE HELD THERE FOR TREATMENT. BURN IT.

Singh dropped the phone from the car window as it sped into the night.

THE *gehenna* WAR

"Elysium is empty of elders, as if a plague had swept over the city, and we ancillae now rule Lisbon as Prince pretenders. Where they have gone no one knows, but we know better than to ask."

– AFONSO ZARCO

This is an exciting time to join the Camarilla. Your abandonment is not unique, my childe, although my fate is perhaps more singular than that of so many other elder Kindred. We all feel the call.

I wished you to have a better understanding of what is going on in the Middle East, so I requested the following documents from a friend who is close to the Ventrue Justicar. A darling that he is, he naturally complied.

These are the surviving diary entries of a recently appointed Ventrue Archon called Hassan Shadid, unfortunately since disappeared.

14.7.2017 - BAGHDAD

I'm back in Baghdad for the first time in twelve years. I left my home in 2005 as a refugee and now I'm back as one of the Kindred. The streets are still familiar but it feels like I was here a century ago. So much has happened. When I escaped, I made the journey to Istanbul, Italy and finally France with my brother. It took us five months. I got lucky in Paris, became a translator and got hired by a company I later realized was a Camarilla front.

The court of Francois Villon needed Kindred who spoke Arabic to facilitate coming dealings with the Ashirra, so they transformed me into a monster. It involved an interview, and for a long time I imagined I was being considered for a very strange corporate position.

When I left Baghdad, my mother said to me: "Don't look back. Make a life for yourself and be happy. If God wills it, we'll join you." I don't think becoming a Ventrue neonate was quite what she meant.

I've been commissioned to make a report of the Gehenna War by Justicar Lucinde and given all the necessary resources to see what's happening on the ground. I'll collect these findings in this diary and use it to compose my final report.

Before I get to work, it's time for the Parisian Success Story to make his grand homecoming.

15.7.2018 - BAGHDAD

I saw my mother, my father, my cousins and so many more people last night, for the first time in many, many years. It was a sad affair for me, although I did my best to conceal my feelings. My sire told me that being a vampire means that eventually all your mortal attachments wither and die under the pressure of time, but I didn't expect it to happen so fast. They all seemed so old, worn down by the war.

One of my cousins took me to see our old house, where we lived before it was destroyed by an American rocket. Almost nothing remained, just a few stones. One of the neighbors came to talk to us, a man I vaguely remembered from my childhood. He gave me a bunch of pages from Das Kapital. My father had been a communist in his youth, and he never threw out the books. When I was a child learning to read, I sneaked to the box where he hid them, seduced by forbidden lore.

The man said he'd found the pages in the rubble and kept them for me in case I wanted a memento.

Perhaps it's better to focus on the task at hand. So, to recap:

The Gehenna War is a conflict between the Sabbat and the Camarilla, fought in the Middle East. The Sabbat are motivated by religious fanaticism, seeking to unearth the graves of the purported Antediluvians, mythical clan founders they seek to destroy. While their goal is imaginary, the process of striving towards it makes them extremely dangerous.

The Camarilla's goal is to contain the Sabbat and protect the graves of ancient Kindred in torpor all around the region. It would be easy for the Sabbat to mistake a methuselah for an Antediluvian, and killing such an ancient being would be a serious loss not only for the Camarilla but all Kindred. Nobody can rival the methuselahs for their knowledge of our shared origins.

Further, the Sabbat doesn't care about the Masquerade, especially when they're fulfilling their eschatological mission. Because of this, it's up to the Camarilla to fulfill its ancient purpose of keeping order in the world and maintain the Masquerade.

All of this is very clear. However, there's another aspect to this that I don't quite understand yet, called the Beckoning. After all, I haven't been Kindred for very long, but even I know that traveling to a war zone to fight the Sabbat is very strange behavior for Camarilla elders famous for being extremely careful with their personal safety.

My plan is to go around the different sectors of the Gehenna War and meet the people who run the war for the Camarilla. But before I can do that, I need to make contact with our allies in the Ashirra.

16.7.2018 - BAGHDAD

She was pretty intimidating, although I don't think she'd been Kindred much longer than I have. She had that old school educated Arabic dignity, the precise British accent, ramrod posture. Saida Jawad was the official Ashirra liaison assigned to assist me on my mission and she seemed determined to catch me unprepared at every turn.

That was how we met: I was in the hotel bar, scoping prey because I was hungry. She and her assistant approached me, introducing themselves just as I was about to make a play for the bartender. It became even more embarrassing when she said they had blood for me at the reception she invited me to.

I think I met over a dozen of Ashirra dignitaries at that reception, held in a palace that had somehow survived the American destruction of the city. I made notes about them and will have to transcribe those later.

Saida is a native Iraqi of Clan Malkavian, or Bay't Majnoon as they're called here.

Here's the thing about the Ashirra: Theoretically they're defined as the community of all Muslim Kindred. If you follow the Prophet and suck blood, you're Ashirra. This was definitely the working definition I learned in Paris and dozens of ethnic French Camarilla Kindred kept reminding me of it. To them, I was a member of a foreign sect.

Turns out this definition only goes so far. When I come to Baghdad as the official Camarilla representative, I'm most assuredly not treated as one of the Ashirra, no matter what my faith is.

I'm still a little skeptical of the official Ashirra story. They're a major sect controlling much of North Africa and the Middle East, a counterpart to the Camarilla conceived as a Kindred version of the Muslim community of faith. Supposedly their leader, a Lasombran ancient called Suleiman ibn Abdullah was brought into the faith by Muhammad the Prophet himself. Huge if true, as they say on the internet.

On the ground, the Ashirra seems to have even a stronger focus on following the dictates of the elders than the Camarilla does, if you look beyond the religious and moral rhetoric. Some of the Ashirra I've met seem genuinely to try to cling to a moral sense of who they are, while others resemble Saudi royalty in their infinite self-regard.

For my work, tonight was very productive. Saida briefed me on the Ashirra side of things and I'll soon meet some of the Camarilla dignitaries recently arrived in the city.

One more thing: I'm a fool for not grasping this earlier but I'm an Archon. I was so intimidated when the established Archons of the Justicar briefed me, I didn't realize I had joined their ranks. I just couldn't believe that someone like me could be one of them. I only accepted it when the Ashirra kept referring to me as such.

20.7.2018 - BAGHDAD

I saw something terrifying tonight that I'm still struggling to understand. Not dangerous, at least not to me. But terrifying nevertheless.

It started at the hotel soon after I woke up. Saida was there to see me. She's helped us a lot these last few nights. Her knowledge of the city is encyclopedic and she's very diligent about facts.

I didn't think much of following her when she said she had something related to the Gehenna War that I should see. We did the same last night, and the night before. This time we drove to the outskirts of the city, to the direction of the road to Basra. The ruins of an old hotel were still there, a surprisingly big edifice the color of the desert. Some of the floors had collapsed but you could climb all the way to the top.

I didn't realize why we left the cars a kilometer away and had to sneak until I noticed the lights of the American military outpost on the other side of the highway, down a side road.

The complete picture dawned on me only when we reached the roof. It was almost as if a rich sheikh had decided to host a picnic among the rubble. There were deck chairs, servants bringing blood, binoculars for those without sufficient Kindred senses.

The Americans had taken over a former government building. It looked like they had fifty people there, soldiers and staff, with Humvees and other equipment. They had been there for a while, probably so they could control the road.

There were five people on the roof apart from the servants, all Kindred. I recognized a few from among the local Ashirra. They bade me warm welcome, assuring me that I would be in for a treat. The Sabbat had infested this particular military installation, using it to quickly establish control over possible gravesites. They had a couple of veterans and fifteen recently Embraced vampires, all drawn from the U.S. military. I'd heard the Sabbat liked to use the Americans because many of them had been Americans in life and because the military's freedom of movement and ability to project force made things easier.

I got scared, obviously. This was the first real sign of the Gehenna War I'd seen and Saida sprung it on me completely by surprise. We were a couple hundred meters from a Sabbat-infested military installation, sipping blood from little glasses with paper umbrellas in them. It was clear some of the Ashirra had done this before, making the war into entertainment.

It was at this point that I noticed the woman. At first she looked like a nobody, just a slight, modestly dressed lady sitting apart from the others, checking her mobile phone. She stood up and something in her posture changed. She became more present. A servant appeared, a deferential young man who helped her take off the outer layers of her clothing. Underneath, she was wearing simple military black.

Everybody was watching her prepare. She didn't seem to care. "What are we using tonight?" the woman asked, the first words I heard her speak. Her Arabic was old-fashioned, like that of a religious scholar.

"A knitting needle", the young man said, presenting her with the needle. She took it and regarded it for a moment.

"What are they doing?" I whispered to Saida.

"Whenever the enemy is too weak to provide a real challenge, she asks her servant to choose a bad weapon," Saida whispered back, clearly excited by what was happening.

"She's going to attack a U.S. military base with a knitting needle?"

Saida gave a little laugh. "That's Fatima al-Faqadi, the Hand of Vengeance."

I had heard of her. She had quite the reputation: She was a thousand years old, she was one of the premier assassins of the Children of Haqim and she'd recently killed the famous Sabbat Archbishop Ambrosio Moncada. And now I was in her presence, just like that.

Fatima walked right past me to the edge of the roof and regarded the American base. She was fingering the needle. In her hand it suddenly started to seem sinister and threatening. "What are the rules?" she asked.

The servant had crept behind her. "The infestation is complete. The Sabbat has Embraced or Blood Bound everyone at the base. Kill all except the prisoners."

Fatima al-Faqadi nodded and vanished. All the Ashirra rushed to the edge of the roof to watch the show.

It's hard to describe what followed. In a sense, I

could see very little. It always seemed like my binoculars were focused in the wrong place. I just saw bodies starting to appear, falling one by one. There was never an alarm. I started to feel sick when it hit me that I wasn't watching a fight but mass murder. At one point, my binoculars were pointed exactly in the right place and I saw Fatima punch the knitting needle through the left eye of a soldier. She gave it a little swish after it had penetrated his brain.

The whole thing took less than ten minutes. Later, we went down to look at the carnage. There had been a soldier watching the driveway to the building. It looked as if the needle had gone through his throat and Fatima had used it to drag his body into a bush to avoid being seen.

I'd never seen a Sabbat hideout in my life. I'd heard horror stories, but they don't really prepare you. The important thing to understand is that the Sabbat doesn't really care about the Masquerade and they don't care about the long-term. They took over the base because they wanted to use it for a week or two, not more. They didn't care about what would happen after that. They'd be long gone, leaving psychotic blood addicts and deranged, traumatized fledglings in their wake.

As I explored the building, I found more and more signs of horrifying moral collapse. There were bodies lying in the basement, Iraqi men, women and children, some drained of blood and others not. The soldiers looked sloppy and careless, physically filthy as if they had forgotten how to take care of themselves. Some of them had old gunshot wounds that had gone untreated for a long time.

Fatima was not the first bad thing to happen to these people. The Sabbat had destroyed them first, in spirit if not body.

I had to get out, and found Fatima leaning against the door of an American Humvee, fiddling with her phone. She looked up at me and said: "The mortals are so inventive. This is a wonderful little toy."

For a second, the genuine delight in her face made her look like a human again.

Saida was waiting for me with a car and a driver. "How are you going to explain all these dead soldiers? This is a Masquerade breach for sure," I asked her,

sounding shrill even to my own ears. I've seen war but never something like this.

"You have your own agents with the Americans, don't you?" Saida asked. "We're partners in this, you and I. We took out a Sabbat base, you do the cleanup."

The message was clear. The Camarilla might come to the Middle East to wage war against the Sabbat, but this was still Ashirra territory. If we forgot that, they would bring out the knitting needle.

27.7.2018 - RAMALLAH

Saida told me that if I wanted to go to Israel and Palestine, the pro tip was to avoid Jerusalem and stay on the West Bank. Apparently, Jerusalem attracts crazies in our world even more strongly than with the mortals. The true fanatics go directly to Jerusalem while the milder fanatics prefer the better havens and excellent hunting of Tel Aviv.

I followed Saida's advice in accommodations but her contact in Ramallah was a bust. I was stood up, but I wasn't alone for long. I was sitting in a cafe thinking whether I should seek further instructions or continue on my own when an intense-looking, wiry young woman sat down across from me. "We don't get a lot of new licks this side of the Wall," she said. "Who are you?"

A rough start, but after I explained what I was doing we started to get along pretty well. She was a local Ashirra called Leila Hamidi, a dissident if I understood her hints correctly. She dressed like a motorcycle courier and seemed to know everybody, but that might have been an act to make me feel even more of an outsider. I'm not sure of her clan but it might be Lasombra or Qabilat al-Khayal. Not many of them in Paris, but not that rare in these parts.

Leila had strong opinions about Jerusalem. She said that in there, the Gehenna War had been going on for a long time, with deranged foreign Kindred arriving on a seemingly nightly basis to pursue their inscrutable goals. The local Kindred population was divided sharply into the young Ashirra, who despised these pilgrims, and the foreigners, who were often too old and powerful to challenge.

Now that the Gehenna War is going strong across the region, all the worst nutjobs apparently come here, determined to fight their ancient religious battles. At least according to Leila. I'm not sure she's a neutral source.

1.8.2018 - JERUSALEM

I think Leila was right. I was contacted by another Archon and instructed to meet with a few people described as "personal friends of the Justicar." I was told they could give me an accurate depiction of the situation on the ground as they were all experienced masters of the ancient machinations of the elders. I would have the rare benefit of listening to the wisdom of these august beings firsthand.

The place: a vast, modernist penthouse apartment with a view over the Old City of Jerusalem.

Present: six elders called here by the Beckoning (so I assume). I calculated their average age at over 700 years.

As you might expect, I answered their questions but otherwise kept silent. If I learned one thing in Paris, it was not to interrupt these beings. So what kind of things do you learn when listening to Princes and Primogen, the great and the good of the Camarilla? Here's a sample:

"...the divine mandate of Christendom..."

"This modern fad for globalism will surely pass."

"The Anarch rabble should be grateful to benefit from our wisdom."

"The problem with the Sabbat is that they don't listen to their elders. Why, after the Convention of Thorns I had a few good friends go over to that side of the divide..."

"The humans should go back to the rule of kings. These new methods are too confusing."

"...the ancient wisdom of the Malkavians..."

If I got this right, they believe some kind of an old Malkavian resides within Jerusalem and the Sabbat are here specifically to destroy it. The way these elders talk about the methuselahs they assume lie sleeping all over the Middle East, it almost sounds like they're a little lost themselves. Many of them don't really know why they were Embraced all those centuries ago, so perhaps they hope that if these methuselahs rise, they can get answers too.

I'm starting to grasp a simple fact about the Gehenna War. Elders, methuselahs and even ancillae from Europe, the Americas and elsewhere congregate in the Middle East. That means that the Middle East now has a preposterous concentration of old vampires.

11.9.2017 - DAMASCUS

From a mortal perspective, the Gehenna War is extremely confusing. The war doesn't map very well onto the human conflicts that plague this area. It would be much easier if we could simply say that the Camarilla supports the regime of President Assad in Syria and the Sabbat is aligned with ISIS. Instead, there's a mysterious web of influence which seems to criss cross across all possible mortal lines of allegiance. The Camarilla, meaning our side, has influence with the Syrian government but also many of the rebel groups. We have our fingers deep in the machine of the U.S. military, but so does the Sabbat and sometimes even the Ashirra.

From a mortal perspective, this is almost impossible to understand. The clue is to see the mortal groups and institutions only as tools Kindred use to work towards their own goals, petty or profound. How petty, I learned when I was given the task of escorting my sire, Mathilde de Tourdonnet, through some of the worst areas of the civil war these last few days.

Mathilde hasn't been a bad sire to me, but she's amazingly self-centered. She's a favorite grandchilde of Hardestadt himself, giving her enormous unearned status in the Camarilla. Because she's in favor with the system, it extends strange privileges to her.

So how does a grandchilde of Hardestadt arrive in Damascus? By private jet, with an entourage of twenty servants, bodyguards and assistants. On the ground, a Russian mercenary company provided her with a security detail of fifty soldiers. I and my Ashirra contacts may have provided the itinerary, but when it came to travel we were just along for the ride.

It felt strange to see such power and privilege in a war zone. I thought the Camarilla had provided me with ample resources for my mission, but not on this scale. Although, I have gotten used to having a jet too. The ordinary strata of Camarilla Kindred are all suffering under the threat of the Second Inquisition. Travel is hard and dangerous, and airports should be avoided at all costs because of the security infrastructure in place.

Thing is, there's another group in the world who regularly bypass such arrangements, apart from vampires: the super rich. The private jet of a billionaire doesn't really get subjected to any kind of stringent security measures, and the most privileged in the Camarilla benefit from this. Most suffer, but those of us who have been granted access to the system at the billionaire level can still fly. Apparently there's not many of us, and I'm amazed I'm in this group, even for the duration of this single mission.

Mathilde seemed like a queen traveling with her entourage. I never quite parsed out if the Russians who escorted us knew we were Kindred or not, but they did a much better job of dealing with security issues than I could ever have. A few months ago, the only

war zone I'd seen was the one in Iraq I escaped from as a mortal. Now, I'm apparently an expert.

So why did the august grandchilde of Hardestadt wish to come to Syria? Why did she demand that we parade through some of the worst, hardest hit, most miserable areas in the country?

I never got a straight answer, but this is what I came up with: She did it for entertainment and power. The Beckoning is said to call the oldest and most powerful of our kind, so she felt she had to at least take a few selfies next to bombed out buildings to suggest that she might have felt the call too.

And of course, the Gehenna War is a big subject of discussion in the Camarilla and the Syrian war among the mortals. She was curious to see what it was really like. The worst was when she wanted to hunt. She told me she had never hunted in a war zone before.

I've seen a lot of terrible things. Most of the Kindred I've met have been monsters of one type or another. But that really got to me, going to all that trouble to inflict herself onto the most miserable people this Earth has to offer. I mean, I hunt too and I have no illusions about what we are, but come on... Making a war zone into your entertainment playground. I guess that's the Camarilla for you.

19.9.2017 - KABUL

I'm still alive, against all odds. If you want to find a place where the Gehenna War has metastasized into a bizarre landscape of adventurers, spies, betrayals and long-suffering locals, this is it. At times, I didn't know if I was meeting with a Camarilla agent pretending to be a Sabbat agent or the other way around. For a while, it almost felt like a game, driving from one armed compound to the next, meeting people whose goals and plans seemed utterly impenetrable.

"Belief in a cruel and merciless Caine creates a cruel and merciless Cainite."

After Syria I felt I could deal with anything. This hubris proved to be dangerous. It was an hour before sunrise. We were planning the next night's meetings at the aid workers' camp where we had our haven on the outskirts of the city.

Someone banged on the door and shouted in Pashto. I'd heard about these night visits from the aid workers: armed gangs kidnapping people, killing them, holding them for ransom.

I opened the door. There were two people, a Pashtun man and a Western woman with all-black eyes. Kindred both. The woman said: "Don't worry, we're not going to harm you." The guards we'd posted on the courtyard were lying in distended heaps of flesh and military uniform.

This is stupid of me, but I never really expected to be face to face with the Sabbat. Somehow I always thought the Camarilla and the Ashirra would protect me.

I turned around and ran, stumbling over the tables and chairs in a panic. I could see black shapes stretching across the floor towards my assistants, blood spraying everywhere, their screams and pain another lesson in what happens to people who serve our kind.

"Fine. Let's make sport of it," the woman's voice said behind me, half annoyed and half amused.

I remembered nothing of the building's layout. The security people who were supposed to get me to safety were gurgling and bleeding.

"You can't escape me. There are shadows wherever you go," the woman called.

Suddenly something yanked me up by shirt collar, through a hole in the ceiling and onto the floor above. Fatima al-Faqadi whispered: "Let's see if we can keep you alive, little vampire."

I was so flabbergasted at her sudden appearance that I just sat there staring. Last time I saw her, she was ripping the Sabbat apart in Baghdad. Now she was here, with no explanation.

"Wait ninety seconds, take the ladder to the roof. I will join you," Fatima said and slipped down the hole.

"Fatima, is that you? What a happy coincidence." The Sabbat woman sounded like she was snarking at someone at a cocktail party. "I've always been a big fan of yours. Love all the killing you're doing. Perhaps we should..."

Something interrupted the woman's voice, followed by a burst of assault rifle fire. I had an urge to poke my head down the hole to see what was happening but then remembered Fatima's instructions. I waited a moment, listening to the sounds of the fight, then ascended to the roof. My head poked up from the hatch just in time to see a man in a UN Peacekeeper's uniform jump down from the roof. Probably Sabbat backup, there to intercept anyone trying to escape.

We'd had a guard on the roof too, but he was dead, impaled onto a satellite antenna.

Standing on that roof, I saw the first light of the morning on the horizon. I was in Kabul, a city I didn't know at all, hunted by the Sabbat, with all my people dead around me.

It didn't look good.

Then Fatima appeared out of nowhere and tackled me off the roof.

We spent two nights hiding in a slum shack the size of a garden shed. Sometimes the local kine

checked in on us and Fatima gave them money. She
was surprisingly kind.

3.10.2017 - BAGHDAD

This mission is driving me insane. I thought the hard
part would have been coming back to Baghdad, the
city I escaped with considerable effort. Or maybe
seeing all the suffering caused by war, dictators, the
endless supply of Western weapons, climate change,
American drone attacks and all the other evils killing
us.

And sure, those things have been hard. But the
worst is having to sit in these air-conditioned rooms
listening to the elders of the Camarilla and the Ashirra
expound on how the real tragedy of the Kindred is
that all the good they do for humanity must remain
secret.

We're not secret benefactors. We're monsters.

I met Fatima al-Faqadi again and she said something about a tomb that stuck in my mind. I'm starting
to think she's the only ally I have. I finally asked her
why she saved me in Afghanistan, and she told me
she'd been shadowing me throughout my entire trip.
She said it gave her something to do after she was cast
out from the Children of Haqim.

5.10.2017 - BAGHDAD

The war between the Camarilla and the Sabbat will
only hurt more people. They will incite the mortals to
fight among each other and kill to sate the bloodlust
arising from each fight.

I've finally understood where the solution to all
this lies: in the very tombs of the ancients the sects are
warring over. Fatima told me that if I was really ready
to embrace the wisdom of the methuselahs, she would
show me something she'd never shown anyone before.

I told her I was ready.

We drove for hours into the desert, swerving
between the eroding craters created by a decade of
bombing. Finally we came to a ruin in the middle of
nowhere and Fatima told me to stop. I'd left my assistants and bodyguards behind, so it was just the two
of us.

Calling it a ruin is an exaggeration. It was just a
little piece of ancient wall, sticking out of the ground.

Fatima offered me a shovel and told me where to dig, waiting by the car while I spent a few hours unearthing a stone slab hidden under the sand. Finally she stopped me and lifted the slab with one hand, turning it enough to reveal a hole leading underground.

Once we had descended the stairs I started to grasp the enormity of the underground structure we were entering. The writing on the walls was indecipherable to me, pictograms of mysterious rites an archeologist would give their life to see.

As Fatima walked behind me, something in her changed. I realized that before this moment I'd only seen what she wanted me to see. The humanity I'd ascribed to her had been a lie. She wasn't like me. I was descending towards one ancient monster, in the company of another.

"I can't come any further," Fatima said. "You must go the rest of the way alone."

I'm giving her these last notes, with instructions to leave them with my assistant at the hotel in case I don't come back.

The Sabbat said this was the Gehenna War. The last crusade. And so it must seem to the thousands of Cainites finding themselves in the midst of it as parasites or almost-defenseless spectators forced to watch from up-close. Fangs and fast reflexes cannot protect even elders against the sudden rains of fiery projectiles falling day and night. Hoary unaging flesh melts away in the heat of white phosphorus bombs.

When the towers fell and the Sabbat went East with the Americans, we figured they were crazy and took their cities. But then the elders started to follow them, proclaiming to be summoned by the ancients or simply disappearing. And the Anarchs joined the struggle for Kurdistan and the uprisings in Egypt, Libya, and Syria, supporting the kine against their oppressors or trying to eliminate their Camarilla enemies in the confusion of it all.

The eldest and strongest of our kind have all been drawn into this hellfire-filled fog of war. Who knows what other powers are hiding there? The corpses of our distant Cainite history reawakened? Or only Sabbat demons embedded deep within human military units,

wearing the uniforms of Navy Seals or the face-covering keffiyeh of local guerrillas? Little information is carried back to us, the abandoned descendents in the West. Still they want us to join.

Lately some of the twisted and soul-tortured veterans of the war have come crawling home. They appear as wild-eyed broken monsters who stalk their own without knowing why or as determined heroes, eager to feed the machine of the Last War by bringing other Kindred to their cause and into their personal hell. Back to the Middle East. Back to where it all began ■

It's always tragic when a young, motivated member of the Camarilla disappears into the machinations of ancient monsters. Fortunately Hassan Shadid had an assistant who was able to provide the Justicar with these notes, so the mission wasn't wasted.

The unfortunate reality of war is that when a neonate undertakes a dangerous task, it may prove fatal. He died for a good cause, the cause of knowledge and understanding.

One last thing: You are wondering about the Beckoning. I'm experiencing it myself, so I can describe it for you. I feel an urge to go to the Middle East. However, it is difficult to me to analyze this feeling. Is this a supernatural compulsion or merely a symptom of the ennui so many my age feel?

I cannot say. That is the problem with being a pawn of beings even older and more powerful than you are: You don't always realize it's happening.

Of course, in my case it's not a common urge to join the war effort but something far more important to our sect and cause.

THE *second* INQUISITION

I realize we didn't actually spend much time together even as I Embraced you and brought you into the Camarilla. You don't know me beyond what I did to you and from these little notes I have left you. Maybe you think me a flippant monster toying with matters of life and death.

Well, when it comes to the Second Inquisition, I am not playing games. They are terrifying and you must take them seriously. Otherwise, you really will die.

I want you to appreciate these words. I have lost many dear friends to the Inquisition and almost died myself. Sometimes we forget the advantage the Masquerade gives us over the mortals. We forget how weak they are made by their ignorance. Once they learn the truth, they are not so weak.

I do not like to talk about this, but I made it out of London when the Second Inquisition started its assault. I was in the haven of a friend when the doors were bashed in. There was sunlight everywhere, my friend collapsing into dust as he tried to claw his way to safety. I was burned badly, and from my wounds they could easily tell what I was. Embarrassingly, I was saved only by my speed and knowledge of the London sewer network. I used to live there, at one point, and the sewers have a lot of history.

After sundown, I made my way to the airport with a view to borrowing Lady Anne's private jet, but they had seized that too. The same happened to me at countless other havens. All destroyed or full of terrifying kine. I soon realized it was even difficult to walk the streets, the damnable cameras the mortals put everywhere detecting me when I tried.

I had to fall back to my oldest tricks. I pretended to be an illegal Russian immigrant on the run from the authorities, and a sweet young man drove me out of the city in the trunk of his car. I was so overcome with gratitude, I gave him a ring I'd had in my possession for two centuries.

The Second Inquisition killed the high and mighty of London Kindred society. They made Victoria Ash run like a dog. If you have a burning desire to fight them, fight like a vampire. Unfairly, and from far away.

*By Manfred Vaughn,
Steward of Arms*

Our ancient traditions, of control and obedience and especially of Masquerade, are our greatest shield against the greatest danger facing us in centuries: a new war of human against Kindred, of sheepdogs against wolves. This Second Inquisition pits our old enemies in the Vatican, the secret police and shadow warriors of a dozen countries, and hunter cells in a dozen more, against not just the Camarilla but against all of our kind. They go to war against us in the guise of their War on Terror, concealing their actions from their own masters in the name of "preventing panic" and "operational security." Already the Second Inquisition has cost us dearly, in Vienna and London and in nameless sunlit rooms guarded by faceless seneschals. Our resources drained, our movements hampered, we must understand our enemies, blunt their attacks, and then turn their panopticon gaze toward those foolish enough to stand outside the Ivory Tower.

The New Inquisitors

The Second Inquisition is a term of art, doubtless coined by some gifted Artiste who wished to emphasize the danger we face, while perhaps reminding us that we have seen such things before. Certainly, to the Vatican this is simply a continuation of the Holy Inquisition established to burn us out of

Christendom eight hundred years ago. The Vatican found it needful to change that body's name to the Holy Office, and then to the still more anodyne Congregation for the Doctrine of the Faith, but the inquisitors' fire, banked though it may have been for a time, never went out.

Similarly, the secular inquisitors keep their true purpose masked behind bland committee-driven titles. Currently, the Second Inquisition operates under the rubric of the Intergovernmental Task Force on Extraordinary Counter-Terrorist Response (ITFECTR), but this name shifts with the political winds and bureaucratic tides. Thus, we refer to the SI, or the Second Inquisition, as such regardless of their official (or most likely, unacknowledged) status.

Such nomenclatural legerdemain also has the doubtless intentional effect of muddying the waters for our tools and other potential investigators. For instance, a Freedom of Information Act request for documents concerning the "Joint Working Group on Transnational Unusual Threat Assessment" never reveals that after the JWGTUTA "disbanded" in 2007 its core membership immediately re-formed as the Multilateral Liaison Committee for Counter-Terror Scenario Planning.

This bureaucratic shell game switches the Second Inquisition from patron to patron, its jurisdiction and budget sloshing between nations, from civilian to military to clandestine and back again. But the core remains the same throughout: five relentless foes hunting us through silicon and shadows, with an ever-growing pack of curs on their leashes.

Project Twilight

The United States government never had an official "Project Twilight," or even an unofficial unified program to hunt the supernatural. Occasionally DEA, CDC, FBI, NSA, or other federal agents stumbled onto our activities and survived to investigate further. Beginning in the 1980s, these investigations began to overlap, and an informal information-sharing network grew up. The agents in this network called their investigation Project Twilight, a reference not to oleaginous interspecies children's romances but to the Twilight Zone of American television fame.

Our countermeasures had almost completely stifled or co-opted these "hunters of hunters" before the al-Qaeda attacks on New York and Washington completely altered the game board. The National Security Agency, freed of its institutional fetters, aggressively acquired control over global electronic communications; the Swiss turned their once-secret records over to the U.S. Office of Terrorism and Financial Intelligence to sift for extremist financiers. Those two developments revealed anomalous patterns of

activity in certain centuries-old accounts: our accounts.

Those who had long advised our kind to stay off the Internet, and to distrust human banks, were proven completely prescient by what followed. OTFI investigations and NSA traffic analysis pierced the Masquerade, and American death squads stormed our havens. The black ops at the spear tip may have initially thought they were assaulting al-Qaeda cells, but soon enough the survivors discovered our true nature. Suddenly the old Project Twilight veterans found themselves called in for urgent noontime briefings in sunny Washington courtyards. Their superiors forgave or wiped clean their irregular records, and promoted them to head up nameless units with quiet authority to task and unleash sudden dawn raids.

As noted, the specifics of the American effort in the Second Inquisition remain hard to pin down — some Princes may even have tried to sic the NSA or FBI on Anarchs and other troublemakers, and then rightfully covered their tracks. However, the general picture has clarified and solidified in the last fifteen years. The American military and black budgets provide these hunters with oceans of untraceable funding, stored in illicit accounts or in tedious-sounding line items. The new Project Twilight comprises three main elements: the Information Awareness Office (IAO) of the Defense Department, a joint

NSA/CIA Special Access Program code-named FIRSTLIGHT, and the retasked and rejuvenated Special Affairs Division (SAD) of the FBI.

The Information Awareness Office

In January 2002, the American veteran secret warrior Admiral John Poindexter established an office inside the Defense Advanced Research Projects Agency with the goal of establishing "Total Information Awareness" of all possible threats to the United States. Every half-baked and experimental program in the DARPA in-box got massive funding, directed to such tasks as analyzing every post or email on the global Internet, identifying specific suspects at long distance using millimeter-wave radar, and most famously briefly establishing a "futures market" in crisis analysis.

Most importantly to us, the Total Information Awareness sentries perceived far more than we had imagined mere machines and algorithms could: correlating random data removed far too much of the concealing fog and doubt around our activities. Poindexter's team prodded at the anomalies in several global economic and political maneuvers until it discerned our outline. When it coupled those analyses with the new OTFI financial profiles, the IAO identified a number of Camarilla assets within the higher councils of American corporations and government. Our tools found themselves slowly cut out of the flow of real power and information — and occasionally, surgically removed from America entirely.

Poindexter had called on his old Reagan-era network of assets and conspirators, now influential administrators in the national security establishment. They freed up platoons of CIA paramilitaries, squads of NRO "security specialists," and even a Navy SEAL team or two. Dominated thralls, ghoul addicts, and even a few foolishly "hands-on" Ventrue found themselves awakening in black sites in the sunny, sunny tropics, invited over holy waterboarding to share more details of the "vampire terrorist conspiracy" IAO had found. We managed to manipulate Congress into officially defunding the IAO over civil liberties concerns in October 2003 before it could wound us too severely. However, we soon discovered that we could not restage the Masquerade.

The various IAO programs simply submerged back into the Pentagon's secret assets and continued under other names. Poindexter's hand-picked successor, Admiral Roberto Farrier, continued and accelerated his work. Farrier personally supervises and unifies the threads of the IAO, keeping it an entirely black project run out of his office in Pearl Harbor without Congressional or Pentagon oversight. He turns promising DARPA projects toward anti-Kindred analysis, weaponizing their findings as they become available. He also coordinates American and other military attacks on us, bureaucratically disguising the operations as "training missions" or "counter-terrorist strikes." Without a direct line to main command authority, the IAO has limits: a few Predator drone strikes or submarine-launched cruise missiles, a company of deniable paramilitaries, renditions to one or two carefully guarded black sites in the Indian Ocean or Micronesia. But the IAO does have a tap into the so-far limitless American clandestine operations and surveillance budget, and willingly spends its lucre on anyone and anything that might burn out one more of our havens.

FIRSTLIGHT

The first wave of IAO strikes in 2002 brought the True Death to, among others, a sewer-dwelling would-be spymistress in Ciudad Juárez named Xóchitl. This may have been the highest-value target the IAO hit in the entire Second Inquisition, because Xóchitl had been slowly grooming her own Dominated tool within the National Security Agency, Associate Director Felicity Price. With her handler gone, Price managed to throw off her condition — the exact methodology she used remains unknown, but was likely something developed early on by DARPA. She "came in from the cold" with first-hand knowledge of not just the Nosferatu, but of the Camarilla's clan structure, traditions, and an uncomfortably large piece of our entire North American network. She gladly underwent every test the IAO could throw at her, even volunteering to be examined by specialists from the Society of St. Leopold. With her bona fides established to the IAO's satisfaction, they returned her to the NSA, her career intact and her access vastly increased.

Over the next year, Price worked with the Society's CIA allies to establish a Special Access Program to sift all U.S. intelligence product for signs of Kindred action. The result was FIRSTLIGHT, an ECI (Exceptionally Controlled Information)-designated compartment within the NSA and CIA bureaucracy. Information flows into FIRSTLIGHT from all over the world, gathered by satellites, informants, and the endless seining of NSA intercepts. Price's team only reads new analysts into FIRSTLIGHT under very specific conditions: full daylight, at the very least, under the supervision of a Leopoldite or other aware hunter. This staffing bottleneck is FIRSTLIGHT's great weakness — there just aren't enough proven hunters to go around.

Price attempts to make up for this shortfall with a

pun-
ishing
schedule of
briefings and
planning, often while
airborne. She habitually
and continually flies west-
ward around the world, holding
rapid-fire meetings at secret airfields
and military bases, remaining in daylight
as much as possible. Each meeting produces
another FIRSTLIGHT tasking, another one of us
targeted, turned over to the IAO, the FBI, or one of
the Second Inquisition's foreign arms to be hunted down.

Special Affairs Division

During the first three years of IAO operations, its
analysts incidentally solved scores of heretofore isolated
murders and disappearances. By this time, the Project
Twilight old boys' network had caught wind of the new
dispensation to hunt down weirdness, and someone put
the IAO in touch with FBI Special Agent-in-Charge
Marcus Questor, who supervised the Southern region for
the almost moribund Special Affairs Division. The SAD
had begun as an anti-Kindred death squad during the
Bureau's war against Capone, branched out to investigate UFOs and Bigfoot sightings in the 1950s and 1960s,
and badly lost the thread during the Bureau's post-9/11
restructuring, distracted by paranoid investigations of
the so-called "demonically imbued."

Questor used the tranche of IAO information to close a number of high-profile cases with plausible cover stories, burnish his bureaucratic credentials, and to covertly unify the old-school "Van Helsings" in the SAD behind him. Within two years, he was promoted to Assistant Director, then to Associate Deputy Director and head of the Division. Questor's pipeline to the IAO provides the Division with hundreds of (sadly legally inadmissible) leads, as well as access to compromised and confiscated Kindred bank accounts when official budgets tighten.

Formally based out of the Criminal Justice Information Services Division facility in Clarksburg, West Virginia, SAD maintains its archives, specialized training center, and armory in a Cold War-era facility dug into the Blue Ridge Mountains. SAD agents operate all over the country, usually under cover in regular FBI field offices. Questor has refocused the Division on anti-Kindred hunts, renditions, and investigations, leaving its former "occult crimes" specialization as a cover against internal Bureau scrutiny. Special Affairs also serves as the formal FBI liaison office to the Second Inquisition's international partners.

The Newburgh Group

In the United Kingdom, the Second Inquisition operates through the Newburgh Group, an informal but close-knit body of highly placed advisors to Her Majesty's Government headed by Sir Simon Newburgh. The Group has no official remit, and barely any official existence — we suspect the hand of the prying Arcanum in its founding. Working through backstairs channels, Newburgh directs the Joint Threat Response Group within GCHQ, Britain's signals intelligence agency and equivalent to the American NSA. The British security service, MI5, sanctions the JTRG to act on intelligence developed by the GCHQ, especially by the Joint Operations Cell created to track sex trafficking and illicit sales on the Dark Web — the overlap between our activities and such commerce is quite substantial, as you will recognize.

Or it was before the JTRG began its work. Newburgh or his Arcanum minders identified Captain Ishaq Khan of the Metropolitan Police as a true believer. Our own records are understandably sparse, but Khan's son and daughter did disappear under circumstances that could imply Kindred involvement. (If they were Embraced, we have not yet found them.) With Newburgh backing, Khan rose to command of the London police Anti-Terrorism Unit, Specialist Operations Branch 13. On paper, SO13 merged with the former Special Branch, SO12, in October of 2006 to form the new Counter-Terrorism Command, SO15. But in actuality, Khan's hard core of SO13 remained an independent unit devoted exclusively to hunting down and destroying the Kindred in Britain. Reinforced by SAS commandos and Royal Marines when necessary, and protected by GCHQ and the Official Secrets Act, SO13 "slayers" burned out virtually every haven in London. In November 2013, SO13 discovered the resting place of Lady Anne of London — you doubtless remember seeing the photograph of Captain Khan holding her severed head.

With London officially "cleaned," SO13 turned its attention to other British cities and began seconding teams of investigators — and occasionally slayers — to Second Inquisition operations in other parts of Europe and elsewhere. The Newburgh assets within GCHQ had long since connected with their NSA counterparts. As two of the Five Eyes partner nations, the U.K. and U.S. routinely combine intelligence and information culled from the ECHELON program of global electronic surveillance. Felicity Price happily added JTRG to the FIRSTLIGHT distribution list, and Price and Newburgh soon identified like-minded partners in the other Five Eyes countries: Canada, Australia, and New Zealand. Their own hunter-slayer teams burgeon on the SO13 model, funded by the IAO or by seized Kindred treasuries.

Eighth Direction

While the Brujah more or less ran the old Soviet Union, their primary enforcement arm was the KGB. Its rival ministry, the Red Army military intelligence arm known as the GRU, remained under KGB control until the convulsions of 1990 and 1991. However, as the fall of the USSR demonstrated, Brujah and KGB control were far from absolute. Within the GRU, covert resistance to the Brujah regime accreted informally at first. At some point during the 1970s, General Ieronim Arkhipov, commander of the GRU Fifth Directorate responsible for operational military intelligence, set up a covert office to identify and isolate KGB influence within the Red Army. That office, the Eighth Direction (восьмое управление), eventually established the truth about the Anarch Soviet and — we theorize — took action.

To what degree, if at all, the Eighth Direction played a part in the fall of the Communist Party, the disintegration of the Soviet Union, and the Baba Yaga disinformation campaign remains unknown. Certainly the GRU has no incentive to reveal its possible role in dismantling its own government. And it has much yet to fear from its new masters. Brujah influence remains pervasive at the highest levels of the Kremlin, as former KGB colonels with archives full of secrets become oligarchs and Mafiya lords with billions to spend on bribes.

Certainly someone close to Putin engineered the abrupt 2009 resignation of GRU head Valentin Korabelnikov, who had been General Arkhipov's protégé. Without Korabelnikov's support and protection, the Eighth Direction — which had eagerly joined the Second Inquisition in 2004 — has been forced to scale back its efforts.

Where it once sent stake-wielding Spetsnaz troopers into havens all over the former Soviet Union, the Eighth Direction now saves up its few "training missions" for the highest-value or most urgent targets. The main exceptions are in the Ukraine and Syria, where the Eighth Direction can operate within the fog of covert Russian military operations, although those theaters carry their own risks. To mitigate them, the Eighth Direction subsidizes and directs several chapters of the Orthodox hunters known as the Akritai. Working through cut-outs is, after all, one of the traits Russian intelligence has shared with us long before the rebels co-opted them.

BOES

Lasombra and Toreador have warred over Brazil for centuries, with the exception of the "Carnival City" Rio de Janeiro, which is open to all clans. Whether Kindred strife or Kindred satiety finally drove the kine to respond, when they did it was with fire and sword. Brazilian national police officers whose faith or hatred outweighed our substantial bribes assembled thick dossiers of the disappeared, the victimized, the kidnapped, the devoured. Possibly tipped off by the Society of St. Leopold, while Brazil's states and cities created elite squads of special police in the 1980s, they formed their own Batalhão de Operações Especiais Secretas (BOES), the Special Secret Operations Battalion.

Funded by seized criminal assets at first, and then by seized Kindred assets, the BOES inserted five- or six-man comandarias within the military police or special operations police in São Paulo (ROTA), Belo Horizonte (BOPE), Rio de Janeiro (BOPE), Vítoria (BME), and other cities and states. Those comandarias scout a city and map out the Kindred turf and activity in it for months or even years. Once this is accomplished, the BOES "flying reserve" squads move in, strike as many targets at once as they can, and then begin clearing the city block by block if need be.

Because BOES for its first decades concentrated on non-Camarilla cities, we paid little attention to their raids. Indeed, it would likely not surprise you to learn that several local Toreador princes put the BOES on the scent of their rivals. But once the Society of St. Leopold brought BOES fully into the Second Inquisition, it became a significant threat to our activities as well. In some cases, BOES platoons have decades of hunting experience, more than any other human fighting force on the planet. The most veteran among them train and radicalize the new recruits to the "Sagradas," (the Sacred, as they call the unit) blunting our kind's weapons of shock and doubt. With U.S. military backing and funding via IAO, it is only a matter of time before they expand their operations outside Brazil: indeed, BOES comandarias may be operating in Bogotá, Caracas, and Luanda already.

Society of St. Leopold

The true core of the Catholic Inquisition, the Society of Leopold — or St. Leopold — has hunted us continually since its foundation in 1231 by Leopold of Murnau and Pope Gregory IX. Its fortunes waxed and waned with our own carelessness: the increasing effectiveness of the Masquerade eventually convinced even the Church that the Leopoldite crusaders were superstitious mad men. By the twentieth century, the Vatican had severed its formal ties of patronage and support, moving its clandestine energies entirely into its centuries-old intelligence organ, the Holy Alliance (known as the Entity since 1930). Denied the cloak of faith and patronage, the society was well on its way to disintegration through backbiting and factionalization. With the escalating reckless piercings of the Masquerade, however, it returned in force.

An Austrian fanatic named Ingrid Bauer, the so-called "Iron Maiden," ascended as Grand Inquisitor in 1998 and began a full-fledged crusade against our kind. Even before the American military got into the inquisition business, Bauer's Gladius Dei shock troopers burned out haven after haven with napalm, autos-da-fé rituals meant as much to build society morale as to weaken us. She reactivated old Cold War contacts between the Entity and the CIA, and with the U.S. military through Italian and Polish NATO liaison teams. When the NSA and IAO uncovered our traces, Bauer's assets were already in place to shepherd their analysts toward understanding them.

The Americans repaid Bauer's efforts tenfold, providing the Society of Leopold with military grade materiel (thermobaric rocket-propelled grenades and mass detection optics especially) and a few deniable billions for the collection plate. Bauer could now sideline or buy off opposing factions in the Society and devote it entirely to carrying out and coordinating the Second Inquisition.

Soon after his elevation in 2005, Pope Benedict XVI brought the Society of Leopold back under Vatican control, recanonized and carefully re-integrated with the Entity and the Church. It now formally exists as a personal prelature, becoming the

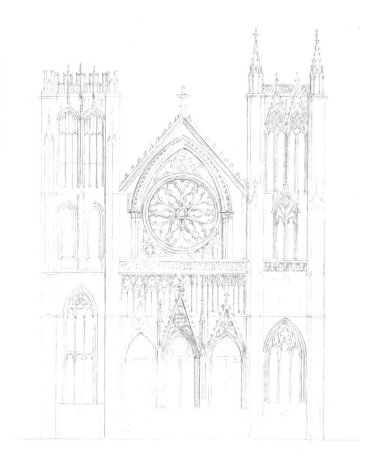

Society of St. Leopold, the patron saint of Austria. (The retroactive assignment must have given Bauer a certain satisfaction.) Its Bishop has directed the entire Entity since 2007. Operationally, the Society's black ops Gladius Dei act as the Entity Special Operations Group (ESOG). Previously, the Entity primarily engaged in conventional intelligence gathering and used the CIA and other deniable agents for direct action; the addition of the Gladius Dei to its ranks gave the Vatican a true covert operations capacity. Unlike the rest of the Entity, but like the Opus Dei (through and with which the Leopoldites and the Entity often work) the Society of St. Leopold can initiate lay and female members, although its higher Provincials are now all Catholic clergy.

Pope Benedict may have resigned in 2013 to protect the Society from its enemies in the Curia and elsewhere, or he may have resigned to serve full time as its true Bishop, with Bauer left in operational command. Since 2005, ESOG has recruited not only the cream of the Swiss Guard, but Catholics from other elite special forces units all over the world, and deployed them to the front lines of the SI's crusades. The even more radical theurgists, unorthodox operators, and other "loose canon" types from the old Society of Leopold became the core of ESOG Team X (or "Team 10" to more secular audiences), a quick reaction force operating out of the Vatican. Armed with hyper-modern ordinance, burning faith, and the records of a 800-year-long hunt, the Society-controlled Entity is the backbone of the Second Inquisition. It must be broken for the Kindred to survive.

Second- and Third-Party Partners

In the last decade, the Second Inquisition has expanded beyond its initial five core members. In addition to the three other ECHELON countries partnered with FIRSTLIGHT and the Newburgh Group, five more nations have provided enough intelligence or muscle to count as "second-party partners" and get seats at the table during operational planning sessions.

France's DGSE intelligence agency had already created a threat-identification system called Emeraude when they joined. Lt. Col. François Senghor had noticed that the anomalous findings from Emeraude eerily fit, of all things, a profile of "most secret threats" assembled by Cardinal Richelieu's Cabinet Noir. FIRSTLIGHT support has allowed Senghor to create the Calcédoine program within DGSE, which has driven François Villon into hiding and begun to clear Marseille of our kind. Calcédoine expanded into Africa in 2011, accompanying French troops deployed to Mali, Niger, Gabon, and Côte d'Ivoire.

Both Israel and Sweden came on board thanks to FIRSTLIGHT contacts with their own national SIGINT groups. Israel's Unit 8211 tracks elders en route to the Gehenna War, and passes along backtraces to FIRSTLIGHT so the SI can hit their now-leaderless cities. (Thus the importance of establishing solid Camarilla succession in a city before heeding the Beckoning.) Sweden's G-Kontoret ("the G-Office") works within that country's shadowy IB military-clandestine apparatus, having reopened the old files of the T-Kontoret founded in 1946 by the occult

scholar (and possible Arcanum member) Thede Palm. It increasingly takes on greater responsibility in the SI's research work, alongside the Newburgh Group and the Society of St. Leopold.

We have almost no information about the SI units inside Japan's Defense Intelligence Headquarters and Poland's domestic intelligence agency ABW, but we can assume that the IAO and Leopold, respectively, act as their "senior partners" when planning actions in East Asia or Eastern Europe. Given the increased frequency and intensity of Inquisition hunts in Japan and Poland, however, it's clear that those two agencies have growing shadow offices suckling on the teats of SI information and finance.

The Second Inquisition has inserted assets and cells on the individual or squad level within all major Western nations and American military allies, but has not yet spawned fully dedicated hunter commands. That said, it is only a matter of time before such commands emerge on the ground there as well. We specifically expect them in Germany (where the Berlin rising may have already triggered just such a thing), South Korea, Czechia (ESOG Team 4 has deployed into Prague for a "cleansing operation"), Colombia, Jordan, Italy, Uganda, Spain (which has excellent SIGINT capacity for its size), and the Philippines (where President Duterte's death squads already include random hunter teams). Local political pressures or turmoil keep the SI from full cooperation for now in Turkey, Thailand, India, Nigeria, and Mexico, although all of them doubtless appear on FIRSTLIGHT and IAO briefing books for the next decade.

Hunter and Hunted

As we must, above all else, keep to the Masquerade, so must our foes. The Second Inquisition cannot simply declare open war, burn us out in urban combat, and corral us into camps for two main reasons: First, the Camarilla still holds very powerful cards within the SI governments (and the Brujah likewise in Russia). We command corporations, senators, newspapers, television stations, whole nations — thus, operational security requires the SI to keep their actions secret even from their own putative masters. The ease with which

we officially dismantled the IAO provides a constant reminder of this. Second, the Second Inquisition has fewer advantages than the First: it does not command the spirit of those it supposedly protects, so it cannot assuage their fears of us. Announcing an "anti-vampire crusade" in the modern night would cause global panic, and possibly the fall of one or more of the governments whose treasure and soldiers the SI redirects. Worse, from the hunters' viewpoint, they could not prevent foolish or self-interested interference on behalf of "undead civil rights," "negotiating with a new species," "the opportunities for knowledge." or any other excuse the kine would make to remain in their comfortable slaughter pen. Even the Pope could not inform his own cardinals of the true threat — how much weaker must be the hand of a faceless bureaucrat in some lower floor of the Pentagon?

How They Hunt Us

Thus, the SI carry out their hunts disguised as operations in the War on Terror or training exercises, or use deniable allies like the Society of St. Leopold and the Akritai. The SAD may have reached an understanding with the remaining "imbued," using them to hunt us in exchange for legal anonymity. The SI may even, in cities where Princely justice is weak or wanting, use self-hating or so-called "independent" Kindred against us. Ever since the disastrous Detroit Hunt of 2012, however, the SI have deprecated that tactic, preferring to vivisect those Kindred foolish enough to try to come in from the cold. Now, when the SI uses our own kind against us, it is through cut-outs or simply by providing haven locations to both sides of a vendetta.

This points up a great advantage on the side of the SI: its complete and total mastery of the global computer network, and its willingness to exploit that mastery to our detriment. The laughable Schreck-Net fell to NSA exploits almost immediately, mayfly humans steeped in silicon culture easily outwitting ancient sewer rats who fancied themselves "hackers."

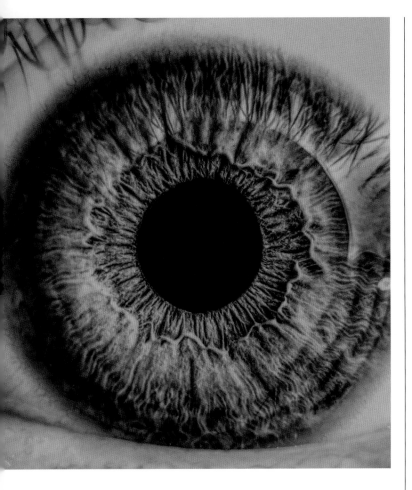

combination of holy relics and ground-penetrating ordnance. The site of the "terrorist atrocity" has remained cordoned off since then, and the SI keeps a permanent bureaucratic presence in the UN Office on Drugs and Crime in the city.

The SI develops more details for its network analysis by pulling emails, telephone calls, indeed every form of electronic communication, into its ambit. FIRSTLIGHT does most of the initial analysis, with backup from JTRG and Unit 8211. The GRU's SIGINT capability rivals that of the NSA, and the Eighth Direction performs its own taskings and analyses, which provides a useful (though doubtless seldom appreciated) cross-check on FIRSTLIGHT findings.

The SI also attempts to channelize our movements. They seldom interfere with elder travel to the Gehenna War front, preferring to prevent lateral journeys from city to city. The early "chaoscope" technology introduced (from unknown sources) in 2004 has now become the somewhat less reliable but vastly easier to mass-produce "Xscope" system embedded in millimeter-wave body scanners in airports worldwide. An SI controller team at the airport keeps an eye out for "blankbody" signatures and alerts either tasked SI hunters in the area or, if need be, the local gendarmerie. Man-portable Xscopes exist, but for now remain almost exclusively in SI hands for field work. The exception is London, where the CCTV systems now incorporate Xscope technology on dedicated feeds to JTRG command posts.

Our activities and relationships mapped, penned up in our cities and leaderless, the SI moves to "cleansing" operations. In London, Brazil, and now Prague, the inquisitors hit as many havens as they can simultaneously, though not all those they have identified. (The goal is, again, to herd us toward places they already have mapped.) Then, if politically or tactically possible, the SI turns to block-by-block clearing with helicopter- and truck-mounted Xscope scanning and follow up raids.

To keep us off balance, and to placate specific interests, the SI launches pinprick raids wherever one of us (usually an Anarch coterie) has been too clumsy or thirsty for comfort. For these actions, they field a hunter team, or if need be embed one or two SI offic-

That trove of data, thanks to the pestilential habit of storing up other clans' secrets with their own, provided FIRSTLIGHT and JTRG analysts with the basis of their network analysis maps. For every city in the world, the SI has at least a general idea of our activities by night in the 1990s and early 2000s.

Every connection one of us has made with another potentially appears on these maps as a link; with enough links, a counterintelligence analyst can trace the pattern even though they have no comprehension of its true significance. That is how the Second Inquisition determined that the Tremere chantry in Vienna was a crucial hub of our activities, even if they believed it to be "the vampire conspiracy global headquarters" rather than the center of one clan's activities. Regardless of their misperceptions, however, the IAO, BOES, and ESOG Team X did in fact destroy the Prime Chantry in 2008 with an as-yet-unknown

ers into a team of special operations soldiers or special police. Raids launch at dawn or noon, depending on local tactical concerns; even the ridiculously confident ESOG and BOES do not relish night combat with our kind. Any survivors — ghouls, hangers-on, or Kindred caught in coffins or otherwise — rapidly find themselves in sunlit rooms for interrogation and then a final combustion before a smirking priest.

What is to be Done

The threat is real, and it is deadly. But it is not existential, not if we fall back on the truths that enabled us to survive the first Inquisition five centuries ago. We must clamp down on the Masquerade wherever possible. Disguise our actions as conventional crime, our feedings as simple disappearances or human trafficking. Resist the temptation to peacock outside Elysium. Shift our funds out of electronically harnessed banks and into gold and narcotics and cash. Get off the Internet and off the confounded cell phones, return to hand-delivered messages or the voices of the night.

We must continue to co-opt the intelligence community, especially those already threatened by the War on Terror agencies' claim to turf and footprint. We must own the legislators (or their over-powerful staffers) who theoretically oversee the inquisitors' home agencies. We cannot weaken the intelligence community outright; we depend on it ourselves for information and control of the kine. But we must break it to our bridle again. Here, we have the promise of power and knowledge, along with secular wealth and gratification of desire, to offer.

In the short term, we can turn the attention of the SI to the Anarchs and the Sabbat. Let them be our hounds for once. Ideally, by pursuing the Sabbat, the SI will find itself drawn into the Gehenna War — surely the American military habit of walking into quagmires overseas can be turned to our advantage. Speaking of the Americans, we can play the other factions of the SI against their overweening paymaster and armorer. Bauer believes her society should hold pride of place, and the Newburgh Group must resent being lectured to by a former thrall. Historically suspi-

cious of (and rightly distrusted by) both the Americans and the Vatican, the Eighth Direction ironically acts as the deciding vote when the two diverge within the Second Inquisition. It should not be impossible to lay false trails in targeted havens to encourage such dissension.

Finally, we must throw the SI onto the wrong foot. Strike where they feel secure, send scouts and even full coteries behind their lines: to London, for example. The inquisitors are awash in money and treasure confiscated from our own coffers; leave behind co-operative "accountants" to encourage malfeasance, embezzlement, and eventual betrayals. Convince them one of their own has turned to us; if we could distract the witch hunters with a witch hunt in their own ranks, that would be both effective and artistic.

For all these tasks, I urge you to consider thin-bloods as possible tools. They can often withstand daylight, and perhaps confuse an Xscope reading. They are eager for advancement in our councils, and will thus perform dangerous tasks without cavil. They seek new territories to hunt in; what better ground to gift them than ground they must retake. Finally, of course, we can lose any number of the thin-bloods if it means weakening our foes. They remain entirely expendable ■

LOYALTY *and* ORDER

A feudal survival. A criminal society. A global conglomerate. The Camarilla embraces all of these models and more. Every Camarilliste believes they behold the true form of our sect, and rage at the blind fools who disagree. And yet, the Camarilla has survived for half a millennium. The Ivory Tower still stands, even after the loss of two foundation stones — and its architects lay new stones to replace those lost even now. The immortals who hold the sect together credit two deeper foundations yet: *Ordem et Fides*, Loyalty and Order.

Alberto Pineda Villa Aka "El Borrado", Lieutenant Of Fiorenza Savona, The Acting Ventrue Premier Of Mexico City, Speaking To A Coterie Newly Assigned There:

You've all heard it. Anarchs who can't afford the IV tubes for tonight's snack bar ask: "Why join a sect where I'm destined to have shit rain down on me?" Let me ask them: "Why are you wallowing in shit for

REPORT #196

TOWER PERMEABILITY
AND HIERARCHY

This group of blankbodies is too tight for simple "watch and grab" operations. They have their own codes, language, and sanctuaries, and analysis agrees we no longer have strategic surprise.

- Historical Section derives the following from the extended interrogation of Subject #37, after consultation with [REDACTED] in Psychological Section:
- The Tower operates along a pseudo-medieval hierarchy with corresponding medieval codes of feudal obligation.
- Internal ambition does not reach outward, but concentrates on internal rivalries. This diverges from historical medieval political patterns, implying a cult-like attachment to the society, possibly immediately upon infection.
- Indoctrination and enforcement of loyalty remain constant, although actual discipline remains arbitrary; another cult parallel.
- Similarly, among blankbody recruits, loyalty goes to "superior" blankbodies before it goes to the self.

The existence of such hierarchical bonds would explain why we find it so difficult to extract information or discover weaknesses within this group, and points again to the value of having an informant infected and planted within the group to assist in gathering information on its size and available resources. less possible information than their peers.

RF14-14 #196

no reason?" The answer they don't want to hear is this: they can climb out of it. You all can. I am here to offer you a ladder.

That ladder has rungs on it. Those rungs have labels. They are called respect, intellect, obedience, and the first rung, the first fucking rung you need to grab onto, and you need to grab it hard, is called loyalty.

"Loyalty is its own reward." So says some corporate head who can't afford a bonus for the staff. Loyalty creates its own reward, because when you grab onto loyalty, it moves you up the goddamned ladder. The Camarilla looks after its own. We hold our cities against our enemies, we avenge a murdered Prince — hell, we avenged the fucking Sheriff of fucking Lawton, Oklahoma and I wouldn't pay five pesos to have Lawton, Oklahoma burned to the ground.

Why did Fiorenza pay much much more than that to burn a bunch of Beast-ridden fuckers? you ask. Because when we protect our assets, we create debts. Debts we own. Forever.

Maybe the Camarilla looks cynical to you now. But it is about the big picture. Be loyal to the Cam, and the Cam will be loyal to you. And that's why none of my rivals, dead or alive, will ever be stupid enough to come for me again.

As spoken by Ambrus Maropis, Camarilla Security Expert for European Domains:

Loyalty isn't something to be proud of. It's not morality. It's not even choice. It's simple physics. Loyalty keeps the Camarilla together, and the Camarilla keeps us vertical and walking.

You don't monitor Inquisition traffic, so you don't know the details. I do, and I can tell you the SI are infinitely more active in Anarch domains. They're clearing out parts of Russia and half of California, as we speak, they're swarming all over Brazil, and they've got a dozen more city-scale taskings on the board. If you were cleared for it, I could give you the numbers.

But here's a number: two. That's the number of truly big scores they've made in

Camarilla domains, in fifteen years. Sure, mistakes were made, but those responsible paid the price, and now we know their pattern, and can use it against them. As long as we don't let adversity divide us.

Loyalty works because the Camarilla does. The Tower is what keeps you waking up in your own haven, not in a sunny room in Puerto Rico. You step outside of that, you're on your own.

The Blood Bond

The Camarilla prefer to cultivate loyalty without the Blood Bond. A Bond is no guarantee — even the most willing thrall may end up turning on their regnant by accident or passion.

Camarilla sires breed Camarilla childer. Anarch sires breed Anarch childer. The Embrace

Many Kindred fear the Blood Bond. They think it will degrade their free will and make them slaves, force them to lose control of their own emotions.

I have been Blood Bound many times. As the decades pass, I cannot even be sure that I remember all of them. You love, and then other things happen and you forget. The person you were Bound to dies, or the Bond fades with time.

We often think that the Bond gives control, but that is not strictly true. We use it to control our Blood slaves, of course, but they're also held in check by the precarious agelessness granted by vitae. They love, but they also need the Blood to stay young and healthy.

With Kindred, a sire can Bond her childer, but risks confusing their need for protection and guidance with their need for Blood. The sire may hold the reins, but be blind to what greed pulls at the other end and helpless to stop the jealous hunger she does not see.

If someone much more powerful than you is bound to your Blood, you might think you have an advantage. But do you? Why did the elder succumb? What did they fear, and what happens to you if their fear — or the Bond — fades? Some elders seek this bondage, desiring to feel the ardor and heartbreak of a real love affair. Emotionally incapable of it otherwise, they hope the Bond will provide the heat they have lost.

In such a situation, you may enjoy the elder's protection, even gloat in their lovesickness — until they want to keep and control you all for themselves. Your Blood has power over them, but in every other sense, they have power over you.

Tegyrius and I shall have power over each other, of course. One wonders whether those who arranged this believe they hold this power over us.

Leges Coterium, per Mithram, 1638 A.D. (Neillson Vernacular Translation)

1. Only a Prince, with the blessing of the Primogen, can form a Coterie.
2. Members must swear a Coterie Oath to one another, and are strictly forbidden to Blood Bond with one another.
3. The Coterie must have a Shadow, to advise them in loyalty and who accepts responsibility for their conduct.
4. Each member of the Coterie is responsible for the actions of every other member: "You are judged together."
5. The members of the Coterie must make Haven together, apart from their sires.
6. The Coterie must, when called upon, defend and protect the Camarilla from all provocations.
7. To become full Ancillae the Coterie members must together pass the Seven Labours.

starts a Bond, sets off innate trust in the monster who just betrayed you. The Stockholm Syndrome alone would be enough to keep most fledglings in line, even without the Blood.

The eldest of the elders know the limits of the Blood. It changes over the centuries, follows its own flow. In the light of Gehenna, it's best to keep subordinates in line with fear and rewards and use the Blood only judiciously.

⋯⋯◆❈◇❈◆⋯⋯

As told by Missulena, self-proclaimed "Head Horror of Australia":

The practice is as simple as bringing a baby's mouth to a nipple. The baby knows it needs it, but it doesn't know how to drink. That's when you use just the tiniest bit of force. You won't have to force it the next time. It will never want to stop.

That's the real pleasure, bringing such joy to their simple wide-eyed face, knowing that I hold that joy in my hand and can crush it without a thought.

Having a mindless toy, a fawning slave, well, that's fine for a week of nights perhaps. But like a baby, you eventually want it to walk and talk for itself. Or rather, for you, as you raised it to do. That takes firm guidance, strong teaching, and yes, punishment when it cries and disobeys.

That's how you raise a childe. That's how you create loyalty.

⋯⋯◆❈◇❈◆⋯⋯

"When you make an oath to the Camarilla, it's expected that you will keep it, little one." Missulena scowled at the young vampire, squirming between two Archons with passive faces as the fledgling wept bloody tears from burned out eye sockets. "Oaths are what keep us whole! The Blood Bond is truly a last resort, for what good is compelled loyalty, where a word should suffice, hm?"

Missulena pried open the new vampire's jaw with one hand, and with some effort. "Some fight remains in you. Very commendable, if ill-timed. Perhaps you should have fought to keep those lips shut last week, when you went babbling to Anarch scum about the Prince's route from haven to Elysium. I suppose I should remind you."

A nod, and the Archons smoothly forced the fledgling to her knees. She had let one of them stay in her haven when he first got to Sydney. It didn't matter. They were loyal to the Horror.

A moment of squeezing, thick Blood on her tongue. Missulena kept his thumb in her mouth for a little while after. "You may wonder at my mercy and generosity. In fact, I'm sure you will. Had you tattled to the inquisitors instead of to Anarch rabble, I would have been forced to punish you."

The fledgling felt herself nod. His vitae trickled down her throat, carrying with it loyalty. Loyalty to Missulena. Loyalty to the Camarilla he represented. She thought about what she had done to betray him, to disappoint him, and nearly vomited in revulsion at herself. She licked his finger, then sucked on it, knowing Missulena could make her vile betrayal go away forever.

> *The methuselah stands alone. The elders stand apart. But the childer must stand together.*

Coteries

Post on Sunburst by Little Lamb:

"If you become a lone wolf, you'll be put down like one." It wasn't my sire who said that, but my dad. He was right. I miss him, and the only reason I still think of him, here in the dark, darker than dark, is because I've got a new family now, and that helps me remember the old one.

As a neonate, attempting to go it alone in Kindred society is an extremely risky experiment, one that almost never works out well. Even Anarchs have learned that they have to cling together in order to survive, although they dress it up in ideological cant about "solidarity." Coteries in their most basic form aren't communes, they're necessary conditions for Darwinian survival in a society of predators.

Of course, the Camarilla has dressed the idea in its own colors. When the High Clans held the scepter,

they promulgated "Laws of Coterie" and sonorous oaths which have mostly died out in modern nights. Inertia and chance keep alive the old rule, meant to hold the Camarilla together in the early years, that each coterie must have members from at least three clans. Modern Princes usually grant relief from this rule and other holdovers like it, however. A coterie willing to come together on any terms and in any composition remains a coterie that can work together to serve the Prince, after all.

Almost every Camarilla regnum still holds to some form of the old Shadow Debut: sires in good standing present their childer to the Prince in Elysium, who acknowledges them as neonates of the Camarilla and assigns them to one or more coteries. Traditionalist Princes (or those who want to be seen as such) might even still exact an oath, and assign the new coterie a labour (also called a mission or a charge) to complete in exchange for such recognition. Even in less-formal courts, Princes appoint a Shadow if a new coterie petitions for one.

Excerpt From Carmelita Neillson's Description of the Tradition of Coterie in "The Bondage Of Kinship":

Coteries provide the irreducible unit of Kindred social activity. Often a supposedly inexplicable occurrence becomes clear when you realize the Kindred involved were coterie fellows centuries ago. To remain in control, the Camarilla has needed to keep these sorts of subterranean loyalties in hand. One text from a predecessor of mine puts it remarkably clearly, for 1862 anyway:

In distant times now long forgotten, Coteries would Blood Bond with one another, but this led to the uprising of the young against the old, for it created loyalties greater between the neonates than between them and their elders, their clans, and the Camarilla. To prevent this from ever happening again, the Blood Bond is jealously reserved for only the eldest of the Kindred to use to protect themselves and the sect from

Blood Makes You Clan
Loyalty Makes You Coterie

harm. We can never again allow the young to join together against the old, for in such union lies the dissolution of all our ancient ties.

Legacy Coteries

Besides newly founded coteries, some groups trace their lineage back to the Convention of Thorns, or even into the medieval past. Such legacy coteries resemble nothing so much as old school societies or fraternities at Eton or Harvard. In theory, each "graduating class" of neonates initiates the new coterie membership before moving on to become full ancillae. Initiation rituals tend to be extensive and painful, even racking, for the most prestigious legacy coteries.

Former members of these coteries from over the centuries often treat initiation as a social occasion, returning to the regnum of their Embrace for the festivities. Often, they take part in the hazing or demand a labour of their own in exchange for admission. Once initiated, however, a legacy coterie can draw on their tormentors for contacts, information, influence, and favors at court or elsewhere in Kindred society. Some legacy coteries, upon initiation, come with resources hoarded over decades or even centuries: a secret haven, relics, occult tomes, or ghoul servants.

Strengthening Alliances

"I will serve you my Master, to the full stretch of my sinews, and to the last dregs of my

human soul. To you I give all my sacrifice and loyalty. To you I give my faith. I swear to

be your companion in both pain and hope; your travails shall be my own to bear."

Loyalty holds the Tower together. Order shapes it. But the architecture of the Tower gradually — glacially — changes as old pillars are broken down and new added; as the world shifts around it, demanding new additions and safety measures. Even the feudal structure

of the Camarilla never ran quite along the clean lines of the plan, overlapping allegiances and secret agreements adding buttresses and oubliettes to the edifice.

Neither age, generation, title, or lineage fully determine the order of the Tower. Younger Princes disdain their elders in poorer cities, a Justicar finds it impossible to remove an Archon building a reputation on the front lines of Gehenna, and the heirs of Hardestadt still act as though the Inner Circle meets at their sufferance. Any of these may guarantee or limit the others' positions. The passage of time and the crumbling of the mortar only further complicates the totality. Neonates who expect either an ossified medieval hierarchy or a clean corporate organization will find themselves lost in the labyrinthian corridors of the Tower. Don't try to understand what our sect really is, or what it would look like drawn on paper. It is many things at once, and there is no reliable map to find, just guides with differing degrees of will to help you. No, take note of the general shape of the Tower, but ask not who should be in charge, but who is sworn to whom, and how.

Immortal Oaths

As explained by Marcel, Follower of Set, Proxy Primogen of Chicago:

What is an oath, childe? A promise? A dedication? Think. If I ask you to make an oath to your clan, to me, or to the Camarilla, what is it we're truly asking of you?

Mortals swear on their mayfly lives, or the meaningless names of their mothers. We swear on the only life with real meaning, an immortal one. Every oath lasts an eternity with us, unless the one to whom it was sworn releases you. Remember that.

We swear on the Blood, and the Blood hears and witnesses. Even if the Blood keeps its own counsel, you can be sure a Herald records it, and you can escape it as easily as escaping your life. Precisely as easily.

Oaths come in many grades, as codified by our good Primogen Critias. He has left us for the East, but his code remains to guide our talons. Even Justicars, who can break oath bonds in need and in service to the sect, hold back at times from disputing Critias. Perhaps they have sworn not to.

THE OATH OF SERVICE

Fall to your knees, pledge your service to another Kindred as retainer, as holder of a domain, as Captain in battle. The oldest of our oaths, sacred within a regnum once sworn unless the Prince revokes it. When Kristof Hutter fled Vienna as the Chantry fell, he deserted his Oath of Service and thus forfeited his fortunes and lands.

THE OATH OF BLOOD

The oath of a childe to sire, of the student to their master. Critias nicely writes that both parties remain bound by this oath, that the master owes tutelage to his pupil, for instance. The Blood wishes its secrets to descend to new generations, and the Justicars sometimes back those wishes. Such was the case of Marisa Namur, who was granted access to the private library of her Regent when he refused to teach her, and who liberated several rare scrolls from the shelves in return.

THE OATH OF DEATH

Called a life boon by optimists, this oath swears willingness to suffer final death in service of another. Those under the oath receive due deference and minor boons from others in service to their mutual liege, a veritable kiss before dying. This oath is often sworn as proof of intention in the face of danger, such as by a coterie to their Primogen before setting out to destroy an overbearing Prince.

THE OATH OF THE TOWER

When a new member is welcomed into our ranks, they swear to abide by the Traditions and obey the Justicars. Often, the Prince takes this oath from neonates when they are first presented at court. When the prodigal childer returns in the shape of a wayward Anarch, the Oath of the Tower is a good way to signal that they have changed their ways, but it usually takes more than words for the fattened calf to be dragged to the slaughter slab.

THE OATH OF ASH

This oath is sworn only to a Justicar before they send you on a suicide mission. As you face final death, all of the Tower must show you courtesy and deference — and if you accomplish your mission and survive, you may name your reward. If you survive without accomplishing your mission, the Tower destroys you and your treasonous get. I know of only three Kindred who have survived swearing an Oath of Ash, and one of them asked only to be forgotten and expunged from all records just as if they had broken it. I shall not dishonor their request by naming them here.

Age and Generation

As told by Talley, the Hound of Clan Lasombra, on a diplomatic visit in New York, to a rapt audience of young neonates:

Not so long ago the Camarilla denied the Antediluvians existed, and now they go to war to protect them, proving that even elders can be fickle and act as Duskborn juveniles. I jest, here among friends. We all know that those who balance the coldness of age with the warmth of humanity excel in your great sect. We can agree to disagree on certain subjects, for a while.

For now, I will give you some advice. A vampire gains much by being close to Caine, especially in your Camarilla, but generation does not guarantee experience, skill, or influence. As age does not guarantee wisdom. Both come with potential, but without training, the Seventh Generation fledgling will almost every time be defeated in most fields by the Twelfth Generation elder who has centuries of practice behind them. You need to know what to do with your advantages to get any use of them.

Stay around for long enough, and you will eventually be closer to gods than men or women. Give the Blood time to thicken and be smart about which paths you choose and what friends... When I was young we were created already as demigods. And we revelled in that power, letting it consume us. Perhaps that has tonight become our weakness, as we struggle to resist the demands of our gods, our cruel fathers and mothers few generations removed.

My advice to you, childer of the Tower, is to plan for what will come. Already, your powers ask for much in return. They will only ask for more as you grow older.

> *"Age beats generation. Cunning beats age. Respect beats everything."*
>
> **– ASCRIBED TO AL CAPONE, EIGHTH GENERATION VENTRUE, CHILDE OF LODIN**

NOTE: According to at least one eyewitness to this conversation, Capone actually said "Power beats everything." – C. N.

Thoughts of Mayumi Shibasaki:

I am told that I am Twelfth Generation. I do not need to be told that I am among the most powerful Kindred in Tokyo.

Do not mistake me. My family is old and excellent, and our Blood unimpeachable. But when I meet a similarly excellent and courteous Blue Blood and he says "I am Hiroshi, childe of Shinobu, grandchilde of Heihachi Kuriyama," am I to research his genealogy? No, I introduce myself likewise, and still neither of us know more than we did.

Of course, I offer no dispute to the Noddists in their underground churches: perhaps being closer to Caine does hold great spiritual significance. But Caine keeps secrets, even from his most ardent kohai.

I am told that the Warlocks or the Assassins have sorceries that allow them to detect generation in the vitae, but I will be ash before I give either group a drop of my own for tasting. And can we trust what they would tell us, should we do so? Sorcery is unreliable, and sorcerers even more so.

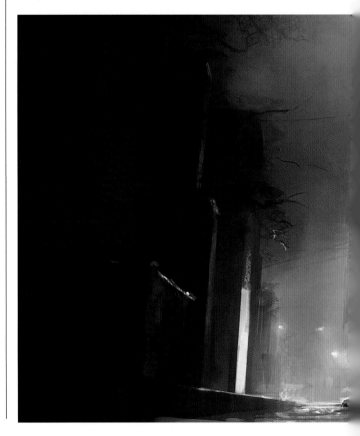

Justice

"You gone done it now, boy." Decker lifted himself from his seat as the other Kindred looked on. As was Decker's rule, the accused party was free to stand without binding and to speak in their own defense. Decker allowed this because he was unafraid of the guilty, and dedicated to the Camarilla. It was important to show people that the Camarilla believes in freedom in security, and where better than the courtroom?

"Not three, but four witnesses have come forward to say you done changed into a fucking wolf in the middle of fucking Brady Street, with kine as far as the eye could fucking see. There ain't much I enforce in this city, but the Masquerade is up there. It real pains me to harm you, but what would you have me do?" Decker folded his arms and tapped his foot theatrically, the court of fellow Camarilla Kindred smiling at the show.

The accused raised his chin up, facing his sire, looking Decker in the eye. "I... I know you won't believe me, but I saw something old, something... ancient and inhuman.

REPORT #182

CAMARILLA JUSTICE

Subject #50 came to us voluntarily. (See Report #182-D for after-action analysis of security lapses.) According to its written account, the Tower Society burned its tongue out for selling secrets to a rival group, and the "Hound" who exercised this medieval justice gouged its eyes out with a heated tire iron "for staring disrespectfully."

The group then impaled it on a wrought-iron fence on the east side of [REDACTED] to be destroyed by the daylight (see current version of Basic Diagnosis Document #3). It managed to extricate itself and stumbled into [REDACTED].

Psychological Section noted the contradiction between the society's need for secrecy (and strong ideological interest in it; see PsyOps Report #1109) and this potentially revealing act of primitive revenge.

Subject #50 confirmed that other "princes" pass other sentences in other cities: private execution, burial alive, and exile being examples.

Interrogation continues under standard [REDACTED] protocols.

RF14-14 #196

It was in one of the windows, looking out at me, and it scared me. It made my Beast... It compelled it to take over. All I ask is you investigate the properties on Brady. You can do what you want with me." The childe lowered his gaze again.

A ripple of murmurs rumbled across the court, before Decker raised his hand for them to stop. "We'll do that, boy. I promise you. I know it wasn't no fault of yours you changing when you did. You're better than that. But, I have to be consistent. And what this shows is you don't have enough self-control to resist our enemies."

Decker let his words sink in before passing the sentence down. "You're hereby exiled to Minneapolis. They know you coming. They're stricter up there, but you'll learn how to do right by the Camarilla. This is a fucking mercy, so be grateful."

As the court dispersed, his childe leaving without a word, Decker slumped into his chair and put his Brewers cap back on. His crown, of a sort. He knew the court would think he was being nepotistic. "Fuck them." If they couldn't show mercy, what good was the Camarilla?

Conclaves

As Recounted by Ambrus Maropis:
You want to host a conclave, and you have enough nous to find me. Congratulations, you passed the first test. You have the resources to hire me for security and logistics. You pass the second test. You have the wit to ask for my guidance. Three out of three.

You can send me your guest list later. First things first: why hold this conclave? Are you meting out justice to some spectacular malefactor? Did another Prince get caught defecting under the guise of answering the Beckoning? Or did some mad ambitious neonate try to set Elysium on fire, like Bogota a few years back?

Or perhaps you have something bigger in mind: a real gathering of kings and queens, powerful Princes plotting strategy in the war, Justicars coordinating policy, things like that. I should tell you right now that if you're hoping the Inner Circle will attend, you hope in vain. Also, I know who

---

Lyon   ACTIVE **28** MINUTES AGO

Have you heard?
The Cam have got some kind of con-clave going in the Villa Florentine tomorrow evening.

Yeah I heard.
Stay clear, and don't talk about shit like this on here.
You know who's watching.

Yeah yeah. Just that wouldn't this be an excellent place to hit them?
Like in Paris and Vienna?

One. That wasn't us. Two. Fuck no.
Conclaves are all the big dogs.
We can't match their firepower.

Mouse of a Gangrel, showing your throat already.
This is the moment we take out a Jus-ticar, man!
Come on.
I got those special incendiary rounds...

No means fucking no. If you act on this, I'll let everyone know it was you.

That just makes me want to do it even more.
Fine.
No fun tomorrow.

would ask me to arrange that conclave, and you're not them.

A judgement conclave tends to the strict and formal. A castle, a bleak industrial complex, a brutalist reminder that the Camarilla has power and the accused does not. If the accused is a methuselah, by the way, you should let me know — those require special wards and you need to pay the Warlocks separately. I'll dispose of the husk for just a half-liter of spillage, by the way.

A grand conclave should have a different feel, especially if you're planning celebrities as guests or as appetizers. Opulence, Bohemian Grove via Russian Mafiya: A-list mortal entertainers (off-menu), high Degenerate fashion, my own guaranteed security contractors. I can give you a Circulatory System contact for the vintages. Budget for more than one night of these. If you want to beat the Convention of Thorns, quintuple that budget.

Why spend like that? To wordlessly explain their position to the Kindred you didn't invite. To plant a little seed of fear: what did those above me talk about? Even judgement conclaves can draw new lines and expect everyone to toe those lines without seeing them drawn.

That's why the Camarilla holds them. I'm certainly not complaining.

As Explained by Lucinde, Ventrue Justicar:
I was there at the great Conclave of Prague, though some call it by other names. It was a grand affair. Representatives of every clan were there to hear grievances, talk of new clans joining our sect, old clans considering changes in their structure, and the way forward in this Inquisition time.

It wasn't our finest conclave, I will admit.

I tried my best to reach Hardestadt as I saw his head knocked back, following the shotgun blast. He was swept off his feet and beaten, shot, and stabbed horribly. I didn't see him crumble into dirt, but the attack was so fast, so relentless...

I lose my train of thought.

The point of the conclave was to show all Kindred present what a unified force the Camarilla is, and can

be. We even had delegates from clans not traditionally of our sect in attendance. Oh, it was a splendid affair, truly. Such a shame what happened to Hardestadt. I have always been so quick, but that night, something just slowed me...

Do not think we will be dissuaded by Brujah treachery. Conclaves are important to a sect such as ours, secretive as we may be. The drones must occasionally see the queen to know why they work. They must bask in brilliance to see what they might attain through loyalty and, ultimately, status.

No, Hardestadt was not the best of examples, but he was impressive while he lasted. I suspect, in a fashion, he might act as an inspiration of a different kind. When old kings fall, new ones rise. What better source of inspiration than to see the old monarch beheaded?

A NOT SO BRIEF AFFAIR:

The Institution of Blood Marriage
by Carmelita Neillson

Legend has it that my clan established the concept of Blood Marriage. Certainly the Toreador Courts of Love in Aquitaine, Occitania, and Aragon arranged and celebrated unions between vampires as far back as 1090. Interestingly, especially in light of current events, the Banu Haqim also seem to have arranged such marriages in Andalusia and Sicily around the same time. The Neillson collection in Burgundy holds a tapestry depicting one such lavish affair embroidered in scarlet and gold. After all these centuries, it is still vibrant.

After something of a lull, Blood Marriages have become more common once again, acting a part of the seeming "return to Tradition" of recent nights. They retain the same basic form as in the eleventh century: both participants declare their union before the Prince or a higher authority (in some regnae formally requesting permission) and share at least a single dose of vitae with each other to consecrate the marriage.

A few theories suggest that Blood Marriages first fell out of fashion due to Victorian puritanism disguised as self-glorification. Now, it is a mistake to

The Blood Wedding combines beauty with tradition, and I am surprised that I have never had one before. After all, this is just the kind of thing I adore.

Our younger Kindred like to think of it as a romantic occasion, free from the sordid taint of our kind, but allow a bride to be honest. Not every Blood Wedding lives up to the fever dream. I have attended a few (and organized a few more) with no greater goal than to entertain the Elysium. You find two neonates who seem like a perfect match and arrange everything for them. Really, it's a gift we give them, the gift of our experience and perspective – during their first decades, so few neonates really understand what's good for them in the long term.

But yes, while pragmatism or politics are often involved, some of these affairs are nothing more than cruel entertainment. I still recall that ridiculous ceremony in Nassau in '72, forcing Angelique and Mario together with false pomp while disguising our tears of laughter as tears of joy.

Perhaps my own wedding is fate's way of paying me back for these little jokes. It is about the joining of two great sects, the fate of our clans, and so on. My personal feelings count for very little, no more than Angelique's did. At least our pomp, our tradition, will be sincere, and I shall see to the beauty myself.

think the Victorians were as they described themselves in literature, but they did enjoy trying. In the age that lovingly embraced the most masochistic ideas of the fin de siècle, the Kindred did not lack behind in framing themselves as lonely beasts of the night, destined to never love or be loved in return.

Naturally, Blood Marriages are not simple love pacts. They sealed treaties in the Middle Ages, and are doubtless as effective in affirming mergers in our current time. Historians easily become cynics; joint addiction explains a great deal as well. But love remains an emotion, as well as an art form in its own right, and we should master it as both. Anger, lust, and fear limit one's palette; paint with different colours every so often.

To return to the current night, the Vermillion Wedding signals interesting times to come. The culture of the Camarilla is changing, perhaps affecting the very definition of what we are and why we carry on. It is clearly a political affair, but perhaps it could be something more as well? When emotions are involved, there is much to be gained, but also more to lose. Let us hope this marriage does not end like the d'Aragona-Piccolomini nuptials of 1490. All married couples quarrel. Eyes wander, and mouths follow. Blood Bound many times over to each other and driven insane by mutual jealousy, Giovanna and Alfonso managed to decimate the population of several Italian cities.

Official Record of the Vermilion Wedding

by Serenna the White, Officiant

There will be many accounts of the Vermilion Wedding. Mine is the first. I was there, and brought it about, and I do not lie.

I saw Victoria Ash in her brilliant white dress, looking more alive than ever.

I saw Tegyrius in his robes of midnight blue, his old eyes gleaming with brightness.

What I saw was a marriage founded on diplomacy, but sealed in love. What I saw, and I believe none of Caine's gifts were used to enact this, was a meeting of minds and souls on a truly glorious night.

The Vermilion Wedding represents more than a bond between Ashirra and Camarilla. It represents a bond between the Banu Haqim and the Toreador. It represents a connection between Tegyrius and Victoria Ash. Perhaps most importantly, it showed that all Kindred are still capable of finding love, no matter how jaded, hardened, and ancient they might be.

For the first time in a century, I experienced hope.

(Record approved by McDonald, Nosferatu Justicar)

The Kindred of Tehran, and a large complement of highly placed outsiders, all stood in attendance as Tegyrius of the Clan of the Hunt and Victoria Ash of the Clan of the Rose linked hands and stared into each other's eyes. They were not a couple

anyone expected to see bonded in a Blood Marriage. Indeed, the two hardly knew each other before the series of carefully choreographed meetings and exchanges of courtship had begun three years ago, following protocols dusted off from the days of Charlemagne and Hārūn Ar-Rašīd. Heirs to their own dynasties, they stood together now, their bare feet in a slowly flowing river of blood.

"Ashirra and Camarilla hereby join in the persons of this Blood Marriage, a sacred union blessed by Haqim and Arikel, Irad, Enosch, Zillah, and The First.

"The vermilion forever marks both you, Tegyrius, and you, Victoria, true color for true union.

"The blood you stand in is the blood of the enemies you slay together, and of the innocents upon whom you both shall feed. Feed now, together."

Serenna of the al-Amin concluded the chant and stood aside, allowing the two vampires to wade into the bloody pool, embrace, and drink of each other's vitae before gorging on the thick flow around them.

The celebrations following the ceremony lasted for several nights, each morning commencing when the servants started washing down the walls and replacing the costly flower arrangements that were decorating every surface not taken up by bodies or meant for dancing. As yet another gift to the covetous bride one of them was allowed to live. Despite all the scrubbing, the building itself was stained vermilion until the city authorities demolished it a week later.

REPORT FROM DAMASCUS
BY SOLEIMAN AL-ISFAHANI, WARRIOR OF THE BANU HAQIM:

Word of the wedding has reached our headquarters. My ghilmän grinned when they heard the news: it explained the new weapons delivered by the warlock I dissuaded them from eviscerating, with some difficulty, last month. Reinforcements, ammunition: something even a ghulam can understand. She and I had spoken in my garden after I kicked the last of the ghilmän out. As their whimpers died away, her voice grew stronger and more insistent. Not all the books had burnt up with Vienna, she said, and certain powers the Prime Chantry had contained could be recaptured with the correct geometries. I of course pled ignorance – a simple warrior, I, no Saahir. Then we spoke of other things, and dined.

But I am warrior enough to recognize an opportunity when it comes, as it has with this wedding. If the Camarilla comes in faith, then dealing in faith can only strengthen us against Gehenna. Thus the viziers say, and I obey. Perhaps I should consider making my own offer of marriage to a warlock who remained unafraid and contemptuous against a dozen veteran ghilmän.

Nevertheless, I recommend the magi we send to the Tremere remain alert for any too-tempting gifts left on the wedding table.

RDAM-14 #188

the COURT

The Feudal Order as Presented for the Fledgling Kindred

Addison Payne continued...

Power comes from presentation. This was how Vlad Țepeș pushed back the Ottomans when they brought 250.000 trained soldiers against his army of 30.000 boys. And this is how the Camarilla keeps its hold on the world. We are strong, but we seem stronger still. We contrive to be perceived as of one mind, omnipresent and united in our mission. However, nothing we do is as homogenous as we present it.

Each of our cities has its own hierarchy forged through traditions developed over generations and oaths made heavy by Blood Bonds. While the tendency of Prince as ruler, Primogen as councillors, and Sheriff as law enforcer has become convention, some cities have multiple rulers or do away with some positions entirely. A few domains even waive the idea of Elysium, declaring it ill-suited to a time where many of our kind gathering in one place carries a potential death sentence.

However carved, the court structure of our cities is important. We impose a feudal rule over our subjects not because we are stuck in the past, but because it remains the superior method of enforcing the stability of our society. The court is the basis of our culture and the reason for our strength.

The Prince

Sovereign, Prefect, Premier, Governor

A common Camarilla adage holds that Princes last forever or crash and burn within a decade. And it is true that once you claim praxis, you must be prepared to spend the

> *"...since love and fear can hardly exist together, if we must choose between them, it is far safer to be feared than loved."*

— NICCOLÒ MACHIAVELLI, THE PRINCE

rest of your time on earth defending it. Few relinquish power willingly, and those who do rarely last to tell the tale of their rule.

The title of Prince dates back further than Rome. Though the role itself has changed in form and function, several principles remain constant: The Prince represents their city, for good and evil. They are in charge of law, governance, and enforcing the Traditions. As those Traditions describe the rights and responsibilities of the

Elder, such as those of the Prince to give or withhold the gift of Embracing another to their subjects or sentence a Kindred within their domain to final death.

Duties of the Prince:

- **ENFORCING THE TRADITIONS.** If the Masquerade flickers in a Camarilla city, the Justicars do not look to those who broke the Traditions, but to the Prince who was supposed to enforce them.
- **TRIALS.** The Prince will either judge all trials or appoint another to the task.
- **GRANTING BOONS:** Hearing petitions from other Kindred and allotting domains and hunting grounds within the city.
- **HOLDING COURT:** Meeting with and formally accepting visitors in the area, as per the Traditions of Domain and Hospitality.

Strains of Kindred Princes

Every Prince rules in their own way, all that unites most of them is a love for playing politics and a talent for exerting control.

- **PROPHET:** This Prince feigns that they speak for a far greater power than themselves. Common Ventrue or Tremere type.
- **DESPOT:** Ruling with an iron fist , they brook no dissent or allow transgressions to go unpunished. Their Sheriff and Deputies are organized almost

like a secret police. Common Tremere or Assamite type.

- **MOGUL:** Detail oriented and obsessed with facts and figures, they care only about results. Common Nosferatu or Ventrue type.
- **SUPREME:** Using entertainments and status games to distract and entice their subjects, this Prince stays in power through the force of their own charisma. Common Toreador or Malkavian type.
- **WARMONGER:** Focused entirely on attacking their enemies and punishing their rivals, they are always on a war footing. Common Brujah or Assamite type.
- **DEMAGOGUE:** Using chaos and flights of fancy to conceal their true purposes, they control their subjects through misdirection. Common Malkavian or Toreador type.

Examples of Kindred Princes:

JOSEPH PETERSON: Elder of the Seventh Generation, Clan Ventrue, embraced in 1972. Prince Emeritus. Joseph is the childe of Prince Lodin of Chicago, and is a former media magnate who still exerts influence over local papers, TV stations, and even websites through his family connects. He served as Prince of Chicago for two months in 2006, stepping up to the role because nobody else dared to do so in a time of tumult. Disappeared from the city shortly after being deposed in a kind of palace coup, with his hated rival Kevin Jackson taking his place. Now resides north of the border, rarely leaving his mansion. He refuses to say what caused his flight from power or speak about his enemies, but it is widely assumed that he must be plotting to return to power.

LOISE "ROUGE ROI" COUSINEAU. Elder of the Ninth Generation. Prince of Marseilles since the 1940s. Best known for being a cold-blooded tyrant who prefers to drink the blood of other vampires and who will mercilessly destroy anyone who defies her. Was called away by the Beckoning in 2017, and now roams around somewhere outside Riyadh, where she has, as it was last heard, joined forces with a traditionalist Islamic sheik-dom in pursuit of unknown goals. Loise still rules her territory from a distance, at least officially. In reality, correspondence from her is becoming increasingly scarce, and whispers have begun spreading that perhaps it is time for a new regent of Marseilles.

RICARDO LUCERO: In these times of change, it is no wonder new pow-ers — or old powers, if you prefer — rise to the fore. The Kalku Governor of Buenos Aires known as Ricardo Lucero had posed as an elder member of Clan Tremere for centuries when prominent Kin-dred of his city vanished almost overnight. He decided then was the time to reveal his true identity as one of the Drowned, belonging

> *"The Ventrue Prophet does what needs to be done immedi-ately, while the Toreador Su-preme only strikes when there is nothing else left to do."*
>
> **– ANNE BOWESLEY, FORMER PRINCE OF LONDON**

to an ancient native breed of much power. Surprisingly, the revelation shocked few Kin-dred. More were alarmed by the sudden gaps where their leaders had once stood. The prince was gone, so Lucero, one of the eldest remaining Kindred, took the role of governor with the support of the remaining members of all sects. They saw him as an inde-pendent who could stabilize the city and prepare it for the inevita-ble Inquisition onslaught. For now, they wait for the true test of his resolve and rule.

The Seneschal
Chamberlain, Advisor, Lieutenant

A Seneschal is the right hand the Prince, empowered to act in their stead. It is not an uncompli-cated position to occupy, perhaps because everyone sees a voluntary Seneschal as a potential Iago. Nevertheless, Seneschal is a tradi-tional court role, and one that is very influential. It is a position in which tacticians, administrators, and advisors thrive, and one worth pursuing if you have a talent for noticing things otherwise over-looked.

Often, the Seneschal will take the role of Domain Steward when a Prince falls to torpor or in other ways becomes unable to perform their duties. However, the crows feast happily on all dead flesh, and few Princes will choose a Seneschal

To be the power behind the throne is ever preferential to sitting upon it. All intelligent Seneschals know this. Overreaching is a fine way to attract accidents. No, he who enjoys existence invests his resources better by passing on information and staying ready to duck out of the way at any sign of trouble.

— ALAN SOVEREIGN, VENTRUE SENESCHAL OF CHICAGO

who look too hungrily in their direction. For this reason most Seneschals have tasted their ruler's Blood at least once.

Examples of Kindred Seneschals:

ROGER DE CAMDEN – formerly of London – served as Prince Mithras' Seneschal and Pater of his cult for near a millennium, including after his own faked assassination. Some claim de Camden was London, as much any Kindred can represent a city, as he served Lady Anne as diligently as he did her predecessor, and still persists to this day while Kindred above him have fallen. Indeed, when Lady Anne was destroyed along with the last of Mithras, de Camden faithfully led his cult to Edinburgh. There he continues the worship of Mithras as Pater and Steward of Edinburgh, and each Kindred who followed him from London hold a vial of Mithras' rich vitae as a treasured possession.

ALAN "THE ACCOUNTANT" SOVEREIGN: A waspish, nasal Ventrue of the 9th Generation, Alan Sovereign is everything a modern domain could want from its Seneschal. As Majordomo of Chicago, Sovereign has served successive Princes as a capable administrator, accountant, and power broker. Commonly seen as the man behind the throne, Sovereign has so far withstood all attempts to discredit him, and for all intents and purposes, he appears to be a thoroughly dull and unambitious Kindred. In reality, Sovereign commands more influence over the investment and commercial banks in Chicago than any other Kindred, and holds the power to close a credit card or empty an account with one phone call. He is the secret landlord behind hundreds of properties, some of which are havens.

ESKJA "THE RED SLIPPER" MÍNERVUDÓTTIR: Born a peasant girl from a fishing family in the fjords of Iceland, Eskja was captured by Barbary Pirates in 1627 during the Tyrkjaránið, and then sold in Istanbul to become the property of a Toreador Prince who so loved her unique beauty that he made her mistress of his palace. Her time with him proved to be painful but very fruitful, because eventually in a fit of passion he drained her of all her blood, and fearing she would die, gave her back some of his blood so that she could live. However, once she had power of her own, she left him to travel the world, spending several centuries in torpor in Iceland. Only within the last decade did she return to Istanbul, now again Constantinople, to serve another of her sire's childer as Seneschal, hoping to revive the Dream.

The Primogen Council
the Senate, the Presidium, the Council of Elders

The Primogen council represents the interests of the clans and advises the Prince on matters of law and rule. Traditionally, it consists of representatives from each of the most prominent clans in the domain — naturally favoring those of the Camarilla, though outsiders are allowed to report any issues to a Primogen not of their own clan. Primogen are often elders, but despite the term (Primogen from Latin means "the first born"), there are no rules in place that this is how it must be. In fact, during the last few decades, more and more councils have seen drastic changes to their structure.

The Beckoning has weakened many domains by drawing away the eldest of our kind. Some Primogen councils now operate on a rotational basis. Others have limited their size to only three or five members, forcing an odd number so votes pass with greater ease. Some smaller domains have even implemented the rule that council members must be under a century of age, believing that clan representatives should be in more touch with contemporary culture and neonate priorities.

Duties and Domains of the Primogen Council:

- **TRIAL BY JURY:** Though the Prince has the sole discretion of punishment, they will often have the Primogen council convene to render the verdict of innocent or guilty.
- **ADVISE AND CONSENT:** Before

a Prince makes any major decision in regards to the welfare of the domain, they are obliged to meet with the Primogen. They can ignore the advice they get, but it would often be unwise. Princes are easily replaced.

Pedigree of Primogen
The notorious Harpy Salamari once said in jest that "there are six pedigree of Primogen councils," and she defined them as the following:

- **THE TRIBUNAL:** Seeing themselves as both judge and jury, they are untiredly trying to find the guilty and punish them.
- **THE CIRCLE:** These Primogen are obsessed with equality and keeping everything balanced.
- **THE DIRECTORS:** They are all business and have no time for frivolity, they consider time spent at court to be time wasted.
- **THE PATRICIANS:** These Primogen are convinced they are the most important Kindred in the city and have grandiose opinion of their status and power. Woe to those who deny them respect.
- **THE UNION:** Believing themselves to be representatives of all those Kindred who do not have a voice in court, they stand up and speak for the "common ancilla."
- **THE COVERT COMMITTEE:** These Primogen do not attend court and rarely if ever meet in person. They are the elders of the city who are still interested in politics but mostly interact with the Prince and each other by letter and proxies.

"The Prince can fall on any night. It's the Primogen who will go on."
– CAPONE, VENTRUE PRIMOGEN OF CHICAGO

Examples of Kindred Primogen:

STEPHEN THUNDERHORSE: Where some domains have Princes or are led by Primogen councils, Providence fields a quorum of Senators including Stephen Thunderhorse. He represents the new money corporate powerhouses of modern Blue Bloods, and to date, he has served his clan well. Despite being a 13th Generation neonate, his sway over Kindred and kine makes him the kind of Ventrue the clan Directorate wants at their vanguard. Embraced in his mid-thirties under false pretenses (his sire thought he was a money launderer but in fact he was a legitimately competent stockbroker), Thunderhorse is already known for his energy and bombastic manner in the Kindred Rhode Island state senate. Many suspect he will go far.

MYLENE "THE PUCK" HAMELIN: It is no surprise the Ventrue hold so many positions of power in these nights, but not all of them are traditional leaders. This 10th Generation ancilla is Primogen of Toronto, but lacks most of the airs and graces of her clanmates. She is a hard-nosed, plain-speaking former solicitor of mixed Vietnamese-Canadian heritage. She still fraternizes brazenly with the kine by dating mortal women (and often does so without feeding), happily swears at her fellow council members when she disagrees with them, and gives out beatings to her own clan members when they fall out of line. Some people think she's called "the Puck" because of her fey appearance. They soon learn it's actually because she has all the subtlety and nuance of an ice hockey puck. Despite this, Hamelin is popular in her domain. She always drives forward her clan's interests and brooks no dissent from Anarchs.

The unbound ancilla known as **IVAN KUTKHA** is one of the most recent additions to the Primogen council of New York. The council is relatively new and larger than in a lot of other cities, as the Kindred community is almost as diverse as that of the kine. Besides representatives from the core clans of the Camarilla, the council also includes members of the independent clans, a loyal Brujah, as well 13th Generation neonate representing anonymous thinblood citizens of the domain. And Ivan, of course. When he first stepped up, offering himself as Primogen, he was regarded with suspicion by most of the council, but his ties to the Russian community in Little Odessa have made him an indispensable addition. Being friendly with the mob makes many Masquerade breaches a lot easier to cover up. To most of the New Yorkers, kissing up to a shady Caitiff is certainly worth it.

Clan Whip

Sometimes a Primogen will choose to appoint a second in command. The Clan Whip is tasked with collecting the opinions of the various members of the clan or faction, and serves as enforcer and advisor to the Primogen.

Example of Kindred Clan Whip:

JASHAN "SWEETMEATS" STANFIELD: Ancilla thinblood and African American native of Baltimore. She serves as Clan Whip for what is left of the Brujah in the Camarilla. When she isn't backing up her Primogen, she controls the illegal gambling industry in her city and has been given right by the Prince to kill any mortal or imprison any Kindred she catches running a gambling operation without her permission. Her greatest weakness is a personal taste for bets and wagers — her name appears on prestation records all over the East Coast, as she rarely turns down a bet if she thinks she can win it.

The Sheriff

Praetorian, Scourge, Inspector, Executioner

The Sheriff ensures that the Traditions and the decrees of the Prince are obeyed, hunts down violators, and delivers just punishment. In the case of minor violations or known enemies of the Camarilla, the Sheriff is usually authorized to act as both judge and jailer/executioner, but when it comes to greater offenses, they will deliver the accused to the court to be judged.

Sheriffs must be superlative hunters and investigators. There are many ways of doing the job, but the best Sheriffs are calculating, sharp, and merciless. After the resurgence of the Anarch Revolt and with the added importance of maintaining the Masquerade, our Sheriffs must be always watching for signs of insurgency, unafraid to strike when they find them.

In large domains, the Sheriff and Seneschal may share the role of Chief of Intelligence, dividing lore and rumors of potential traitors between them. A domain in which the two work together in unity is quick

You think I take pleasure from hunting down lawbreakers and miscreants? You think I enjoy cutting their heads off in the traditional manner, putting their skulls on spikes outside Elysium for everyone to see what happens to deviants? Well, you'd be right. They should've thought about that before they broke our laws.

– SISTER JANE, SHERIFF OF COPENHAGEN

to strike down on anyone spreading lies about our order or attempting to ignite revolt of any kind.

Duties of the Sheriff:
- Protecting the city against itself.
- Locating and punishing lawbreakers.

Examples of Kindred Sheriffs:

JOSEFINE ADELBRANT: Former Gothenburg cop who found out a little too much about the Cainites while working the city streets and fled. An Anarch pack she had been investigating pursued her to Stockholm only to fall afoul of a Camarilla watchdog coterie that was keeping tabs on them. She was protected for a time, and then Embraced in 1985 by the leader of that coterie, who later became Sheriff (or "Brandvakt") of that city. Josefine was his loyal childe until he perished in a fire started by Anarchs who disliked his methods, and she only barely escaped with her unlife. She has since taken over his position as Sheriff. Shrewd, sternly attractive, and a fierce combatant, she is highly intolerant of liars, criminals, and fast-talking Anarchs.

NICK KILPATRICK: Neonate of the 12th Generation. He worked as a bail bondsman in the family business before being Embraced in 1994 by his brother Arthur (now missing). Kilpatrick serves as Sheriff of Cincinnati, guarding the city against all manner of chaos and foul play. He loves his job and is known to be eager to punish any form of transgression, not always waiting for the Prince to pass judgment before doing so. An adept criminal himself, despite his "day job" as Sheriff of the court, he still does occasionally use his safe-cracking skills to pop open a vault. Prone to bouts of depression, he can sometimes be suicidal and deeply ashamed of his addiction to feeding off of crack addicts and other drug users in order to get his fix. His large family is his main weakness. He tries to hide them as best he can, but Kilpatrick Bail Bond is a well known company, and on one occasion his grandmother was kidnapped by an Anarch gang. While he didn't recover his nana alive, the gang completely disappeared without a trace.

The Herald

Whisperer, Harpy, the News, Ambassador, Voice of the Prince

A Herald acts as the voice of the Prince, proclaiming decrees to Kindred subjects and carrying messages to and from other rulers. In this time, where we must fear the use of technology, many Heralds are still well-connected outside of their domains, endlessly finding new ways to communicate, and giving us a way to reach our kin despite the dangers. At Elysia, there will often be a Herald telling tales of Kindred activity, celebrating our victories and sharing news of enemies and allies in far-away-territories.

In some domains there is no Herald as such, but inevitably certain individuals, who happen to be sufficiently inspiring or charismatic, will gain the confidence and attention of the many — and the control over status and truth that follows with that. By those who appreciate them, they may be given the title of the News. Others will, echoing Virgil, whisper about the insatiable Harpies.

An important task in any domain is maintaining the records of prestation, the system of favors traded, offered, won, and used. The Herald responsible for this is known as the Chancellor.

Prestation

The system of prestation replaces feelings of isolation and hunger with something to strive for, with favors and rewards that can be won. The beauty of the system is in its simplicity. Whenever a Kindred publicly asks another for assistance, the Chancellor diligently records it. In this way favors become loans to be paid off, investments in the future. Paying back is a matter of honor, and those who refuse find themselves hunted and despised.

Duties of the Herald(s):
- Announcing the decrees of the Prince.
- Keeping the records of prestation.

Examples of Kindred Heralds:
KRYSTYNA "THE PEACOCK" KOWALSKI is the celebrated and much-beloved Herald of Warsaw. Since her embrace in 1910, she has revolutionised the city for the Kindred, leading the way in cultivating the increasingly pulsating nightlife and developing a system of information trading that benefits the domain. From her haven in the Opera Club, she acts as the hub of news and rumors, and anyone who wants influence over what new tales will enthuse the city's Kindred and send them into dizzying fits of intrigue come to

"My favorite part of my duties is declaring the Blood Hunt. Seeing the greedy fire of justice light in the eyes of Kindred starved for entertainment and hanging on to my every word. Being a Herald is a magnificent responsibility."

**– KRYSTYNA "THE PEACOCK,"
TOREADOR HERALD OF WARSAW**

her. Kowalski's position could easily get her in trouble, but she knows how to play the game. Her schemes are just serious enough to keep nightlife interesting without ever threatening the domain itself. The Kindred of Warsaw love it and adore their Herald, who always dresses decadently in vibrant colors and fabrics, reflecting her light-hearted attitude toward the world.

ARKADY "THE CENSUS" VOGEL: A 12th Generation Gangrel from the domain of Belgrade, Vogel has existed in the background of the city's Kindred affairs for centuries, rarely interacting with other vampires. His preference, as a former scribe in service to Belgrade Fortress, is to stay out of everyone's way, taking copious notes on everything he sees and every target he wishes to hunt. He is, in his own way, an accomplished biographer. Only when the Anarch Movement resurged in recent years and his clan departed the Camarilla did Vogel stand up and say "no." He despises the chaos and danger of the Anarchs, craving Camarilla stability. With that in mind, he offered the Prince his services as city Herald, knowing the workings of local and distant Kindred. As a result, he is one of the oldest Heralds in Europe. The small, wiry Gangrel despises the sobriquet of "harpy," and is rumoured to carry a grudge against anyone who dares use it to describe him.

Principal of Faith

In times of strife, Kindred and kine alike turn to faith for comfort and guidance. The Principal of Faith is an ancient position that has recently come back in vogue in certain domains. The title covers a bewildering array of courtly advisors on matters of the soul, from the Christian preacher reminding the Kindred of the domain of their humanity or learned Haqimite advising the Prince on matters of cultural diplomacy to the methuselah-cultist trying to teach respect for the ancestors. Some are intolerant fanatics who seek to root out heresy, others represent a broad congregation of believers, seeking deeper meaning from within the traditionally secular government of the night.

The Principal has a varying degree of power, from

officiant of courtly rituals that no-one really puts much stock in, to being able to override the Prince on matters of faith and forgiveness. Some Principals are even consulted in matters of interpretation of the Traditions. Usually the Principal is appointed by the Prince, but they may also be a popular preacher lifted to official power by their congregation. The faith of a powerful Principal often becomes the official religion of a domain.

Since the twisted priesthood of the Sabbat have left most of their cities, faith, religious titles, and worship have become more accepted in the Camarilla, but even now, few dare use the tainted Catholic nomenclature of Bishop, Cardinal, Priscus, and Templar. Even the Church of Caine prefer to use titles from Islam, or Orthodox and Protestant denominations like Imam, Alim, Pastor, Archimandrite, Preacher, Hierodecon, or Protopriest. When the Principal represents the cult of a methuselah or another uniquely Kindred faith, the titles of them and their underlings are of course drawn from the traditions of that specific blood cult.

Examples of Kindred Principals:

DOYLE "ASSISI" FINCHER is a devout Catholic born to Irish immigrants, and at an early age became a butcher in the infamous slaughterhouses of early 20th century Chicago. He was extremely proficient at his job, but highly unsocial with his human peers and was only comfortable in the slaughtering of animals. Those he was able to calm and dispatch without pain, with supplications to St. Francis. His efficiency inspired Inyanga, the Gangrel primogen of Chicago, to hire him as her "tracker and butcher," testing him on various

"Tonight, we will teach you how to commune with your soul, your Blood, your Beast, and to understand what you can become if you decide to try."

– DANIEL ANDERSON, CONSUMPTIONIST OF THE 10TH (PREVIOUSLY 11TH) GENERATION

hunting expeditions and treks. She was so pleased with his performance that she embraced him. Like his sire, Doyle has always preferred to feed from animals, claiming spiritual connection with them in their moment of death, which he experiences as a moment of communion with his patron saint. This is one of the reasons he serves as the Principal of Faith to the current Prince of Milwaukee. Fincher currently owns a large stockyard on the South Side and, using several ambulances for transport, sells a huge selection of animal blood to other Kindred. During various conflicts within Milwaukee, he has become known for providing Kindred of all types sanctuary in the sub-basement of his factory, including Anarchs and other outsiders.

CILLIAN KYBER is one hell of a charismatic and well-spoken neonate, but what would you expect from a Toreador? The 12th Generation Kindred has no great impact on the world stage, but is something of a celebrity in his own select circles. As his most recent invention, he has become the self-proclaimed Noddist of Belfast. How he came into ownership of a copy of the Book of Nod and fragments of the Jyhad Diary are his best-kept secrets, but he is uncannily convincing when he, with a smile and a wink, declares that he can work out exactly where in the world each Antediluvian is buried and where Caine currently wanders. He even says he's met the Dark Father personally. While most experienced Kindred dismiss Kyber as a bombastic liar, he has the younger neonates of his domain lapping up every word.

"Put down your lanterns. It's time your eyes got used to the dark."

– MARTHA, MOTHER OF THE LOST, SHADOW TO MANY

The Shadow

The Shadow is formal advisor to a coterie, assigned by the Prince to shepherd them through the minefield of Kindred society. The Shadow does not lead the coterie, and has no special ability to punish or discipline its members. They are typically a much older Kindred with unique wisdom or talents, worthy of guiding the young, or alternatively someone who has angered the Prince but cannot be openly punished, instead receiving a thankless task. A wise Shadow nurtures their coterie into a loyal and useful team of allies — but whether Prince or Shadow scores the first hit is unimportant, as long as the Camarilla wins.

Examples of Kindred Shadows:

LEA "GOLCONDA GIRL" SUAREZ is an 11th Generation Kindred, Embraced in 1864. It is said she once had a loving husband and four children, all of whom are now dead for undisclosed reasons. Lea never abandoned her Catholic faith, though she has modified it a bit, and she is prone to preach to other Kindred when they least desire it. It is well known that she has turned her parish priest into a ghoul and rules over the congregation like a wrathful angel, using the parishioners as her ears and eyes in the city. She now serves as Shadow to a coterie known as the Avenging Angels. They operate out of the vicarage and are often seen dressed as priests and nuns.

One of Suarez' core beliefs is that living 100 years without succumbing to frenzy is the key step on the path to Golconda. In only a few months she will reach that full century without her Beast even once being brought to the fore, and she is going mad with anticipation, expecting immediate results from her long toil when the day comes.

YURI "KOSCHEY" KOSTYUSHEV claims to be a distant cousin of the Romanovs of Russia. He was Embraced in 1916 by a Nosferatu he met while attending one of Grigori Rasputin's lavish and carnal feasts. He is haughty, arrogant, authoritarian, and a firm believer in striking before you are struck. These years he is Shadow to a motorcycle gang coterie named the Cossacks. He personally recruits its members from among young Kindred with some sort of blood tie to actual Russian Cossacks. The coterie sometimes work with their allied human motorcycle gang, the Night Wolves, to carry out missions for Yuri.

The Keeper of Elysium

All weary nightwalkers sooner or later find themselves drawn to Elysium. We carry such burdens, and Elysium offers rest and momentary forgetfulness. Pure joys on a darkened path. A place for contemplation and to socialize amongst ourselves. This is what the Keeper guards.

Appointed by the Prince, and often closely allied with the Heralds, the Keeper of Elysium is tasked with hosting ceremonies and social gatherings and maintaining a sanctuary where no strife can enter. Some Elysia we share with the kine, and here the Masquerade must be upheld. Others are highly-secured Kindred-only locations where we are free to drop our masks and wear the faces we want.

In any Camarilla Elysium, the Keeper will welcome inside only those who are already allowed in the city, by command of the Prince. Anarch clan members are only welcome in our Elysias on rare occasions or if they have renounced their sect and sworn allegiance to the Camarilla. As thin-bloods are offered no protection under our laws, they are as safe inside Elysium as the kine.

"It is a great honor to host for my Prince and his court. I am inspired every night to please my fellow courtiers and to mediate conflict and debate. There is no higher praise than to know I am trusted to perform this role."

– GYÖRGY KOVÁCS, TREMERE (TRADITIONALIST) PEACEKEEPER OF BUDAPESTY

Examples of Kindred Keepers:

MICHEL "CAMP-VAMP" HOULE has been the Keeper of Elysium since 1986, as well as host and something of a dandy at the Revival Burlesque and Queens Club in Toronto, which is considered, along with the entire city block around it, Elysium. A true impresario and ringmaster of chaos, Houle is and will always be an entertainer. His stage name is "The Scandalous Camp-Vamp Glitter-Queen" and he is famed for his ostentatious, theatrical and very funny nightly shows in which he deliberately doesn't follow traditional ideas about what is considered in good taste. Despite his eternally good mood and flirty manner, he has many enemies, for he is ruthless in enforcing the peace of the Elysium, which is perhaps why he has not left his establishment in nearly 20 years.

DELIA DAWES is known as "the Pin" because without her the domain would explode. The fledgling, psychologist, and avid clubber was born in the 1980s and Embraced in the British city of Bath one year ago. By no means should the fate of a domain be the responsibility of one so young. Yet, Dawes quickly realized that she'd been Embraced into a city about to fall to civil war. On her first night at Elysium, she discovered that the Tremere were planning a coup on the Prince, her sire Jackdaw. She also realized the Ventrue and Toreador would send their ghouls to burn them from their havens if they carried it through. She acted on impulse when alone with her sire and discreetly slew him herself. The coup neutralized before it began, she immediately began her campaign of distraction. Believing that what the kindred craved was entertainment, she became fixated on providing it for them, and she organizes masquerade balls, raves, historic tours of the city, and anything else they might like. She believes that if she fails, Bath will collapse. Though a beautiful young woman, Dawes often looks stressed with unkempt hair, yesternight's clothes still on, and a hungry look in her eyes. She doesn't like to feed while others in the domain are still hungry.

Celebrated Elysia From Around the World:

ficult to leave. Something about them make you lose all sense of time. It's delicious. Last rumored to have taken over an abandoned waterfront building just outside of Helsinki, End of the Line goes wherever the crowd is hungry to lose itself in the feeling of the beat. Word of mouth is spread from KitKatClub in Berlin to Bassiani in Tbilisi, ensuring that even if mortals have no idea what happens here, they want to be a part of it. Flowing with the music is a lot like having a pulse, and Kindred conduct is hidden by studious ignorance — the code of clubs all over the world: mind your own business. We do as we please as long as the party only lasts for a night at a time.

THE ART HOLE is an avant-garde gallery in Queens, New York, and I mention it because you will never find yourself feeling more lost in the visuals than at this crassly named Elysium. It's actually run by an elder of Clan Brujah, so I'm told, though I've never met the elusive Ms. Weise. Perhaps the Beckoning summoned her. Either way, her gallery remains open, displaying some of the most vivid and daring works of this age. Mostly by such as you and I, although right now I believe they are showing a series by Fábio Magalhães. A quiet alternative for the more contemplative Kindred, you could call it.

Just as legend suggests, **THE LABYRINTH** is within the isle of Crete. Long held by the native Toreador and Nosferatu, it's said it was one of the first Elysia ever constructed specifically for our purposes. I cannot attest to it ever holding the Minotaur, but its impossibly intricate design does guarantee confidentiality. The Labyrinth is a place where shadows pervade, and secrets can be exchanged or stored away. It's a favored meeting place for those who enjoy the dark, but a word of warning: it's easy to lose yourself in the many rooms full of curiosities and attractions attentively selected to captivate the visitor. The old Keeper will attend to your every spoken and unspoken wish while you are inside, but they are notoriously uncaring once you find yourself outside on their doorstep, hours later than you planned, and the sun is about to rise over the horizon.

PONTE CITY is a tower block in Johannesburg and the inspiration behind The Traveling House Party, which happens whenever and wherever a Keeper of Elysium seizes residential property and declares it sacred ground. This kind of party is increasingly popular in this era where we often prefer to stay indoors rather than risk open spaces. It may take place in the Keeper's own haven, that of another Kindred, or in a mortal's house after the mortal has been suitably brainwashed, Blood Bound, or rendered unconscious so a home invasion can happen. Keepers who host these events rarely leave witnesses to tell the tale, and always change the location before the next event. The only exception is Ponte City, where the Kindred in the tower have slowly been draining all kine residents dry.

THE CATHEDRAL OF TRIER in Germany is one of the oldest church buildings standing in Europe, and I'm told the infamous Ventrue Ilsa Reinegger built a haven beneath it. History aside, the genuine sense of respect and comradeship among those who attend, the peaceful sermons, and the choir song sparks something in even my wizened heart. All arranged by the Keepers but found no less holy by the unknowing congregation. On empty nights, it's restful to gather your thoughts here, but blood is scarce unless sourced from vagrants

brought in from the cold.

CONGRESSO NACIONAL is perfectly suited to Camarilla use. This massive structure in Brazil is designed mainly for political negotiation, and its surveillance is notably under Toreador control. I've lost count of the number of Kindred meetings that have taken place right under the noses of the Brazilian government, but the wonderful thing is, there could be 20 going on at once and we would never know, as the building is big and remote. The Ventrue especially appreciate this type of Elysium, as hosting in such a location guarantees debate will occur, and solutions may be reached without violence ∎

The Elysium is your place to shine. Your battlefield, the stage for your greatest joys and most mordant sorrows. You will be trashed and humiliated, driven out in tears. You will engage in stratagems so subtle your enemies will never realize you were behind their misfortunes.

For me, Elysium has always been the heart of the Camarilla. My most natural environment.

There's an aspect to Elysium I've always found highly amusing. In most cities, Elysia are free from violence. We are not allowed to physically assault each other, or sometimes even use the powers of our Blood. A wise restriction, to be sure. But does it make Elysium into a peaceful place, a venue for diplomacy and reaching common ground? I think not. The restrictions on obvious harm only mean that we can put into play much more grievous plots.

I trust you are starting to understand why I love it so!

Whatever you plan, it cannot be obvious. If you wish to harm someone, do not go directly against them. Instead, target their assets, friends, loved ones, mortal relatives. Then, offer to make peace with them and help them against this mysterious assailant. Frame another enemy for the deed, or better yet, one of your allies, just to make the plot harder to penetrate. If you execute a move like this properly, you'll find yourself holding the hand of your enemy as he cries about the family he has lost.

Sometimes I leave it at that.

Conventional wisdom of Elysium says that you attack the powerful for profit and the weak for fun. Many do this, and seem to enjoy themselves, so I won't say it's not something you should do. Personally, I have always found it unsporting to destroy the vulnerable. It is too easy, and I like a challenge. There's a real thrill in humiliating someone much more powerful than you are and escaping any consequences.

The mightiest of the Kindred style themselves ancient and wise, but most are still perfectly susceptible to common flattery. They have egos like the rest of us, and if they think themselves immune to manipulation, they are even easier prey. Still, consider sometimes taking the risk of being contrary. For most elders, having anyone speak against them is a rare occurrence. They surround themselves with sycophants who hang at their every word, so they may find a young rebel exciting. Of course, this can also get you killed.

To really convince people of your sincerity, you must act with your heart before you betray them. Let's imagine that a rival has destroyed your chances of fulfilling your dream of becoming the Keeper of the Elysium. Can you go up to them, flirt, apologize for your presumptuousness, and confess you have always admired them? Can you look them deep in the eyes, tell them you love them, and mean it?

A word of warning about these kinds of emotionally charged revenge plots: If you want to be believable, you have to allow yourself to feel. If you do so, you may find your original objectives changing. This has happened to me countless times. I remember once when a young neonate, a slip of a girl, seduced a lover I was cultivating at the time. I was furious. No child is going to get the better of me! I went to her, spoke very sweetly, and before I realized what was happening, I was having an affair with her. I stopped caring about my original plan for revenge because I was enjoying myself too much.

Why do so many Kindred seem superficial, obsessed with appearances to an embarrassing degree? The answer is simple: For protection. If your peers think you mainly care about sporting a fresh new style every season at the Elysium, they won't find out about your mortal lover, your secret childe, or your commitment to the Catholic faith. Every time the people at Elysium find out you care about something, you have a new weakness. They will know where to strike.

The trick is to show only what you want them to see.

The City

While the Blood broadens your possibilities, adding abilities and connections you'd never have imagined to be within your reach while mortal, it also does limit you. Once you have it, once you've appeared on the radars of the secret dead, there's no escape but the final one. With great power comes also a great deal of interest in what you get up to, and if you think only the Second Inquisition is watching you, you're mistaken.

The Camarilla has feudalized the night-side of the world, as manifested in each of their cities and those of their allies. With creation into their ranks — our ranks — you are awarded a position and certain responsibilities. These gifts are not to be simply refused. And with them your city becomes both

prison and temple. You are kept within its borders by our rulers, and forced to stay by those who would destroy you if you left. In other words: the city of your second birth will swallow you up before you can take your first steps as a new being. On these pages I have gathered, you will read accounts by Kindred who have traveled all over the world. But these are the privileged, who have seen centuries pass. Most of us never get to leave.

Your city is your world, so you should learn its ways and limits.

From the local politics — who openly and secretly rule among the living as well as among the dead; to the ways in and out and who guards them. If what stands between you and escape is a moistened path through Nosferatu territory, you better keep on good terms with the sewer rats. Learn what systems are bugged by the SI or other mortals (being chased down for manslaughter by the cops can be just as destructive as being watched by agents of the world conglomerate command). Make sure to earn a few

well-placed favors from influential members of your city. And familiarize yourself with your local domains, who owns them and what rules they enforce on their grounds.

You will be granted a domain for yourself or at least the right to make haven and hunt within that of another. It all depends how well-liked you and your coterie are by the Prince, who sired you, and which areas of the city are currently available and in need of protection. You shouldn't cross into the domain of another without permission, nor should you hunt outside your own, unless specifically granted the right. Trust me on this.

The difference between one domain and the next largely comes down to the quality of hunting within it. The Rack, the Red Light District, and the slums make for the best and safest hunting grounds (the carefree, the desperate, and the paperless are easy feedings), while the suburbs, military bases, and very religious communities are either highly risky to hunt in or do not include enough subjects to feed from. Impress the Prince, and you may be given access to the university dormitories and the endless supplies of anonymous self-discarding blood dolls also known as visiting students. Make a nuisance of yourself, and you risk having to beg for your share of unpoisoned blood.

Anarch Free Zones

The Camarilla presents a façade of zero tolerance to the Anarch Movement, but in truth the sect would rather have the Anarchs peaceable but at a distance than warring for control. In many city domains that recently held sizeable Anarch populations, our rulers designate parts of the city for Anarch use alone. We are forbidden from going there, but the free zones tend to be placed within the least hospitable parts of the city, and we wouldn't be welcomed anyway.

The hope is, I think, that the next couple of decades will see the free zones abandoned as the rebels either give up and declare for our side or go elsewhere, where conditions are better.

Camarilla Embassies

Similar to the Anarch free zones, the Camarilla hold what is styled as embassies in some Anarch, Ashirra, and even Laibon domains. I imagine that Kindred assigned to these territories vary between ultra-conservative loyalists and turncoats waiting to happen, as diplomats cast withering looks at their neighbors while plotting their downfall, or make overly-close alliances with the locals. Regardless, the Inner Circle considers it important, our leaders declare, to have representatives from our the sect in almost every vampiric city, so they might at least encourage the Masquerade, maybe even affect a change in politics and philosophy. These are early nights yet, but in undecided domains, the ambassadors hold some sway. Or so I'm told. The influence of the Ivory Tower is not so easy to resist.

Naturally, not all Kindred want this honored, Justicar-assigned, role of envoy. The embassies may be for the greater good, but they do make fine excuses to send troublesome competition into hostile domains.

The Wilderness

The culture of the Camarilla-owned city may be strict, but Kindred without accommodation are under constant threat. Beyond the city walls and outside the court's protection, danger increases by a great magnitude. Whether struck down by environmental hazards, the sun being the greatest enemy, or simple bad luck in the form of a car breakdown or collision, being away from our havens for too long can prove fatal. Travel by plane, train, or boat always comes with the risk of delays, but these nights, strict border control, XScopes, terrorist alerts, and concerned citizens on the lookout for suspicious activity make the risk of setting off an alarm with the nearest SI operative overwhelmingly large.

And if the SI doesn't get you, or the sun doesn't find your unprotected, lonely flesh, there may still be other threats lying in wait, too great to face on your own. They howl at the moon or paint their faces with vitae in the honor of Caine, the first kinslayer. I'm sure this doesn't complete the list. If there's one thing I've learned from all this: there is always someone, or something, worse.

– LEO, NEONATE CHILDE OF ADDISON PAYNE

Important Cities In The World Of Darkness Tonight

Aleppo

It was the constant song in my head that drew me here. Not to Aleppo, exactly, but near...

It is just that there is so much blood, pulsing in the people, running in the streets, splashed up the walls. I smell it everywhere I go.

I only wish those explosions had not rent my coterie's haven asunder. Now I am alone, left to feast on gruesome remains like an animal.

It could be worse.

This song. It calls me still. Deeper into the land before me. The Kindred who are here hide from newcomers. They fear what is to come. I believe we are responsible for the terror they face. Their ruler is a tyrant, their would-be liberators are little better, but it is us who carry this wave of carnage throughout their city.

You know, I saw some of the natives gather the kine to them like orphans to a nurse. They said "we will protect you with our gifts." I thought maybe they are better than me, better than us.

But no. We are monsters from beginning to end. It does not take long for any vampire to see a herd as a herd. Nobody is safe here. Mortals, Kindred, the things in the ground, awaiting our fangs... Nobody is safe.

– GHOSH, ELDER OF TRIPOLI, FORMERLY OF THE PRIMOGEN COUNCIL

Berlin

Berlin holds a lot of lessons for our sect. For a long time it was known as a divided city. The two Princes, one in the East and the other in the West, struggling for control against the backdrop of the Cold War. The Berlin Wall fell, but the Camarilla civil war only got more intense.

In fact, we became so focused on our own power struggles that we became blind to what was really happening out on the streets. I'm not pointing fingers. I was as blind as anyone. I wanted to be the Prince, and waited for the others to clear the playing field so I could make my move.

We always knew there were Anarchs in the city, but we didn't really care. The Princes thought they were irrelevant, useful only for a moment's cruel entertainment during a boring night in the Elysium. We didn't realize the pull Berlin had in the mortal world, and the power a dream could have over a recently Embraced vampire.

If you became one of the Blood in some stuffy, claustrophobic little town and had to try living under the local tyrant, you dreamt of Friedrichshain, its parties, the art scene, fetish clubs, whatever you wanted. Many young vampires escaped and came here, and nobody in the Camarilla really bothered to keep track. After all, how could an Anarch really affect the magnificent political struggles of the ancients?

The last Prince of Berlin died in the street, torn apart by an angry mob of Anarchs.

That's something to think about if you believe that the Camarilla is forever, or that the young, naive Kindred of the Anarch Movement can never present a real threat. Berlin was one of the great strongholds of the Camarilla heartland, until it wasn't.

The Berlin of today still reels from the violence of the Anarch revolution. Power is in the hands of different gangs like Red Liberation and the Stirner Gang. Kindred overpopulation means the Masquerade is in more danger than in most places, but at least the locals are used to seeing weird-looking people on the street.

Berlin is a perfect town if you want to go someplace where the rules are in flux, where a young vampire can make their mark. Just be warned: Nobody owes you anything, and there's no Prince to protect you.

One last thing. I know what you're thinking. How did I survive? How can a Tremere Chantry still exist after all that rage?

I did something the Princes could have never done. I had the humility to understand the revolution would not be stopped and prioritized my clan over trying to keep the Camarilla in power. You can judge me for that, but I lived to see another night. And I'm still here, in Berlin.

– MAXWELL LDESCU, THE TREMERE REGENT OF BERLIN AND THE LEADER OF THE CAMARILLA REMNANT IN THE CITY

Brussels

I've heard the Kindred call Brussels the City of Wastrels, and it's not a compliment. There's a lot of power in Brussels. It's one of the hubs of the European Union and NATO. If you want to influence mortal politics, this is the place for it.

From the standpoint of Camarilla elders, however, Brussels is a small town that became a city but recently, a mere two centuries ago as the nation of Belgium was born. They see it as a shining modern metropolis built in the shape of the new system of global political power. They like to send their childer here to learn how to influence mortals and work their politics to their advantage. The idea is that after a couple of decades in Brussels, the childe of a Justicar or a Prince will have the necessary experience to start really working for their sire.

The only problem is, the childer tend to be over privileged, pampered, arrogant twits. They might not have started that way, but living too close to the power of their sires has made them so. These wastrels don't spend their time in Brussels working with politics. They party, fuck, hunt, do drugs, and engage in bizarre vendettas with each other while ghouls like me do the real work.

The Prince of Brussels is a Nosferatu vampire called Nikolaus Vermuelen. He's an ancilla, too young to be able to stand up to the progeny of the Camarilla's great and powerful. However, he does have a talent for not being around when trouble starts. The wastrels get killed but the Prince lives on.

For the Camarilla, the real importance of Brussels is in the work of lobbyist anointed like myself. We make sure that Camarilla interests are represented on the level of European Union politics. While the wastrels invent new cruelties to amuse themselves and the indigenous Kindred residents of the city try to endure as best as they can, we wield the vast financial power of the Camarilla to serve the political interests of the undead.

The interesting part is that most of the time, nobody really bothers to check what we're doing.

– HENRIK KORHONEN, RETAINER AND A PARTNER AT THE CAMARILLA-CONTROLLED LOBBYING FIRM WRIGHT+MOREAU STRATEGIES

Budapest

It has been some time since my last visit to Buda, or indeed Pest, but I assure you it is worth the trip.

Few domains contain as vibrant a history as this one, and it is carried quite openly. Even the stories of Kindred warring for the city's control - which long remained under Ventrue dominance with such fallen icons as Bulscu and Rikard - are shared between mortal historians who do not know the truth of what they speak. Bodies lie still, beneath the cobbles or beneath the Danube, biding their time to wake and do battle once more. Think of the rich blood in those still veins.

Ah, but I get away from myself. What is there now? Opportunity. This is a domain the Warlocks would dearly love to claim, but they find resistance from the Clan of Beasts and their Nosferatu allies. Yes, the sectarian lines are skewed here. Fiends once posed a threat in this region, but they seem peculiarly absent in any number these nights. That is something worth investigating.

So yes, opportunity. While clans clash for the kingdom, others of us move in to channel the power of vitae layered within this domain. Budapest is a glorious trove of lore, just waiting to be uncovered. I daresay the revelations we might find could disgrace many of Eastern Europe's oldest Princes, when their ancient pacts are revealed.

– COUNT JOCALO, MINISTRY INFORMATION BROKER

Cairo

Other cities claim to be domains of peace and prosperity, but few can stand up to Cairo. Have you ever been? You will find more mortals than you know what to do with, you will find yourself rubbing shoulders with Camarilla and Ashirra diplomats alike, and you will come away with more baubles and trinkets than you can pack in your case.

I see it on their faces. Every time an outsider comes to Cairo, they are staggered by its brilliance. We are a jewel, maybe the biggest in Africa. And we are unassailable. We see the activities around us - where the mortal fanatics detonate their bombs and the Sabbat attempts to control their mania - and you know what we do? We laugh. Cairo is above such trivial behavior.

Yes, we have lost many of our strongest Kindred to this Beckoning, but more always arrive. The Ashirra now takes a great interest in Cairo, but promises to respect its neutrality as the meeting place between sects. If Prague holds that title for clans - and I doubt that, by the way - we proudly hold ourselves as the place where anyone may break bread, no matter their philosophical leanings.

Am I concerned about the increase in Cainite activity throughout North Africa and the Levant? No. I am confident that when all is said and done, the thrum of blood in this city will cool the tempers of any Beasts. It is impossible to stay angry here, when you can drink your fill and never be noticed for doing so.

Here is the trick: We Egyptians do not like to admit it, but we worship death. Not like the clan of that epithet, but our culture has forever been tied to it. When we find a body in the streets, we handle it and dispose of it, with all due ceremony and respect. Do we question the means of death? Rarely. Too many die to waste our time with the cause. What we focus on is the life that was had, and the afterlife a spirit will experience. That is enough. Some say Egyptians are all members of a great death cult, and they are not far mistaken. The kine worship us, whether they know it or not. We worship the dead, whether we know it or not. We are above petty differences, when all of us face the reality of death nightly. It is in our culture, our architecture, and our vitae.

All who come here must make a sacrifice to the dead. It is a simple transaction, but one that keeps Anubis content.

– MUKHTAR BEY, CAITIFF PRINCE OF CAIRO

havens. Even Capone was here. We were the template, see? Ventrue, Tremere, and Toreador on top, Brujah, Nosferatu, Gangrel at the bottom, Malkavians... ehh. Who knows with them, right? Anyway, the domains around us took notice.

Things have changed. Since the Camarilla tightened its belt, we squeezed the Anarchs into pits like Gary, Naperville, Joliet, and the city remained ours. Pure Camaril-

foot square of territory in Skokie, you should be fucking grateful.

This is the promised land, friend.

– BRET STRYKER, CHICAGO HARPY

Chicago

I know what you're thinking. It's my kind of town, right? Chicago is different to how it used to be, friend. We were swimming in Anarchs and Camarilla, duking it out over the Rack, over territory, over fucking nothing. Still, it kept the nights warm. Old gangster shit, running and gunning, setting fire to

la. Law and Tradition honored on every street. We keep things tight.

We've turned this city around, made Chicago great again, you get me? We drained the swamp and it left us gleaming like pearls. These nights, if you're invited to Chicago to meet with the Prince, brought to attend Elysium with the Primogen, or you're given leave to have even a

Constantinople

The mortals call it Istanbul, but we still refer to the City of the Dream as Constantinople, in honor of Michael, our savior, our dreamer, our hope to this night. It was the last city in which all clans came together, unified, and dedicated to finding a way of existing without torment and enslavement to the Beast. It was glorious. Michael led the way. The Trinity — of which he was a part — consisted of him, the transcendent Dracon, and the architect Antonius. They built great things. They lifted us to new heights. Even following their destruction and torpor, we Kindred of Constantinople strive to attain them once again.

It has been a long road. Few domains have been through as much tumult as ours. Leadership rises and falls. Philosophies are learned, applied, and discarded. Newcomers are welcomed as elders are banished, then elders are put in power as newcomers are regarded with suspicion.

We cannot help it. The Dream was a wonderful concept to experience as a vampire. It was a time when mortals gave themselves willingly, where guilt was a forgotten nightmare, and the Jyhad just stopped. We crave a return to that time. We need it.

Now there is a new Trinity, the Camarilla and Ashirra leaving Constantinople to allow their rule. Michael awakes again in Mary. The Dracon takes a new form. The third… The third…

Constantinople will be the beacon for all Kindred. Come, answer our call. Learn of our dreams and let them change your natures.

— AZRA, KEEPER OF ELYSIUM

Dubai

What is the difference between the needs of the vampire and those of the super rich? In Dubai, there are none. Both want their private playgrounds, to keep the people under control, and to build pointless monuments to their own vanity. This is a place where the hubris of some mortals exceeds the ambition of most Cainite elders.

Dubai is possibly the most restrictive Ashirra domain in the world. The dominant clan is el Hijazi, who have been closely intertwined with the Al Maktoum family for decades. They helped Sheikh Rashid bin Saeed Al Maktoum build the city in the 1960s, and are close also with his sons. Indeed, through Sheikh Mohammed Bin Rashid Al Maktoum, el Hijazi have their hands around all of the Emirates. They say even the Minister of Happiness is a ghoul.

The only Cainites who can really stay in Dubai as permanent residents are members of el Hijazi. All others must declare themselves on arrival. If their business is deemed legitimate, they can be given permission to stay for a set period of time. Some are allowed to stay in the city for a few nights or weeks. Others can stay for years, even decades. Eventually all will have to leave. And only el Hijazi are allowed progeny. If any other Cainite wants to make a childe, they are welcome to Embrace in another city. The only saving grace of Dubai's repressive regime is that executions are extremely rare. Cainite offenders are typically banished from the city, disposed outside its borders like pieces of refuse.

Since the turn of the millennium, a significant number of influential Ashirra have moved to the city, even if only temporarily. In their palaces, immense wealth protects them from the scrutiny of the mortal population. To them, Dubai is a safe place to out the chaos of our time. Not that they deserve that.

— LEILA HAMIDI, PALESTINIAN ASHIRRA DISSIDENT

Jerusalem

Despite what they tell you, it started here when we unearthed Him.

Jerusalem is a city of madness. Have you heard of the Kindred exposing themselves to the sun, walking into holy buildings, frothing at the mouth and declaring their being vampires in public?

This holiest of cities finally got to us. It finally got in our heads and made us wake up.

It's all madness. We now clash in the open here. Those who could hold on to their heads got out when they could. Many came back, drawn to the rave.

It is like one of those movies, where all the characters go insane in space. Jerusalem is like that. I'm sure there's much a vampire could gain here. What a city to control. What a people to access. What history to pillage. What vitae to drain… But remain here and not go insane? That is simply impossible.

This is the fountainhead from which the blood of Malkav sprung. We drank it and made the rest of the city fall to ruin.

This is heaven. Embrace the insanity and be the Beast you are meant to be.

— MORDECHAI LASLO, RABBI OF THE BAJ'T MAJNOON, NOMINALLY OF THE ASHIRRA

London

The story of London is long and winding, childe. It would take a mortal lifetime to tell it. You are here not to hear of the tale of the Thames, however, or the architecture, or the Great Fire, or even of the Blitz and the rebuilding though, are you? You wish to know of Mithras.

For many centuries, the city was synonymous with Mithras, our Prince, our God-Emperor. He was our deity and our liege. Harsh, but ever fair. I served him for most of my existence until the time he decided to die, and after that as well.

It is a mistake to say London was a Camarilla city. It was a Mithraic city. It is just that Mithras of Clan Ventrue saw more use for the Camarilla than he did for any other sect. Other Kindred remained there under his mercy, and those who wished to claim power entered his order, or cult, if you will.

London was one of the strongest Kindred domains. Whether ruled by Mithras, one of his seneschals, Anne Bowesley, or indeed Mithras again — upon his reawakening — it was the hub of European power. The city was a throne. Upon it, Mithras had complete control over the British Isles.

This mortal Inquisition rose up recently, and we laughed at it until our Prince said it was time for our cult to decamp as unstoppable danger approached. We were to make for Edinburgh,

where provision was in place for the continuation of our worship. The cultists, including myself, headed north. The remaining London Kindred, hundreds of them, Queen Anne, and Mithras too, faced the Inquisition as the kine led a purge of the city. The Kindred had no clue what was happening. I caught glimpses of Mithras' face in my daysleep, however. He was smiling as the end came. This was the war and the death he wanted.

Mithras was the Unconquered Sun. London was the unconquered domain. He finally fell to a worthy opponent, and hundreds fell with him.

We continue his work from Scotland, and will never stop worshipping his name and deeds. London is empty now. No Kindred make haven there, and none shall, for fear of disturbing Mithras' tomb. Some say the Duskborn are the exception, but this only serves to prove their contaminated state — all true Kindred who pass through the city come out terrified, or not at all.

– LORD ROGER DE CAMDEN, PATER OF THE CULT OF MITHRAS, SENESCHAL OF LONDON, PRINCE OF EDINBURGH, ELDER OF THE THE LINE OF CAPPADOCIUS

Miami

What a den of shit. I apologize for my lack of eloquence on the subject, but few cities appall me more than this one. The Sabbat held it since its foundation, and it shows.

There's still too many shadows here, too much flesh, too many drugs, too much needless bloodshed… I get away from myself.

It is difficult to rattle me, but Miami does it. The mortals see it as some sunshine paradise with cocktails on the beach from 8am. I see it for what it is. Every Kindred who comes to Miami loses something. Their compassion, conscience, or perhaps just their humanity. Their eyes deaden, they see everything as a bag to drain, and even better when they can add some designer drugs to the mix.

I came here investigating the Circulatory System. I believe this is where that odd little industry started. All I've found are bodies, piles of ash, and recordings of experiments I wish I could forget.

I have killed more people than I can count. I would kill all the Kindred in this city if I could. It is rotten.

– FATIMA AL-FAQADI, VOICE AND BLADE OF THE CHILDREN OF HAQIM SCHISMATICS

Paris

The Camarilla is sometimes called the Ivory Tower, and if there is one city in the world that represents that Tower, it is Paris. The old Camarilla stronghold used to be defined by the triangle of London, Paris, and Berlin. With the fall of London to the Inquisition and Berlin to the Anarchs, we are left with just Paris, but the City of Light is as strong as ever.

Strong, and in many ways, incredibly repressive. Paris is a bad place to be if you are Anarch, clanless, or even a Camarilla Kindred without good references. Prince François Villon has ruled the domain since forever. He has only officially been Prince for a few centuries, but he was pulling strings and getting his powdered hands all over French court, living and unliving, long before he seized the throne for himself. He has now gotten so comfortable on it, he likes to be called king.

No matter what happens in the rest of the sect, Villon seems to become only stronger. And with this he becomes more picky, more demanding. Kindred from faltering domains are these nights coming to seek asylum here so often, that even an elder might get shown the door if Villon does not like their face. You can say, that the pre-revolutionary ancien régime never ended for the Kindred. It is just as with the Sun King, as Villon tells it. The court has become very degenerate, you might say, but there is true power hidden under this corruption. You cannot defeat it by being very strong or old. The thing to be in Paris is interesting. Pretty will get you in, but smart will keep you alive.

– DAHLIA GAUDIN, SKILLED SEAMSTRESS, THIN-BLOOD TOREADOR, AND MISTRESS OF PRINCE (ROI) VILLON DE PARIS

Prague

Our city is the most important battleground in Europe tonight. Too many eyes focus west on the void that is London or the decadence that is Paris. Others look east in fear, at Moscow with its rattling sabres or Sevastopol with its current problems. Prague is something more. Made symbolic by the treason of Bell, it's ground zero for the War of Ages. All over the globe, the unbound are empowered by this telling blow against our sect. But here, where it happened, we still stand. That should tell you something about how hollow their victory is. The blood still flows down in Elysium and old Vasily sleeps soundly under the floors of Pražský castle, undisturbed by the ruckus.

If you believe the propaganda, what we have achieved in Prague cannot be understated. It's no Anarch bastion, nor is it a Camarilla tyranny: Prague is the city of neutrality through division. A place we watchfully share. Our Camarilla Scourges patrol the streets of the inner city, maintaining order and stability. Meanwhile, the suburbs and the south of the city has become Anarch free zones. In this way we keep any political unrest contained, as the unbound are busy spreading their international propaganda among the local activists.

All Kindred are welcome in Prague if they know their place. We have our own traditions here, of hospitality, concealment, peace, and our own symbols marking our leaders, our enemies, and those from which we can freely feed. The city is in balance, for now.

Truth is, we are a neutral city because we are torn between extremes. Our new Prince is busily expanding his collection of weapons and has been fortifying the havens of his allies. I know what it means. Perhaps it will begin tonight?

– KIRILL, PRIMOGEN AND SCOURGE OF PRAGUE

Rio de Janeiro

If you want a good time, you come to Rio. If you want an easy meal, you come to Rio. If you want to live life like it's your last night, come to fucking Rio! Come to Rio for a whole new experience, my friend. You don't trust me, huh? Just look at the way this city's set up. The Lasombra control the clubs, the high life, the tourist scene, the beaches. The Toreador are in the favela, the shanties, scrumming around with the beggars on the streets. Doesn't that just seem crazy to you? You haven't seen the half of it. This city is one of freedom, but believe me, we got rules. They just ain't your Paris or Chicago Camarilla rules. Imagine the Camarilla fucked the Sabbat, or no, the Sabbat fucked the Camarilla, yeah? Rio's its little baby. We share blood, we have a good time, we don't give a shit about what happens outside the city. This is where the party never stops!

So, uh, one other thing. Don't leave the city limits. I mean it. Get high on the Praia de Copacabana, open up a tourist's throat, dance in the spray — whatever. Just don't go out of sight of the city lights. There's some bad shit out there. Not Sabbat, not Inquisition. They might be Kindred, but I'm not sure. They snatch up anyone who goes off the path, my friend. They hang in trees and linger like corpses, just waiting for someone like you to trip up.

Just have a good time in Rio, that's all I'm saying!

– "DIZZY" BARRETTI, MALKA-VIAN TOUT

Stockholm

Calling Stockholm a Hellene city is not entirely wrong. The Camarilla here have an almost Anarch fascination with the political systems of the kine. The dominant Brujah and Ventrue have their fangs sunk deep into the dying democratic socialist ideal of Folkhemmet ("the peoples home"), hiding their feeding accidents as statistics in a vast system of elderly homes, daycare centres, and hospitals. The typical Swede trusts the state to take care of them, and it really does. It makes sure even their blood is taken care of. The dozen or so unbound and Anarch leeches of the greater Stockholm region call the slightly fewer but older Camarilla Kindred Gråstaten ("the Grey State") and both fear and ridicule them. The Grey State is just as isolationist and elite

as any western Prince and their court, but makes a great show of pretending to be the most refined undead democracy in the world, and it kind of is. Unknown to all living Swedes, they elect their own undead masters when they go to the ballots every four years. This means every Grey State ancilla and elder is attached to one of the major political parties of Sweden and they are allowed to use any means they see fit to help their party into a position of government. The Kindred attached to the winning parties score seats on the Kindred Urtima Riksdagen ("the Untimely Council") that still gathers every month in an underground chamber under the parliament.

The young-looking but ancient Hellene Gustav Sörensson and his Social Democratic Council alternates with the noble-born Renaissance Ventrue Christina and her capitalist/nationalist Alliance, traditionally fronted by the conservative party Moderaterna. The most recent election has been nightmarishly even and has the potential to change everything. Gustav has disappeared to the East (his will is now represented by a coterie of young caretakers who seem to hate thin-bloods especially) and Christina is supporting the populist nationalist Sweden Democrats, violently opposing the Ashirra and the Banu Haqims' recent rising influence among the unbound in the region.

The Anarchs of Stockholm are used to thriving as outsiders and have never been a part of the Camarilla. These coteries and autarkis come and go, their unlife-expectancies counted in decades rather than centuries. The Others, as they sometimes call themselves, attach to the illegal party scene and the pseudo-criminal groups, weird congregations, mosques and collectives in the suburbs, or find other specialized niches where the Grey State can't find or threaten them.

– ARVID OLOFSSON, NIGHT WRITER FOR OMNI

St. Petersburg

For the longest time, the rest of the world thought St. Petersburg was a graveyard for Kindred... Someone went around telling tales that Nosferatu boogeymen kept scouring the city clear of our kind, so everyone left us well alone. Even the Brujah Council in Moscow stayed clear of the city, leaving it to my sire to rule, and then me. It was a pretty simple life...

But now the doors are open. It's time for change, they say. I've never felt too much like a Camarilla stalwart. But then, I've never felt much like an Anarch either. I like to march to the beat of my own drum, as they say. Some consider me simple... That's not nice. I am anything but. What sets me apart, is I don't get involved in other domain's shit...

Now read these words: You stay the fuck out of my city or I will hunt you down with my army of Sewer Rats and feast on the blood in your cold, crusted heart. Petrograd has no place for you.

This is the city of the Tsar. This is my city, and you will play by my rules.

It's all a game, you see...? Isolation can be terrible. It can make one lash out. Please, come and visit. There aren't many of us here, but there are plenty of kine.

– NIKOLAI, VENTRUE PRINCE OF ST. PETERSBURG

Tokyo

I stayed in Tokyo recently to visit the Regent there, and give them the low-down on activities post-Vienna. I can honestly say, I have never experienced a more intense fortnight in all my time.

It seems everyone is a tourist here. Life in Tokyo is... weird. I think weird is a fair assessment. I made the mistake of assuming the domain was like everything I'd seen on TV and online, but it's more than that. It's a total mind-fuck. A vampire can get dizzy in a city like Tokyo. There's so much heat, but it's a cold heat.

I'll explain. I did that thing tourists do, standing in the street while the sea of Japanese people flow past you. I did not feel hunger once. Not once. It's like something here subdues it. I can't explain it. I asked my fellow Tremere about it, and even they have no clue. Everything here is measured, calculated, precise. It freaked me out so much I ducked into a pachinko parlor (some stereotypes are real) and finally felt the thrum of life again. Some poor old bastard felt my confused, raggedy bite that

night, metal balls dropping from his hand...

So, there is a strong Camarilla presence in Tokyo, but I've no idea if they send word back to the Inner Circle or the Justicars. I know in this age, everywhere is accessible, but Tokyo and Japan in general are so technology-dependent, it now feels utterly cut off with Inquisition eyes on our emails and messages. This makes the city pretty autonomous. The Kindred here order themselves into set levels, determined by age, and once they reach a certain point (I think three centuries undead?) they are expected to relocate to Kyoto. All but one have, without a fuss. The one that remains is some gnarly Nosferatu made of scabs and scars, and nobody wants to argue with her.

If anyone is in charge of this domain it's Mayumi Shibasaki. She doesn't rule, technically, but ensures order is kept and tribute flows upstream. She's of the Old Clan, so she says, but has no issues with the Tremere.

Like I said, Tokyo is weird. I recommend everyone tries it, but don't get caught here. Almost every vampire I encountered seemed detached, or vacant, like something was inside them riding their bodies.

Probably nothing.

– LILLE HAAKE, TREMERE MAGISTER, HOUSE CARNA FACTION

Venice

Clan Hecata keeps a lid on their Venetian activities these nights. My contact, one Lydia di Giovani, tells me it is because they wish to avoid the attentions of the mortal hunts so rife at this time. I seriously doubt her family have too many worries, however. My own research tells me a whole bunch of the famiglia have ties to the Inquisition, and lay low like cockroaches until the worst of the fires burn out.

Another contact tells me the Hecatas have gone to ground to conspire on some grand scheme several years in the making. They are opening some gateway beneath the Mausoleum (that impossible skyscraper they invest half a fortune in keeping erect, given the water table below it), and need to work together to bring something through, or send something back.

What I do know is this: you can visit Venice, you can feed there, and you can even have your convocations there. The attack on the Camarilla Inner Circle some years ago was a blip, I believe, and though rumors hold of the Brujah losing their representative (I am shedding no tears since their betrayal) and one of the Nosferatu disappearing somewhere beyond the veil, I feel the city is entirely safe. Ten years without an incident is not bad for our kind, and anyway, if you hang around long enough you may be able to report back to me what the Clan of Death is doing in the city's bowels.

– KARL SCHREKT, HIGH PONTIFEX OF CLAN TREMERE, TRADITIONALIST FACTION

Vienna

For a long time Vienna was the seat of Tremere power, a place that drew the childer of the clan into itself but welcomed few others. Rumour had it, Tremere himself slept uneasily beneath the city, controlling most everything that went on in there. As the tale goes, around the turn of the millenium, he awoke and began some grand ritual or communion. I wasn't there, and I can't claim the veracity of this statement, but it certainly holds up with what happened next.

The Prime Chantry was attacked.

As I recall, this was the first time we found evidence of a new, organized Inquisition. Somehow they knew about us, they knew our weaknesses, and they knew the greatest secrets of the Tremere:

where to find them, which to hit them, and how to destroy their strongest bastion.

The news reported explosions throughout the city, but it would be more accurate to call them quakes or disintegrations. I never saw flames in any footage, just buildings collapsing rapidly. And from one moment to the next, the Pyramid was dissolved, Tremere and his Inner council supposedly turned to ash for good.

Now the city is without leaders. The bewildered Warlocks have been forbidden by their elders from stepping foot in it, the Inquisition has cast its gaze in other directions, and the Anarchs have begun to move in, making their havens in dusty rooms left hurriedly a decade ago.

My limited understanding puts the chantry in the center of some U.N. quarantine zone, telling me

there's something worth salvaging in there. Think of Vienna as if it was the Vatican City of vampires. So many powerful Warlocks with secure havens, well-equipped staff, and secret magics tucked away in every nook and cranny. And no one really to look after it anymore.

The one thing that bugs me about how Vienna went down is the inconsistency. I can believe the Inquisition were behind this, though don't ask me how they did it. But — and it's a big but — why did they only target the Tremere? And why did they then up the ante in London by purging the whole bad batch? Something doesn't add up. I kind of wish the Tremere were still a solid enough unit to ask to investigate the whole thing.

– AMBRUS MAROPIS, HACKER, WEBMASTER, AND TECHNO-LOGICAL SAVANT

KINDRED *clans*

The Camarilla was founded as an accord between seven great clans. Five of those remain. In the last decade one more family of Blood, the Children of Haqim, have proven themselves worthy of our attention. As the union between Victoria Ash and Tegyrius the Vizier has been sealed in blood and through Blood, and while the metaphorical wedding sheets are still damp, we prepare to welcome the Clan of the Hunt amongst our own.

While clan unites Kindred of the same ancestry all over the world, clan organization and legislation is almost entirely local. Society-wide edicts, like the exclusion of the Brujah from our gathering and the appointment of clan Justicars are the exception. Many Princes sanction or apply interpretations of the Traditions based on clan: "No Toreador in my city may Embrace this decade," or, "The progeny of Malkav may kill anyone outside their clan who feeds on the inmates of LA County Jail."

In seeing the clans as social units, nations of the dead, or at least as subcultures with their own shared values and propensities, we do simplify reality. By permitting Primogen to speak for all Kindred of their line, we disregard how complex every clan's internal structure really is and how it differs from domain to domain. We accept and enforce these generalizations for a good reason. They work. They bring order. If we would not treat the clans as political entities, with whom contracts and agreements can be made and laws can be created to control, we would be inviting chaos.

By treating the clans as nations, we also follow the precedent set at the Convention of Thorns. The governing structure of our society, with Justicars, Primogen, and other offices held by representatives of our clans aids clan coherence inside our sect. When we say Clan of the Rose, we refer only to the Toreador who have sworn oaths to uphold the Traditions and our glorious union, not to their fallen brethren scurrying outside the light of our Traditions.

You can argue that not all Ventrue are ambitious, proud, or wealthy, and that our view of the clans as cohesive and organized groups disregards outliers. But such a comment misses the point. Individuals who step outside agreements made between the Camarilla and the clan elders are meaningless to us.

And before you waste time repeating clueless thin-blood concerns that the clan system forces us to be what we are not or sorts us needlessly into racist categories, ask yourself why your clanmates share your obsessions. The Blood will tell. It makes you what you are, no matter how unique or individualistic you perceive yourself. And thus we build our union first from clans and secondly from individuals.

The Anarchs are ready to spill Kindred Blood to defend the idea that clan should be rendered meaningless compared to individual conviction. To ask about heritage, or even worse, to make a ruling against the entirety of a clan, is not acceptable among the unbound. This is their folly, and it makes them weaker than us. Anarch Brujah have loyalty only to the kin they know, not to Brujah next state over or to a grand tradition of (dubious) accomplishment dating back to Carthage and beyond. Their idealism states that "a bat is a bat," but we all know that's untrue. Comparatively, most Gangrel scoff at the idea of hiding their lineage, as they are proud, and the way their bestial nature asserts itself in physical changes would reveal them even if they tried.

It is understandable that the abolition of clan politics, laws, and ideas of common personalities and flaws can be appealing thoughts, especially to neonates embraced during the last 30 years. The problem is that our condition is not rational. The Blood unites us on a level that not even the most brilliant Hemetic scholars yet understand.

Where others deny what they are or even fight it, we give our great bloodlines structure, direction, leadership, and power. We

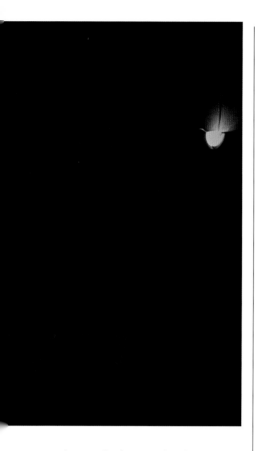

The Blood always tells, I suppose. I am Toreador, and thanks to the Embrace, so are you. Sometimes I wonder about the influence of the Blood on our destinies. Our clan is known for its refinement and taste. We are the most beautiful, sensitive, and glamorous of all Kindred.

I don't believe in false modesty, and I think I epitomize all of these qualities. Few Toreador are as perfect examples of our clan as I am.

There was a time I was ashamed of my mortal life, but that is long past. I have ceased to care about such things. Had you seen me in my mortal days, I don't think you would have thought that girl would become the queen of high society. I was the bastard child of a tavern-keeper's wife. I left home young to follow armies and fuck soldiers for a little bread. I don't think many Toreador would be able to see the refinement and glamour in a quick coupling in the mud.

I survived. Thrived. There's a modern term for what I used to be: sex worker. I hustled. I worked. I recreated myself as the situation warranted. I had a talent for being a chameleon, becoming like those around me, or what they wanted.

My sire was a pimp named Maximilian. He started feeding me his Blood until I was addicted. I served him for a long time, and I think he forgot that Blood addiction is not always the same as real love. I saved his life and he Embraced me. The second time he was about to die, I couldn't help him, instead escaping with his enemies to America.

I left Europe as the illegitimate childe of a pimp. I arrived in New Amsterdam an aristocrat, a refined Toreador ingénue eager to see the wonders of the new world.

Did I make myself into the perfect Toreador on purpose? Did I know of the image of the clan and seek to conform to it? Or did I just follow my instincts? Was it my will, or the voice of the Blood? It's been so long, I don't remember anymore.

honor the history that has come before our own and we strive to act in unison with our clanmates, or at least with respect of our shared past, flaws, goals, and role in the world. For this we are superior, realistic, and pragmatic.

Let those who would devalue the importance of our great clans rage or bicker as they please. Soon enough they will face the truth of the Blood in themselves, as well as final death at the hands of their wiser Camarilla loyalist clanmates.

Praise your blood. Respect your elders. Embody the ideal of your clan and know your place in the hierarchy of night.

For the Tower and the great union of clans!

VENTRUE

I'm going to be honest with you. I'm happy to be old enough that I never have to date another Ventrue again, unless they're an exceptional individual.

The Ventrue seem like good partners if you're young, insecure, and just starting your Camarilla career. They're powerful, dependable, wealthy. Many of them don't mind having an elegant Toreador trophy wife or a showcase husband to orchestrate their little parties for them.

I won't judge you for choosing to be addicted to the Blood of an autocratic tyrant. It's safer than many other ways of being one of us. Easier, at least at first.

There's even a trick to it, if you want to learn it. The Ventrue look to you to provide something interesting in their lives. Tedious themselves, they want to feel the dark majesty of our existences through you. If you want to seduce one of them, you can never be boring. Be flighty, temperamental, passionate. Always keep them on their toes. Every time you make them feel something – anxiety, love, jealousy, arousal – it keeps them interested. The problem is, you can't keep this going forever. I don't think even I could do that. Once they get bored of you, the nature of your affair will change. You will become just another servant among many.

The Ventrue in Kindred Society

```
<LuJu added FSav0>
LuJu: Subtle chat, got it?
FSav0: As crystal.
Jackson: Good. Don't need more shit raining down on the city.
LuJu: Excellent. We need to discuss our role in the society.
Jackson: Same as it ever was. We on top.
LuJu: We would like to think that, but with the recent defections to
    and from our country club, our position is precarious.
FSav0: While I agree we've now got rivals to our seats from the Sau-
    di, nobody trusts them. We're a known quantity. We have ever swum
    in the seas of influence. Sometimes we manipulate it from behind
    the throne, while at other times we take the crown and scepter.
    Whenever there are reins of power, we have at least one hand placed
    firmly on the strap. Ever since we crushed the B in C'thage, we've
    been in charge. Everyone knows this.
Jackson: She right. We considered to have the wealthiest individual
    clan members, though obviously we practice a society of motivated
    self-interest as Sovereign says.
Jackson: Not like we be lending resources to each other. We buy in-
    fluence, silence opponents, hire help, and live opulent existences
    from our penthouse suites and private jets.
LuJu: We need to consider if that opulence is a risk. We stand strong
    as the country club's figurehead and we do this by identifying to-
    day's trends and emulating them to great success. The question has
    to be whether this puts a target on our foreheads.
LuJu: We're at the front of the club.
Jackson: Yeah it ain't perfect, but better us up front than our Vien-
    nese friends or the dancing trash.
FSav0: Agreed. We're at the front of the club because we're the only
    ones who can handle it. We don't ask for power. It is our duty.
LuJu: So you two maintain that despite recent events, our position
    remains unchanged? Still kings, still duty-bound to rule, still go-
    ing to be recognized as the country club's poster kids?
Jackson: Hell, if it's that or Anarch ignominy, I'll choose that.
FSav0: Fuck, that's a damn buzzword. Log off. Get away from your cur-
    rent location. Now.
<Jackson logged out>
<LuJu logged out>
<FSav0 logged out>
```

The Ventrue in Mortal Society

Ventrue consider themselves a cut above Kindred of the other clans, reflecting this opinion in the mortal company they keep. Where some vampires would comfortably rub shoulders with kine on the street, Ventrue share a private booth in an exclusive club, meet mortals across boardroom tables, or outright own their kine through wage slavery or bonds of Blood, and have them tailored to their needs. Most Ventrue have little interest in forming meaningful relationships with lowly mortals. Time is money. The mortals with whom they associate often share the same feelings.

Ventrue enter mortal society in positions of power, controlling corporations openly or as silent partners, forming societies and clubs with restricted memberships, and involving themselves in mortal politics as much as they dare.

Many Ventrue wear sharp, expensive fashion. They lean toward the practical and declarative suit or dress, always bearing a designer label, or a custom outfit created by a tailor on staff. Less inclined to dull formality, the Ventrue are more drawn to dress like the husbands and wives of popular politicians, drawing the eye and maintaining the attention of the viewer. Their outfit will remain immaculate — obsessively so — adorned with a brooch, tie clip, or signet ring that denotes

deeds or titles to other Ventrue. They know other Kindred look to them as the Clan of Kings, so they usually keep numerous mortal servants to ensure no hairs fall out of place, no creases appear, and a change of clothes is always available in case of embarrassing blood spillage.

The Sins of the Ventrue

To the as yet unnamed Childe of Fiorenza Savona,

Congratulations on finding the second letter. You will need this if you are to prove yourself worthy of the Directorate some night.

You will have already determined

that some blood tastes like vomit and ash on our tongues. We Ventrue have incredibly particular tastes. We do not settle for anything but the finest vintages. Yet, those vintages will differ from Blue Blood to Blue Blood.

It becomes apparent in these nights of increasing scrutiny that our "restriction" or "preference" is harder to cater for without drawing the eyes of interested mortals. Therefore, many of us now surround ourselves with the herd from which we feed (if you ever question why one of our infamous stockbrokers or investment bankers spends several hours every night in the soup kitchen, I assure you it is not out of charity) or we make deals with groups such as the Circulatory System to procure us the vessels we need.

In truth, the latter option is the more civilized. Better to have your favoured vessel delivered to your door than having to hunt among the vulgar and the vermin.

Do not give the System too much information, mind you. They made that mistake in Chicago when the service initially arose, and now everyone knows their feeding styles. My recommendation is to order an assortment of vessels you want, and surround them with similar, but not identical kine. You will know which ones to drink from, and you can always donate the leftovers to your associates and subordinates.

- S.B.

Property of the Circulatory System

Clan Ventrue are among our best customers. Their restricted palates prevent their drinking blood of certain types, with restrictions often varying between individual Kindred, though said restrictions (preferences, as our Ventrue clients like to say) may be passed from sire to childe. See below for a sample of feeding restrictions listed for the domain of Chicago:

- **H. BALLARD:** Members of his own family.
- **A. CAPONE:** Women born in Italy.
- **Z. FORGE:** Sleeping men.
- **F. GAUGHAN:** Men born in Italy.
- **HURRICANE:** Unknown. Possibly a single mortal.
- **K. JACKSON:** Members of mortal gangs.

- **L. MATTHEWS:** Individuals with hallucinogenic drugs in their bloodstream.
- **E. NEALLY:** Opium/heroin addicts.
- **J. PETERSON:** Mortal journalists.
- **J. SCHUMPETER:** Recent victims of physical assault (one week?)
- **A. SOVEREIGN:** Mortal employees of the financial sector.
- **B. WASHINGTON:** Mortals in the shower.
- **E. YORK:** Blue-eyed mortals.

As you can see from this well-researched report, feeding restrictions fall across multiple spectrums. Gender, place of birth, employment, situation, appearances, and blood quality are some of the sectors we must examine.

Of interest are the feeding restrictions that appear manufactured. The recently returned to society F. Gaughan is said to only feed from Italian males due to his loathing for sire, A. Capone. E. Neally is suspected to have been a drug addict in his mortal days, and E. York only dated men with blue eyes (according to anecdotal evidence).

Ventrue are known to do anything to get the blood they require, for the simple reason that without it, they expire. If you wish to examine a Ventrue's capacity for sin, dangle one of its favored vessels out of reach. Many Ventrue, such as H. Ballard and A. Capone are known for their greed and pride. Both corral their vessels in greater number than is required, and both take exception to those same vessels receiving harm from another source. On the same note, expect a Ventrue to behave with heavenly virtue if they think it will get them what they require. F. Gaughan sacrificed himself to torpor for the sake of his herd.

With all this in mind, be certain that the Ventrue are our best paying market. Tease them, carefully, but placate them.

Toreador

Many Toreador think that to be truly understood, you must find your lovers within the clan. If you want beauty and refinement, why look anywhere else?

They may well be right.

Yet... I prefer to have my romantic escapades outside our own clan. God knows we've all done that thing where we fall in love with a mortal, Embrace them, and then it falls apart because it always does. Romance inside the clan has always felt to me like an extension of that, a little too incestuous for my taste.

This does not mean I haven't loved other Divas, of course. My very first vampire lover was my sire, after all. And you will find our clan full of pretty girls and handsome boys Embraced because one of our peers decided they were drawn to something lovable about them. If you look, you'll be able to see it too. At least for a little while.

The Toreador in Kindred Society

The Toreador are predominantly members of the Camarilla, and will proudly tell any Kindred who ask that they are responsible for its formation. According to Arikelite scholars, it was Rafael de Corazon of their clan who suggested the sect name, the Traditions, and the hierarchy in each domain. The sect serves the clan, as it enables them to mingle with and prey on humanity without the vulgarity of having to be an obvious monster. To most Toreador, the Anarchs are boorish cretins with misplaced priorities, and vampires of any other group are what happens when excess runs a little too far.

The Toreador occupy an important role in domains, their finger on the mortal pulse allowing them to keep Elysium contemporary and update other Kindred on social mores and cultural changes. As mouthpieces for the Kindred, they are often called to voice the proclamations of the Camarilla, and spread legitimate news and destructive gossip throughout

The Toreador in Mortal Society

"TOREADOR" AMONG US

REPORT #98

The blankbodies who belong to the "Toreador family" hold a startling depth of influence in mortal society, though we believe this is an afterthought to their true aims. The family, or subspecies, focuses on the popular in culture and society. They bury their fingers in the media, influencing television, popular music, rolling news, and vast quantities of online porn. They open galleries and nightclubs, salons and wine bars. The Toreador are entrepreneurial, likely owning more properties and businesses globally than any other blankbody group, besides possibly the "Tower" (see Report #68). This dedication does not automatically translate to wealth, as a Toreador will only stay with a project for as long as it holds interest. We have observed that blankbodies of other groups sometimes come in as partners, to ride the Toreador's success and then hold the reins of a business once the Toreador loses interest.

All this tells us that for all the Toreador success among the human world, they merely seek to enjoy it rather than control it. This allows their shallow ambitions to compliment the more dangerous ones of the Sombra and Venture families (see Report #212).

Where there is reason to suspect Toreador activity, look for eccentric but popular individuals who surround themselves with objects designed to make an impression on the viewer. Clothing, cars, and even personal assistants will stand out, while the Toreador blankbody itself will likely be stylish, but not necessarily a very colorful individual.

TOR98-3 #98

their cities. Some make art of their messages, conveying the tale of a Prince's fall via stenciled art in the alley outside Elysium, ridiculing a Tradition-breaking neonate with a crude song, or celebrating a Camarilla victory with a parodic stage-play. Typically, mortals remain none the wiser to the true meaning of this art.

Art's recent widespread accessibility through media and museums with low cost entry, allows the clan to finally relate to vampires of other bloodlines, and kine from poorer backgrounds. Historically, the Toreador always remained aloof of those they perceived as less "cultured."

While the elders of the clan resent mingling with riff-raff, the neonates and ancillae embrace a period in which their works are now available to all.

The Sins of the Toreador

Krystyna Kowalski to a guest, over a "Bloody Mary" in the Opera Club:

I've spoken to many Kindred your age and I can tell you, our feeding methods haven't changed much over the last millennium. We Divas still enjoy the thrill of love and the passion of lust. Those emotions break through our jaded facades, making the feed an exhilarating experience. We turn on the charm, seduce the vessel, and take blood from them as we take them in other ways.

Sin

I walked the night,
a glistening rat.
I preened and whined
and cut and cried,
a most splendid rat.
I emptied a man's pockets of
his talent,
his empathy,
his trust,
his blood.
My face looked back at me
from a shop window pane.
I was coated in
glory,
love,
loyalty,
liquids.
A moist,
A most beautiful rat.

No, we have not developed a genuine desire for sex in itself. I believe that will always elude us as we grow older, such is our curse. But the combination of feeding while kissing, drinking while fucking, gorging on blood while experiencing the closest we get to orgasm is intense. I do not know why the other clans balk at such practices.

Of course, there are those who believe to feed and fuck is vulgar. Those are the kinds of Sensates who favor a single vessel, and work on them for years, just drinking a mouthful every week or so while spending the rest of the time admiring the mortal as their muse. Those relationships never end well. They think it's love, but it's just obsession. Eventually, that muse runs out of whatever drew the drinker in the first place. The Sensate moves on and the mortal is left a hollowed-out shell. Most kill themselves without their Diva sponsor.

WHEEL *of* FORTUNE

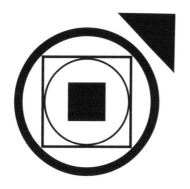

TREMERE

I know what you are expecting. You think I am going to tell you the Warlocks are boring, pointless to romance.

And yes, that is often the way. Theoretically their passionate focus on the mystic powers of the blood is compelling, but in practice... It feels as if they understand the acquisition of power, but not what you need it for.

Still, I have had a few rather eye-opening experiences with older Warlocks who have spent one or more lifetimes in the stifling hierarchy. It does strange things to them, gives them interesting predilections and surprising sexual tastes. I have seen and experienced most this world has to offer in terms of people and their intimate desires. I'm not easily surprised, yet in these interactions with the Tremere, I learned something new. It wasn't always to my taste, but sometimes you make love not because you're into it, but because curiosity makes it impossible to stop.

All that aside, it would be worth pretending to love one, just to get a look at their libraries of vitae.

The Tremere in Kindred society

Our Thaumaturgy sets us apart from all other clans. We alone rule the miracles of Blood. The outsiders crave our Hemetic magic with jealousy. For all their antiquity, the methods and beliefs of the elder clans are mired in superstition rather than an understanding of the hidden structure of creation.

We were long the strongest pillar of the Camarilla, and we will be again. But for now, we are seekers. We sense the Blood speak to all clans, and it will be us who master communion, control, and destruction, if necessary, of the forces that rouse within us. We may be divided as a clan, but our cause is the same: master the secrets of eternity and keep them away from the eyes of the ignorant and unworthy.

Clan Tremere goes by many names these nights. We refer to house before clan, though most of us still occupy the Camarilla. Until our recent fall, we even threatened Ventrue rule over the great society of night. Now our Pyramid is fractured, two great cracks splitting us into three houses. It is sad, but necessary. Change is required for growth to occur. The change in us mirrored by a change in the world. As above, so below.

Our role in this grand play of curses and blood is a simple one. We are the clan who will make every sacrifice necessary for immortality and power over the vitae. The Camarilla has always been the best alliance for achieving this aim. We loyally serve the other clans, rarely taking praxis for ourselves. Why bother with temporal rule when we have eternity for experimentation?

We recognize the importance of numbers. Three and seven. Clan Tremere used to be one, with seven heads. A hydra. Now we have three heads and three bodies, but the Blood does not change.

We were the strongest of clans until I launched my little schism, though I can't take all the credit. My bond to the clan weakened because of what was going on in Vienna, I'm sure. I was just tired. Tired of being told when to kneel, when to bow, when to give up my vitae or take the vitae of someone else.

I realized there was a better way. The old way. Commune with the land, the spirits of the earth, with life and with death. All of this through the Blood. That is the way of House Carna.

Schrekt maintains that House Tremere will rise once more with him at the head, and his new council of seven. Perhaps he is correct. Maybe the old bonds will once again be enforced.

While I disagree with Schrekt, we find common cause in keeping the Tremere strong as a clan. Our reputation for strength and unity cannot be shaken further.

- CARNA

THREE HOUSES

REPORT #139

Our understanding of the blood manipulating blank-bodies known as "warlocks" is slim, despite several close encounters. What we have have uncovered of late might allow us to question one of them in greater detail, and perhaps provoke a response. It appears the infected of this group ascribe to one of three factions. Our preliminary definitions are as follows:

TREMERE: The core faction. Strict hierarchy. Very secretive. Attack B313 appears to have damaged this faction significantly.

CARNA: A fringe faction. Cellular. Very secretive. Difficult to target due to their widespread nature. Ingratiated in multiple feminist magic cults.

GORATRIX: A fringe faction. Strict hierarchy. Difficult to ascertain numbers. One informant swore (under questioning) that the leader has died twice over and risen again in recent nights.

The three factions are unified in the loosest sense, but rivalry makes it possible that we can use them against each other.

TH-44-67 #139

The Tremere in Mortal Society

The Tremere sphere of mortal influence is highly specialized. Where other clans may look at a sector of the city's infrastructure and plant a flag to declare that group their territory, the only area the Tremere call their own is academia, making it common for Warlocks to make their havens inside universities or on campus grounds. The clan members love attending night classes, learning up to date theories, engaging in private debate with favorite professors, and then feeding from the great mind sat with them.

Beyond intellectual circles, Tremere influence overlaps the arcane realms of occultism, witchcraft, and human secret societies. They embed themselves in groups like the Rosicrucians or the Golden Dawn, both based on Hermetic thought, sleep beneath freemason lodges, and study alongside mortal hedge magicians. Scientology is one of the more high profile occult groups known to be under Warlock influence, and though the New Age movement is usually the domain of the Lunatics, the Tremere are believed to have played a major role in the catastrophic attempt to establish the spiritual commune known as Rajneeshpuram in Central Oregon in the early 1980's.

The addition of House Carna to Clan Tremere has created new avenues for the Warlocks of tonight. Tremere of House Carna — known as Blood Witches — may be less formal than the Pyramid of old, but glowing with the fierce determination of those who have recently discovered how different power tastes when you are the one who wields it, they are no less intimidating for their resourceful creativity. The witches burned by our forefathers have risen from the ash, and when they enter mortal society, ripe with vengeful fantasies and sanguine cravings, it is to liberate new sisters and teach them how to bite before they are bitten.

Feeding Practices

If you are reading this, you are of the Blood. If you were not of the Blood, you would not be able to read this.

As a member of Clan and House Tremere, it is imperative you follow these instructions:

- Never drain the vessel dry, for expiration prevents their future use.
- Do not Embrace the vessel without permission from the Council of Seven.
- Ensure a quart of blood is saved from every vessel for ex-perimentation, and dispatched to your nearest chantry.
- If possible, remove all memory of feeding from the vessel's mind. If not possible, ask a sen-ior member of the clan to do so, or recruit a herd of mortals who won't talk.

Previous region-specific restric-tions on feeding only from intel-lectuals and those of esoteric focus are waived during the clan's time of recalibration. Further instruc-tions will be issued.

Sins of the Tremere

My dearest Aisling,

Through winding winds I trust this letter reaches you, where'er you tread these nights. I write this to you now, knowing our communications online must halt. May this short, guided letter find you without disruption.

Our recent turmoil following the devastation in Vienna brings to mind talk we once had on the nature of sin, and whether we are creatures of same. I am an atheist as you know, so belief in God and some heavenly arbitrated sin sits wrong with me, but I can share my observations of recent years. Really, it should have been clear to us all along.

We Thaumaturges suffer greatly from hubris. Throw cocksuredness, vanity, tremendous ego, and pride in there for good measure. We are not divinely stricken with these conditions, for they are of our own making. For too many years we were the runaway success story, but our situation now is due to the afore-mentioned sins and follies.

Vienna collapsed because we made no secret of the chantry's placement there.

The clan splintered because we all felt we were wiser than the next of us.

We were so sure of our unassailable position in the Camarilla, the Assa-mites are now sneaking in to replace us.

We must return to form, and fast. We will not be a small wheel in the Camarilla's grand mechanism. We will surpass our former heights, using knowledge of our previous failures to help us reach our destinies.

For this I require your help. It is time for you to consider the worth of a rolling chantry and the power that it could accumulate through constant movement. I believe it is time for you to give up your seat in the Chantry of the Five Boroughs, and embrace change.

Change is greater than both of us, and our visions said to follow this broken path.

Windham

I have broken more hearts through the centuries than I have suffered heartbreak myself. When I have, it's often been the fault of a Malkavian.

I am very good at the social games we play, but sometimes a Lunatic will beat me. Their advantage is that they don't always know they are playing a game. The sincerity just hits me in a weak spot, I suppose.

Many Toreador like to play with Madmen the same way we do with the Lepers. Exploit their weaknesses, fake a romance, see if you can get them to destroy themselves for love of you. I shalln't judge if you do this, but I have never been able to enjoy it. I am too sentimental.

There is one more thing about the Lunatics I feel I should mention. There's a rumor which says that if you drink too much of their blood, you will lose your mind. I have drunk enough to suspect it's not really true, but I like the idea. It gives a Malkavian blood orgy that special frisson of excitement.

Malkavians in Kindred Society

The Malkavians are proud members of the Camarilla. They benefit from the Masquerade, has ever had a firm relationship with the Ventrue and Toreador as counsels and muses, and just have a feeling that the Camarilla are right. Abandoning the support of the Camarilla exacerbates a Malkavian's mental illness, though long-term Anarch Lunatics state this heightened madness provides greater insight still and is the clan's true calling.

Rationally, our sect should not tolerate unstable supporters. Yet, the Children of Malkav thrive with us. It is as if their mental ailments allow them to circumvent the Traditions without breaking them, somehow letting them remain unnoticeable, despite their abnormality, in the darkest parts of the city, where civilization fears to tread. We all tend to overlook what we find uncomfortable... And often enough, they put on good faces, acting as easily-trusted advisors to Princes or even ascending to praxis, before anyone recognizes their self-assured authority as megalomania and obsession.

Though few coteries comfortably house the Lunatics, they make their way by attaching their loyalties to

REPORT #112

THE APPEARANCE OF THE MENTALLY COMPROMISED

The family of mentally compromised blankbodies known as "Malkavs" share a notable feature of appearance. When in the same city, we believe they coordinate without communicating. In extreme cases, they are seen wearing variations of the same outfit, leading to a club filled with, for instance, Armani suit-clad blankbodies. One informant talks of an AA group where three members always wear their left trouser leg rolled up. More commonly, Malkavs in a city share a feature they subconsciously apply to their outfits. A color theme, a pocket handkerchief, the same brand of mobile phone, or a signet ring may denote that these are the mentally compromised blankbodies of the city. Carefully note the appearance of all blankbodies you encounter, and look for common features.

PSY-EV-7 #112

any Kindred willing to do more than just dismiss them offhand. And they can be exceedingly useful. Lacking normal systems of self-preservation, the Malkavians act as pioneers in new explorations of the Blood. Our kind has always been aware of the differing properties of blood, but it was the Lunatics who started identifying the reasons behind the fact. They managed it by using many of their own bloodline as test subjects. Though we shrugged at first — it would be their loss if their members suffered — the clan's gamble paid off. They now corner the market in blood trafficking and research on its mystical properties gained via consumption of mortal resonance. This fact vexes the Tremere no end.

We have often looked down on them with pity or from fear, letting the Nosferatu act as their shepherds when others would take advantage of their infirmities. But in recent nights the Lunatics have shown themselves more than capable of looking after their own.

Malkavians in Mortal Society

My daughter is such fun, but you should not listen to her too closely. She plays with her hand concealed, you see. Some of us feel the need to purge words from our minds as if they were a poison. I speak readily because I play with an open hand. My daughter, less so.

She and her sister are interesting studies in how we interact with the kine. My childe runs a nightclub, rubbing flesh with mortals of all kinds. That throng of meat, dancing and pounding feet, pulses thumping, blood rushing. We enjoy being in places full of kine. After hours parties, hospitals, universities, other less hospitable institutions. Why, I know an Oracle who makes his haven in a rehab clinic just to get a little sight from those poor, afflicted mortals who have spent a little too long dancing to a chemical tune. He claims their blood tastes enlightening.

We surround ourselves with those who are already disturbed (at least as far as other mortals consider), and blend in as well as we're able. Sometimes we take positions of authority: board member of the hospital, chief psychiatrist in the clinic, leader of a cult of street kids. Our spheres of influence encompass healthcare, the realm of conspiracy theorists, fringe religions, and of course, addicts.

Cynical Kindred believe we tell our herds what they want to hear, but our vessels are more loyal than others. Obsessively so. The aging, demented population falls within our reach. Where other Kindred dismiss aged mortal minds as addled beyond use, we alone pry intelligence from the degenerated, and they love us for it.

Any mortals in need of support will find it with us. They can lean on us, and we take the weight, and their blood with it.

Sins of the Malkavians

Yes, I'm still here. I'm everywhere now. I'm in my head, I'm in yours. I'm beneath Manhattan and on a mountain in Wakhan. But enough about me, what about you? Where are you going to get a mouthful of blood tonight?

It's not easy for us. The Clan of the Hidden makes a lot of noise about their difficulties, what with their unconventional faces, but imagine how it feels to go to feed only to suddenly be reminded of your mother (you know, the one who didn't hold you enough), when you catch a whiff of a vessel's perfume, or your father (you know, the one who made you a man), when you feel the scratch of beard against your cheek, or your crushing self-loathing, when yet another mortal rejects you.

It's not easy knowing you, your brothers, sisters, parents, and children (in a Kindred sense) are all touched, as they say. Mortal psychology doesn't even begin to understand the nature of mental illnesses in their own kind, and our condition is another thing entirely, so while entertaining, therapy doesn't exactly help. Nor do we have the option of seeking support and solidarity from our friends — we can't even tell strangers on the internet these nights. The only thing we can reliably do is self-medicate.

So how to feed? I know Malkavians who acquire their blood in bags, stolen from donation vans. I

Dolphin B. ACTIVE NOW

What do I give a fuck about the SI? Bring them on.
If they can find me, they're welcome to me.

I still suggest caution.
They will be monitoring this channel.
So only type what you want them
to see.

They think we're all sinners.
They're right.
I've sinned. My whole family's sinned.
Feeding from the mentally ill? Not a sin.
They're not helping anyone anyway.
It's what we do to the healthy.

Tell them this. They need to know.

I fucking hate those kine without a care in the world. I fucking hate their cheery, unknowing face.
I want their lives. I want their normality.
Now, I know I'll never get it.
So envy. Envy, anger, jealousy, spite. I let it all out on them.
Here's one for free, you SI fucks:
There's an old abattoir just outside Batimore, used to be O'Tolley's slaughterhouse.
It's where I've been storing all the norms I've been revealing a bit of the world to.
A bit of truth.
If you're lucky, one or two may still have some blood in them.
But you'll have to be quick!
Blood drains fast when you stick a blood bag on a hook upside-down.

It's not their fault.

No, it isn't. But it isn't mine either. Let's just say "the voices tell me to do it." That always works.

know Malkavians who create highly specific herds that won't set off or exacerbates their various ailments. I know Malkavians who throw caution to the wind and let their full derangements manifest on whatever poor mortal they stumble upon in their moment of need. My advice to you is simple: determine what you need to score this night. Do you want the memory of all that trauma from years ago? Maybe so. Maybe it enlivens you. Do you want the anonymity of stalking the coma ward in a hospital for calm melancholic blood? Possibly. Maybe you feel less guilt that way. You want to make the voices stop for the night? Then you find a chunky vessel and take more than you require, just to let your eyeballs float. My point is, never go off half-cocked. Malkavians who survive are those who don't break down during feeding. Honestly, there's nothing worse than having to explain to some jumped up Sheriff why there's a mortal with their throat open, blood all over the cop car, and right outside the Prince's haven. Really, there's nothing worse. Unless you want it. You might.

⋯⋯✦⋯⋯

"I've been watching you, Persia. I see how you struggle with your condition." Ozzy stroked his clanmate's hair as she sat there, still as a statue. "Our condition. We all suffer. But I have a nepenthe. It will not last forever, but it will break your reverie."

He pulled a plastic, crinkled bottom from his satchel, its contents a thick burgundy-brown color. "I'm sorry it's a little clotted. I've had it on me since last night. I was going to use it myself, but... I think you need it more." He attempted to unscrew the tap, glued as it was to the bottle neck. With a little exertion, he twisted it free.

"Drink up, Persia. Allow me to tell you a little secret." He poured the claggy liquid between the still Oracle's lips. "You've been raised to only take your fill, and nothing more. You've been so good at that. Well now you break free. Medication exists for our kind, and it comes through the blood. We can stave off the voices, the dirge, the fugue, and the mania, we just need to drink a little more than the others. We need more than a mouthful. We need to fill our bellies."

With one hand he gripped the back of her neck, while he squeezed the fluid into her mouth with the other. "Some will call us gluttons, but we must heal ourselves. The only way, the best way, is by consuming as much blood as we want. Tell all the Visionaries you know: the more blood you drink, the quieter it becomes. Once we get tired of beauty, we want a taste of the grotesque.

Nosferatu

Every Toreador should have an affair with a Nosferatu at least once. There's something so touching about how grateful and sincere they are. They look at you like at a gift from God. They introduce you to their Vagrant friends who watch your affair with meek envy.

The very first time I did this, there was a young man, my lover's childe, who became so jealous he kidnapped me and demanded I love him like I had loved his sire. It was all quite thrilling! He tied me up, made speeches about his love, wrote poetry, brought me humans to feed from.

After a week I got tired of it and killed him, but I still cherish the memory. It's rare to see such commitment.

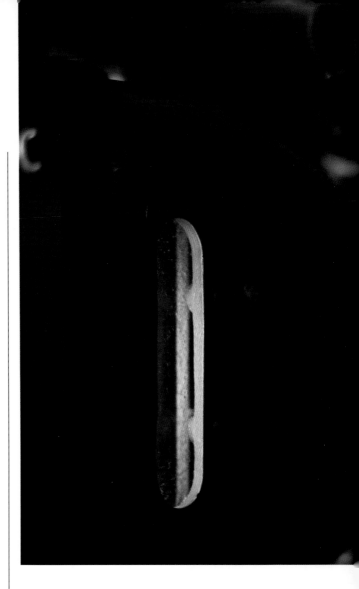

The Nosferatu in Kindred Society

This is Ambrus. If you can stand to listen to this recording without destroying the machine it's playing from, let me tell you how I sorry I am that it came to this, but let me also tell you why we did what we did.

Necessity forces action. We joined the Camarilla because the benefit of being able to hide from humanity was greater than the allure to rule it. We're a grounded clan, so far as it goes, in touch with those who struggle against great odds, even if we prey on them regularly. We've always been better at hiding than seeking.

So as the Camarilla started tightening its noose around Kindred who weren't 100% bona fide Camarilla, you expected us to inflate the life raft for both our clans, for when we jumped overboard. We even told you we would. We told you that the Camarilla would do nothing but subjugate our clan at a time the sect was under more scrutiny than it had ever been. We said the Anarchs were the best fit for us.

I hate to tell you this, but we lied our asses off. We let you jump, and even gave you a little push, but we never had any intention of joining you. We saw the Brujah following the Gangrel and realized the Camarilla would need our information, intelligence, networks, and raw strength more than it ever had before. Your absence created a vacancy. The Camarilla prized us for letting them know about the Rabble defection.

So are we arseholes? Almost certainly. But our position is stronger than it's ever been. The Camarilla needs us, and we need them. I wish you luck in the Anarch Movement, Theo, but I think you'll come to regret your decision.

⊷⊶⊷◆⊷⊶⊷

Appearances are everything, my dear. One could argue it doesn't matter what we wear. A stylistic setting won't turn a lump of coal into a diamond. But a little thought to detail never hurt. Even if you can't ever be beautiful, you can still appear impressive, intimidating, influential, tasteful... And as such, our clan tends to be more conscious of presentation than any of the others, even the Degenerates. Some adorn spectacular masks designed to hide their form, while others heighten the horror with makeup and gruesome accessories that cast doubt on what is real and faux deformity. In Elysium, most of us wear our curse with pride. Sometimes too much pride, as neonates still reeling with the pain of subjugating themselves to our abhorrent condition revel in their misery, showing up in bizarre creations made from trash and second hand leftovers meticulously crafted into haute couture getups that would be worthy of the catwalk if they didn't stink of piss. There are exceptions, of course. The Nosferatu known as Cleopatras attempt to look as sexually appealing as they can, grooming the more normal parts of their bodies and concealing the rest.

Our afflictions run the gamut between skin diseases to grossly distended facial orifices, and bulging organs and bones to unnatural clumps of hair, cartilage, or tumors. I don't remember much from my mortal days, but I remember I used to obsess over the cellulites on my thighs. It is a charming memory. I was so beautiful.

As our transformation usually takes weeks or even months to be complete, some Kindred theorize that we are the most living of all our kind and that our deformities are the visible signs of the body's attempt to sacrifice parts of itself to stave off death. Like cauterizing a wound. I like the idea. We are like the "Moroi," the living vampires of Eastern European folklore. We look more like corpses than any of our Camarilla cousins, but in contrast to them, we still feel what it was like to be human. We still carry the spark of day inside.

The Nosferatu in Mortal Society

Nosferatu struggle among the kine. While any mortal Embraced into the clan has the same social capabilities as they had the night before the bite, the hideous countenance or bodily deformities that comes with membership in this clan makes interacting directly with mortals difficult. To make up for their curse, they adopt creative methods to help interaction. The simplest is to associate with outcasts and those afflicted by medical conditions. A Nosferatu with a caved-in nose and bleeding gums would fit better into a meth rehab center than they would a champagne and caviar party in a penthouse suite. A Nosferatu with constantly shedding skin would perhaps find respite in a medical facility, while one that bears scabs, sores, and appears streaked with grime may stand proud in a homeless shelter. The unlucky ones that sport truly monstrous deformities like elongated skulls, all-black eyes, large pointed ears or rodent-like countenances are forced to seek circumstances where they can wear masks or trust their mastery of obfuscation to hunt. All their decisions, from choice of feeding grounds to retainers and trusted servants depend on the severity of their curse and with what level of skill they hide it. In most cases, they are likely to hide behind several layers of subterfuge, preferring always the path of most resistance to that which is the most well-lit.

Of all the clans, the Nosferatu are the least likely to directly associate with former mortal connections. Few would understand the sudden degeneration in looks, and many Nosferatu could not bear to show their faces to loved ones from a previous life. However, most bear no such resistance when it comes to Kindred society. Here, they often revel in the revulsion their unhidden appearance causes in their fellow monsters. "We show them what they really are," as the saying goes.

Catfish Alert!

Watch out all you online dating addicts, as there's a catfish epidemic sweeping across Europe! But wait, don't you know what catfishing is? Let's explain:

Some users of dating services like Tender and OkCupid craft fake personas using photos sourced elsewhere. They use these artificial profiles to tempt hopeful men or women (mostly men) to contact them, engage in pseudo-relationships online, and eventually arrange to meet with their prospective date.

In most cases, that's where it ends. The guy discovers the young hottie he was looking for isn't who she said she was, and goes home angry and betrayed.

Not so much with the latest incidents.

Reports from dating site metrics for cities such as Athens and Rome state catfishing is up in a big way, but the men who report meeting these fakers come back with real horror stories

of their dates. While we don't judge people by their appearances here at RED-Buzz, accounts tell of real freaks waiting for these guys, somehow disguising their diseased and malformed condition until the last possible moment, at which point they show their horrible faces! One even attempted to bite a prospective boyfriend!

DateDice in Greece has announced they're investigating whether this is some coordinated prank for a reality TV show. If so, we can't wait to see the reactions on these guys' faces. Apparently, the makeup on the catfishes faces is so good, it caused one guy to faint and wake up in the hospital!

Sins of the Nosferatu

Each clan possesses legions of sinners. The Nosferatu like to hide, act as martyrs, and care for the unwashed and unwanted, but they are far from virtuous. Their shepherding of select mortals is just another form of exploitation. They brainwash the kine into believing they are the only ones who care for them, only to sink their teeth in once their victim no longer has anywhere else to go.

Their cowardice and recent turncoat behavior puts them at odds with the Brujah and other Anarchs, but such is their pride and arrogance, that it makes them look out for their own before they see to any others.

Ironically, the vice most Nosferatu succumb to is vanity, as it is rare for a Leper to be fully at ease with their ugliness.

The Clan of the Hunt,
Assassins,
Children of Haqim,
Saracens,
Mediators,
Lawmen,
Assamites

BANU HAQIM

This will shock you, but until now, I have never had a Haqimite lover. In a few cases a Child of Haqim has tried to pursue me romantically. Stern, serious young men, and once a woman too. The tragedy was that sometimes it's more pleasant to be wanted than to give in. With these individuals, I sensed their devotion and need, the intensity of their emotions. There was something pleasurable in their frustrations, and it would have passed if I had accepted them.

In time, they get over it.

Word of warning, though. It's fun to pit suitors against each other. Their jealousy of one another is entertaining to watch, often good for a laugh at the Elysium. However, and I speak from experience, it can be dangerous if one of them is a Haqimite. The woman who pursued me challenged my lover to a duel and killed him. An altogether romantic display of ardor, but unfortunately she was sentenced to see the sun by a Prince who did not understand the finer points of violent love.

My future husband will be a Haqimite, so I will finally complete my set.

Young that you are, you probably want to ask why I'm going along with this. The great alliance between the Camarilla and the Ashirra will be made official though this wedding, with me as the symbolic offering. Why accept such a role for myself?

You must understand that we exist for a very long time. Many things can happen. I have resolved to be the main character in my own story, and with this step, I move from being a mid-level Camarilla celebrity to the center stage. It requires me to take a certain role, but it also propels me upwards.

For a mortal, a choice like this would define the rest of their life. This would be their final fate.

For an immortal... Well, I do not wish to disrespect my future husband. I will cherish him for the rest of eternity. After all, what kind of a person would act dishonestly at their own wedding?

"I was dead, then alive.
Weeping, then laughing.
The power of love came into me,
and I became fierce like a lion,
then tender like the evening star."

– RUMI

The Odense Pact

By Aisha Talwar, Vizier of the dispossessed Children of Haqim

The circumstances surrounding the Banu Haqim entry into the Camarilla are little known, but here is what I heard:

The sorcerer known as Ur-Shulgi, back in Alamut, began a purge of all the Children of Haqim his inhuman mind deemed unworthy. This judgment extended to any who abandoned Haqim in favor of Allah. Some say his refusal to disavow the book of peace destroyed Jamal, who held the title of Eldest at the time, but we cannot prove this.

As you would imagine, many Children of Haqim balked at the idea of abandoning faith. They absconded, falling on the Camarilla's mercy. These vampires — the entire Vizier Caste and many of the Warriors, so I understand — pledged to serve the sect where the Brujah and Gangrel had failed, having made several entreaties to this effect over the last two decades. The groundwork was already laid down, you see. The obstacle had always been the clan's mutual enmity with the Tremere.

Three things happened to make their admission a possibility: the first was the Brujah departure; the second was the Tremere loss in Vienna; the third was the Sabbat's Gehenna Crusade, that gave us a common enemy on the battlefields of our homelands. When many of our faithless siblings seemed to join, or at least assist, the Cainite unbelievers, our dedication to this pact grew hard as damascus steel.

You see, the Camarilla felt weakened by the war and the rise of the Inquisition, yet in a position of negotiating strength all at once. The ancient enemy of the Banu Haqim, the Tremere, were hamstrung, and a vacancy awaited the Assassins' attendance. It may surprise you that the Camarilla held meetings with both the accursed Followers of Set and us Haqimites on the same night, to decide on which of the two would join. The "Ministry," as they style themselves these nights, met Justicars in one city while we Banu Haqim met the sect's representatives in some kitchen in an irrelevant Danish town. Their meeting was opulent and hidden behind a NATO gathering in the same hotel. Ours was ignominious and out of sight.

Theirs blew up. Ours did not.

The Camarilla laid the deaths of those Justicars at the feet of the Setites. I am more inclined to believe it was us. We knew exactly what they were doing, and secured our position in the sect.

Oh, do not think the Banu Haqim were innocent in destroying the Tremere. Someone slipped the Inquisition the exact location of the Tremere sanctuary in that capital. Someone has hated the Tremere for half a millennium. Someone benefited from the Tremere injury.

I bow to the strategists among the Warriors. We always considered them murderous fanatics, but lacking in nuance. It appears they played the Jyhad better than anyone.

———————◆———————

The Judge enters the city in secret. The night reveals patterns of misconduct to his patient gaze. Monsters with human faces steal innocent blood. Blood-tainted ambition crush divine dreams of justice. The streets overflow with wickedness. That one is a murderer — a monster. And the woman over there sold her own child — she is a monster. And also the soldier there — he serves an unjust King. Someone must bring balance. Someone must point the finger and decide what is right and what is wrong. It will be Haqim. A decision is made. To hunt monsters the Judge must become a monster himself. The father listens and grants Haqim his wish. But like all such things, it's a test wrapped inside a curse. The Judge knows that no court is unsullied. His code is to always drink souls of the guilty, to feed the cause of justice with the blood of the wicked. King and Queen are his first targets, but it doesn't end there. In fact, it never ends at all. There is so much evil to gather in his burning veins. So many black souls to drink. He can't do it all by himself, so Haqim begat Ur-Shulgi and its siblings to make war on the rest of their unjust kind. As the second city fell, he led his children to the hidden mountain fastness Alamut. Centuries pass. Justice is meted out and the deaths of the guilty are planned and performed in exchange for a Blood price. But who is guilty? "Every last blood drinker," says Ur-Shulgi and turns on his brothers. "Only those that break the law of God," says the mortal Prophet and looks straight into the Judge's eyes. He wavers. Vigilante or holy warrior? Psycho-killer with a code or righteous bounty hunter? Assassin or divine executioner? Personal or universal justice? Hunters of their own kind, with traditions leading back to Solomon and beyond, the Children are my last and only hope. Let them come for me. On my knees I pray: "Just Haqim, make me and my kind pay for what we have done, so that the Earth may turn unperturbed, no longer marred by our hungry shadows". An absence of sound tells me my prayers have been heard.

Who are the Banu Haqim?

The Judges of the Banu Haqim are torn between their hereditary thirst and their passion for justice. The Judges have long set themselves apart from Kindred society to better deliver their soul stealing capital punishments. That is about to change. A schism divides the clan between followers of the newly awoken methuselah, Ur-Shulgi, and the Islamic Warriors and Viziers embraced long after the clan abandoned their merciless blood worship. Alamut — the Children's hidden base of operations somewhere in Afghanistan — has fallen entirely to the blood cultists, who prepare to deliver their judgment on their kin, and most sensible Haqimites are now exiles fleeing their old home. The majority of these have joined the faithful sect of Muslim Kindred: the Ashirra, or are seeking asylum and full membership in the sect's western counterpart — the Camarilla.

Whether they are cultists or warriors for justice, all Children of Haqim adhere to a strict code of some kind, be it Ur-Shulgi's blood laws, a personal vendetta,

the American constitution, some obscure variant of Islamic law or even postmodern theories of oppression. But no vampire is free of self-interest. The uncomfortable truth is that the Children hide their uncontrollable lust for diablerie behind a strict idea of right and wrong. To the Judges someone is always guilty. And the guilty must be punished, their souls sucked out through their arteries to make the Judge stronger in preparation for the next justified murder.

The Banu Haqim include a diverse array of hunters, judges, and killers. Though the clan's focus on judgment frequently manifests in the act of dealing death, the mortals Embraced into the clan are as often qadis, strategists, and law students as they are bounty hunters, soldiers, police officers and trained assassins. The clan's geographical ties likewise make most of the members embraced between 600 C.E. and the early 20th century of one of the denominations of Islamic belief. Older Banu Haqim tend to worship the Blood over any mortal faith. Young members of the clan hail from any place or culture in the world, and while some convert to Islam after their death, most modern Haqimites keep the faith of their breathing days and are respected for it.

In modern nights, Banu Haqim target mortals capable of assessing and handling threats, enforcing law and tradition through force of personality or skill, and of course, killers who would contribute to the clan's aims. The Banu Haqim keep a look out for war veterans, especially those disgraced or wounded in war. They offer them immortality, a chance at redemption, and purpose. Such mortals become prized neonates.

The Banu Haqim are more than a clan of murderers descended from al-Ḥashāshīn, though they have adopted many practices from that mortal sect. The Viziers and Warriors of the clan descend from different broods of Haqim. Each feels compelled to Embrace different mortals, with the Warriors tending toward the martially inclined, while the Viziers drain and turn those with political and legal power. The connection between the two is law. Banu Haqim within the Ashirra and Camarilla strive to maintain and enforce law, making their choice of prospective fledglings critical.

The Banu Haqim in Kindred Society

I was called Fatima al-Faqadi in life and it is the name I wear in death this night. I am Banu Haqim, a judge of monsters and men. Like many of my kind, I am also an exile. But we are no longer outsiders. The Camarilla welcomes us, and we welcome it, as the time has come for the law of Ashirra to guide the ranks of all Kindred.

You have heard the Banu Haqim are divided. This is so. Most of our warrior caste cling to Alamut and the old ways. But the Old Man of the Mountain is dead and the assassins now worship the blood god Ur-Shulgi and have revived the archaic ways of blood worship. This is the code that tells them to slay and consume the souls of all vampires outside our bloodline. The rest of us refuse to give up our mortal faith and morality. We recognized long ago the danger of slavish service to an inhuman being and found purpose in the infinite scope of Allah's mercy. Ours is a code of killing for peace and the greater good.

Fleeing alongside our kine, escaping the madness of the Gehenna War, we risk everything to find new homes. We beseech the Camarilla for sanctuary, and for the most part they grant it. We are grateful to them for their respect. In this they are much better than the increasingly Islamophobic kine of the West. We pray they will not turn back to the intolerance we have come to expect from European and American elders. Perhaps the opposite is true. This union of ours can be the first step towards an age of understanding and justice for both the living and the dead.

We are the judges of all. We must deliver sometimes unpalatable sentences to our fellow Kindred. It is a role for which we are feared and respected, and one of which I am proud. A daughter of Haqim, I serve my kind as an instrument of justice. As a creation of Allah, I feel remorse for every slice of the blade, every scorch of flame, and I question every ounce of satisfaction that comes with ending the lives of the unworthy. The Prophet's are words of peace and community. I am cursed to lead a life of war to make them manifest. Such is my role, and who am I to question it?

The Clan of the Hunt were once mercenaries, bounty hunters, and hired killers among Kindred. When a vampire wanted a final death sentence carried out on a peer, with no connection made to the hit's source, they contracted the Assamites to dispatch a killer. For a fee of vitae sent back to the clan's ancestral home, the Child of Haqim delivered the sentence without moral qualms.

These nights, the clan's global role has changed. The Banu Haqim who worship Ur-Shulgi and have turned their back on Islam still practice internal clan

rituals relating to the sampling and storing of Kindred vitae. Rumors of mass diablerie fuel the fear that the clan wants nothing less than the end of all their kind. These loyalists, hidden in the fortress of Alamut, have driven more than half of the clan to break their bonds to their blood soaked past. In doing so, they have attracted the attention of our sect. The Banu Haqim are once more seen as a potential pillar of the Ivory Tower. Camarilla-sworn Banu Haqim groom sectors of our domains, specifically gaining influence over the kine involved in law, and the breaking of it. The

Islamic Banu Haqim, steadfastly keeping themselves outside the influence of the Ur-Shulgi are known as loyal Ashirra champions, and as Western and Eastern Kindred find common enemies in Sabbat and Anarch uprisings, the idea of the Camarilla seeking an alliance with the Clan of the Hunt seems more and more reasonable.

The Children of Haqim have ever claimed their founder was the judge of all vampires. Within the Camarilla they maintain his legacy, claiming herds and retainers within police departments, security forces, and border patrols. They also hold dominion over segments of organized crime. The clan grooms kine within these sectors, some for the Embrace, some for service, but mainly to hold a valuable card in Camarilla cities. When the other clans want a problematic mortal shut up, the Banu Haqim exert law's grasp via the kine.

The Banu Haqim in Mortal Society

As spoken by Aisha Talwar, Vizier of the dispossessed Children of Haqim:

A common mistake other Kindred make when assessing we Banu Haqim is believing we have no sphere of mortal influence. They say, "the Assamites are a clan of Arab vampires who feed on vampires and live in a vampire fortress away from mortal eyes." This fool's argument is the primary reason the Ventrue and Tremere still object to our admission into the Camarilla.

Of course, there are also barriers based on our faith. Many Camarilla members still express a learned hostility to Islam, either from the misrepresentation of our faith in modern nights or due to them holding the reins of power all the way back a time when the wars against the Ottoman Empire or even the Reconquista or the crusades cast us as enemies of the Christian world.

We have always held sections of mortal society in our grip. While the lawmakers (and sometimes breakers) are the obvious sectors, consider also the ethnic groups within which we masquerade. It is not racist

REPORT #52

RELIGIOUS BLANKBODIES
PART B

In Part A we covered the interaction between the
blankbodies and the Catholic (and Anglican) faith.
Here we discuss the matter of these creatures and
their connections to Islam.

It was an incorrect assumption made around the
time of our formation, that blankbodies hold sway
over the living followers of Islam on a systemic
level. Due to Islam's cellular nature and lack of
formal hierarchy, the faith's resistance to undead
manipulation is, in fact, remarkably strong. While
violent Islamist groups are susceptible to manipulation from blankbody threats, these are fringe
elements of the Muslim community and their power is
rapidly diminishing outside active conflict zones.

Agents have noted that while many interrogated
subjects swiftly abandon their belief systems after infection, those who ascribe to Islam cling to
their faith to a greater degree, manipulating the
ritualized practices of the religion to suit their
needs.

One strain of blankbodies calling themselves
the "Children of Hakim" (the whereabouts of this
Hakim are unknown, but we suspect it to be a cover
name for a key leadership figure) have in earlier
records been described as a globally Islamic species of predator. Correction: While the Children
of Hakim exist in great number in countries such as
Syria, Turkey, and Iran, they are as capable of in-
fecting non-Muslims with their condition, and there
are indications that there are many non-Muslim
Children of Hakim, possibly due to foreign inter-
vention in the conflicts in Iraq, Afghanistan, etc.

Connecting Islam to a single group of blankbodies is an erroneous link. As with the uninfected,
faith can emerge anywhere and among any people.
Our records show the group calling itself "Ashirra"
(see Report #6) is largely driven by faith, with
Islamic leanings, but still resists the stereotype
of a single religion.

Always keep in mind that no matter what faith it
practices, each blankbody twists its religion to
fulfil its needs.

to admit our clan is predominantly one of many hues.
Do not be mistaken: all clans originated from the same
part of the world as we, but our diaspora has come late,
resulting in a greater number of vampires of Eastern
African, Arabic, Bedouin, Persian, and Indian background, among a host of other ethnicities not "White"
or "European."

Of course, such a gamut of origins provides a wide
range of mortal areas to influence. Millennia of prejudices and influence over the wealthy families of Arabia
give us ease of access into petrochemicals (incredibly
useful for gaining resources), banks and finances (incredibly useful for restricting the resources of others),
telecommunications (you will consider that sector of
use when trying to hide cell phone use from the Inquisition), and luxury hotels. Yes, stereotypes still exist,
and we are not above capitalizing on them.

The Sins of the
Banu Haqim

*The good old southern boy puffed pointlessly on a cigarette as
his elder peer cleaned her weapons in his garage. It was only a
fleeting visit, but a rare opportunity for one Child of Haqim
to ask questions of another. "So doll, what's our sin?" Hopkirk
smiled at Fatima as she ignored him, continuing the massage
one of her blades with an oiled rag. "You seem to be convinced
all other Kindred are sinners. So what's ours?"*

*Fatima stopped what she was doing, tucking her cloth
into her pocket as she raised the blade, looking past it at
Hopkirk. "Must you ask? Our sin is plain for all to see. It is
the Blood. We have it on our hands. We have it on our lips.
We have it down our throats. We bathe in it. We relish in it.
We love the Blood." She held the long dagger out, balancing it
with her arm.*

*"That ain't one of the seven deadlies, is it? I mean, I guess
it could be wrath?" Hopkirk spat the cigarette to the floor,
stamping it out with his heel.'*

*"Abandon your narrow view of sin. The Quran forbids
the consumption of Blood and the handling of the dead. In
speaking that truth the Prophet, peace be upon him, spoke
also of our kind. We were not unknown to him. He knew our
relationship with the Blood is all sins. When blood is near, we*

hunger, we lust, we take pride in our kill. We will not stop until we have drank the body and soul of our victims." Fatima wiped the blade down again with a clean cloth, before gently placing it in its sheath.

"So where does that leave us? Everywhere I go I hear about how we're beyond mercy. Do you really think that way?"

Fatima smiled, but it was a sad smile. "We are tested nightly, my brother. For as long as Ur-Shulgi exists in Alamut, he will pull on every one of our sinful urges. He will toy with us until we return to him and his mercy. We must pray for strength and fight to resist. Until we are free, our clan is sin incarnate."

We are judges over Kindred and kine, so appointed by Haqim and Caine. Our terms of judgment may cling to tradition and ancient law, but they are as exacting and true now as they were millennia ago. We feed on those unworthy of the blood in their veins. The most sacred punishment is for the Judge to drink the blood and soul of the criminal, making his demise strengthen the lawgiver. There are many roads to our drinking: besting an opponent in combat, delivering judgment on a sinner in the process of the sacred Blood Hunt, stealing from those cursed as we are cursed. Every feeding is a ritual. We do not take blood lightly. It must come from a source who needs to relinquish a liter of life.

Banu Haqim Archetypes

LAW STUDENT

The Banu Haqim value understanding of law and tradition, frequently Embracing legal experts to help modernize (or at least make relateable) the clan's expectations of all Kindred. This Child of Haqim was still studying law when turned into a vampire, and suddenly the boundaries changed. No longer restricted to 21st century versions of mortal law, they are now an expert in Kindred law. Such a Child of Haqim commands respect among the Viziers.

UNION CHIEF

Knowing when to put feet to the streets, when to arm and take down the man, and when to hold back and simply refuse to aid a tyrant sets this Child of Haqim apart from the stereotypical law abiding members of their clan. The Union Chief came from a background where knowing legal loopholes and how to encourage others into action was integral to their success.

THE ARBITER

This Child of Haqim may have been a Sheriff in life or in undeath. In some way, they were an enforcer of judgment, perhaps holding a position of moral power such as priest, imam, or community leader in a small town or commune. Their ability to wield laws led to the eventual Embrace.

HIRED GUN

In their mortal days, this Child of Haqim was a killer, plain and simple. Perhaps with a military, law enforcement, or security background, but just as likely to be an individual with murderous urges. At least one lethal act drew the attention of a Banu Haqim sire. Now this character continues to live by the gun, or the knife, the poison, or the severe beating, but with all the legitimacy of a hired mercenary.

BLOOD SCHOLAR

The Banu Haqim are known for their obscure blood magic and reverence of the vitae, but this vampire was a blood scholar before the Embrace. Whether a member of a Sufi study group, a cultist in a fringe religion, or a ghoul in the service to a thaumaturge, this mortal's activities drew the Banu Haqim's attentions, and they were put to work interpreting the will of the Blood, along with ways to subvert it.

Disciplines

Blood Sorcery: The power to poison vitae and use the Blood as a weapon against others, as well as sifting truth through the manipulation of Blood. The Banu Haqim keep the secrets of their Blood Sorcery close. The warriors of the clan typically pursue a form of blood magic

known as Quietus that provides its practitioners murderous abilities, while viziers delve into versatile ritual aspects, gleaning secrets from their Blood and others'.

Celerity: The ability to move and react quicker than humanly possible. The Children of Haqim use Celerity to terrifying effect. Many are skilled in its use before all other Disciplines, to rely on speed of judgment before doubt can slow a blade to the throat. Hesitation leads to a vampire's demise. When feeding, the Banu Haqim dance a dervish of drinking from their favored vessels, darting in and drinking their fill before disappearing as quickly as they appeared.

Obfuscate: The ability to melt into shadows, craft an illusory appearance, or fade from plain sight. The Banu Haqim stalk their prey clad in shadow, whether as a means to feed discreetly or deliver final death to a target without ceremony of formal challenge. Some Banu Haqim utilize this Discipline to witness a target committing a crime, before delivering judgment.

Bane

Banu Haqim are drawn to feed from those deserving punishment. This is especially true for vampire Blood, the very essence of transgression. When one of the Judges tastes the Blood of another Cainite, they find it very hard to stop. Slaking at least one Hunger level with vampiric vitae provokes a Hunger Frenzy test (See Core Rules p. 220) at a Difficulty 2 + Bane Severity. If the test is failed they attempt to gorge themselves on vampire Blood, sometimes until they diablerize their Kindred victim. This presents many problems as the Banu Haqim integrate with the Camarilla, who tend to see the Amaranth as anathema.

Clan Compulsion

BANU HAQIM: JUDGMENT

The vampire is compelled to punish anyone seen to transgress against their personal creed, taking their blood as just vengeance for the crime.

For one scene, the vampire must slake at least one Hunger from anyone, friend or foe, that acts against a Conviction of theirs. Failing to do so results in a three-dice penalty to all rolls until the Compulsion is satisfied or the scene ends. (If the one fed from is also a vampire, don't forget to test for Bane-induced Hunger frenzy.)

Rituals

Level 2

ISHTAR'S TOUCH

The blood sorcerer can convert a dose of their own vitae into a touch-activated narcotic that renders a victim uninhibited and vulnerable to Disciplines such as Presence and Dominate, along with attempts at mundane manipulation, coercion and interrogation.

- **Ingredients:** A small amount of hashish or other narcotic substance
- **Process:** The chosen substance is mixed with the user's Blood and rubbed between their fingers as the incantation is read (or whispered). The Ritual only takes a couple of minutes to prepare.
- **System:** The user makes a Ritual roll vs. the Stamina + Resolve of the target mortal or vampire after they make contact with the affected vitae. For the remainder of the scene, the victim suffers a dice penalty equal to the margin of win on the Ritual roll on all resist pools involving Composure or Resolve. (Apply the penalty only once in case the pool involves both Attributes.) The narcotic vitae retains its potency until it is touched, up until the end of the scene.

Level 3

ONE WITH THE BLADE

The Banu Haqim connection to the delivery of harm and death is such that they can speak to a weapon and command it to strike with increased accuracy and lethality. Many Banu Haqim are known for their dedicated weapon, which in some cases are carried with them for centuries of use. Such a weapon never rusts or dulls for as long as it remains in the vampire's possession.

If someone else physically claims it as their own, it ages much as a ghoul denied vitae would do. In the case the weapon is still useable following this degeneration, if it is used against its original owner — the blood sorcerer — it inflicts grievous harm in retribution for them having lost it.

- **Ingredients:** A melee weapon and enough of the caster's vitae to fully immerse it.
- **Process:** The vampire submerges their chosen weapon in their own vitae and speaks a mantra dedicating their life to the weapon. The weapon must remain submerged without interruption until the following sunrise.
- **System:** Once the Blood is exsanguinated and the weapon is submerged, make a Ritual roll. On a win, the weapon becomes mystically dedicated to the user. It remains of immaculate quality unless subjected to focused harm when outside the caster's ownership. Additionally, if anointed by the Blood of the user it gains a two-dice bonus when used in combat. The anointment takes a single turn, forces a Rouse check and lasts for a full scene. A vampire can never possess more than one weapon dedicated this way. In order to perform this ritual on a new weapon, the previous dedicated weapon must be destroyed first.

The vampire with this weapon must ensure it never leaves their possession. If stolen and used against them, it cannot gain any additional dice but deals Aggravated damage against its owner (the one who originally performed the Ritual).

THE ANARCH CLANS

The Camarilla has many enemies. Perhaps the most tragic of them is the Anarchs who imagine they can survive outside the protective reach of our great project. When I think of their chances for survival and experiencing the true blessings of immortality, I almost weep.

The Camarilla has withdrawn behind our natural borders, so to speak. We do not pretend to represent every mangy little blood sucker anymore; we have come to demand a certain level of refinement from our members. But while ridding ourselves of the Gangrel was only reasonable, I must admit that it has made our Elysiums slightly too proper.

There is a little game you can play if you get tired of the endless politics of court. It requires a modicum of modesty and an ability to give up center stage, but I assure you it is worth it.

Many vampires know my name, but few actually know what I look like. It is easy for me to reinvent myself, and it will be even easier for you.

This is what I do: I invent a new identity, a backstory and style. The last time I did this, I was Jasmin de Lacy, a poor little rich girl who had fallen into the clutches of an evil Toreador elder and only barely escaped an addiction to his Blood, only to find herself alone and vulnerable on the streets.

Jasmin was a great success. The Anarchs were averse to my upper class background at first, but started to warm up to me after I told them many horror stories about the vile things going on at the Elysium. I cried tears of Blood, as I did my bravura reenactment of how the elder had bound my mortal parents to his vitae and forced me to witness their addicted degradation.

The key to success with this kind of a ploy is to avoid making yourself the center of attention at all times. I know the temptation to be real, because it's so easy. However, the more people pay attention, the greater the risk of failure.

With Jasmin, I settled into the role of a girl the rebels had heroically rescued from the evil sect which would control her. I went to their parties, played around with their mortal friends and followers, had a bunch of affairs and just generally got back in touch with humanity again. It was lovely. They were so young and so earnest. Every moment with them gave me more will to go on existing.

You are thinking this story will end with some grand betrayal where I called in the Archons to bring fire and fury to these young upstarts.

It does not.

I left after the wedding plans started to take up most of my time. As far as those Anarchs know, Jasmin de Lacy is still out there, a hapless little unbound creature fleeing the wrath of her vicious sire.

The History of the Anarch Movement and why our lost childer should remain so

by Fiorenza Savona

The Camarilla is the best hope for all Kindred. Never forget this. The actions of Anarchs — showing off in front of the kine, getting overly invested in their ideological struggles — push our kind toward extinction. We know this because it has happened before and almost destroyed us, back when our great-grandsires were simply fledglings. In the period we remember as the Burning Times, the Anarch Revolt and the Inquisition came to be great threats to us, nourished by each other on our flesh and vitae.

The Anarchs of tonight like to say we were at risk then of absolute destruction due to our elders throwing us into their wars without care. But this is not so. We became vulnerable due to Anarch disloyalty, idiocy, and self-absorbed rebellion.

The Camarilla is still a young organization, at least compared to some of our elders. They — in all their aged wisdom — established our sect when they recognized that the best way of surviving the progress of human culture was to become a more civilized type of predator. We had to give up on the idea of acting as lions or wolves, loudly proclaiming our strength, to withdraw to the shadows as snakes or spiders, watching and leading our prey without their knowledge and leaving almost no trace of our presence.

Pride would that some disagreed. The Anarchs and their allies believed us to be cowards. For them, power was not enough, they had to be praised as well. How frail their grip on reality, how childish they were.

The Movement's Beginnings

My great-grandsire was Prince of a vital domain named Frankfurt, in what is now Germany. From the era we call the Dark Ages through to the time of the Revolt in the early 15th century, she held that city in a velvet grip. Her style of rule was informed by a decent understanding of humanity and it was both soft and firm, yet everyone obeyed Julia Antasia — for that was her name — and she led her domain into an era of prosperity unlike any other in her region.

But while we of the Antasian family attempted a moderate rule, encouraging the fair and compassionate treatment of the kine while keeping in mind their role in our long unlives, some Kindred felt that wasn't enough. These vain leeches wanted to lord over mortals, torture them, be heroes to them, and in some cases, become their gods. Perhaps it is worth noting that in this, next to the Tzimisce, Lasombra, and Brujah, stood also the Children of Haqim. These clans pushed and prodded the kine mercilessly, appearing to them as gifted heretics, devils, witches, and faithless tyrants. They played with the faith of the humans, driving their fury and fear, as they become both the leaders and targets of hysterical mobs of farmers and disorganized local uprisings. Still, we saw them as troublesome but not a real threat. That was, until the Albigensian Crusade changed everything. We did not know it then, but what began as a war against the cosmopolitan lords of Languedoc started a fever, an obsession, a flame that almost snuffed us out.

Like all holy wars the conflict was grounded in realpolitik. Occitanian nobles' tolerance of Jews, Muslims, and heretics had made them wealthy on trade, and they were the envy of the lesser men of Île-de-France. Made bold by successes in the Holy Land, the northern lords beseeched Rome for permission to wage holy war on their southern brethren and received it. The decades-long war that followed annihilated the Cathar heresy and almost destroyed Occitanian language and culture, but that tragedy is fairly irrelevant to our kind. What does matter is that the inquisitors sent to root out the Cathar heresy in the wake of the crusade found something much worse than ascetic Gnostic fanatics. They found us.

Hidden among the ranks of the Cathars, Kindred heretics were claiming to be angels and Perfecti who had transcended the flesh. Arnaud Amalric, the papal legate, studied them and sent detailed protocols of their weaknesses to Rome, and in response Innocent

III founded and financed the Shadow Inquisition, and by extension, the Society of Leopold. Its agents, led by the infamous Cardinal Marzone, spread slowly, in secret, from Carcassonne and Rome to root us out wherever we could be found. For two centuries they hunted us under the pretense of combating heresy, allied with victimized peasants all over Europe.

When the Anarch rebellion started in earnest in the late 1300's, it quickly spiraled out of control and set off the most deadly religious witch hunt the world has ever known. Inquisitors and mobs launched attacks on us during the day, when we slept. They burned out entire domains of ancient Kindred. These kine — so empowered — declared that the time of monsters was at an end. And what did the Anarchs do? They celebrated! They led hosannas for their success in destroying the established system — a system that had been working. They danced in our ancestors' ashes as the world burned around them.

At the start of the 15th century, our lost childer finally decided not just to attack their sires and grand-sires, but also their clan founders. In this event, to their credit, the Children of Haqim were quite absent. The Tzimisce, Lasombra, and the Famila Giovanni all attempted to destroy their Antediluvian progenitors. Whether these venerable creatures were indeed the first of their bloodlines or just immeasurably ancient elders is unclear, and nor did it matter much to their ungrateful childer, who were eager to free themselves of everything that had come before them.

This Great Betrayal caused chaos among all who participated. The Inquisition they had set off levelled its eyes on the now impossible-to-control Anarch Movement. Thousands of pyres flared up across Europe as the Inquisition engulfed the late medieval world. The centuries of struggle that had preceded were as nothing compared to the sheer scale of the destruction wrought by Torquemada and his contemporaries. And all of a sudden, the squawking, raving Brujah and their kin came to clans like ours, cap in hand, asking for salvation and a better way.

We formed the Camarilla in response. We should have crushed the Anarchs completely, but we did, in many ways, see them as childer. They drove us to the brink of final death, and still we opened our arms to

them, when they were ready to return to us for guidance and protection, and because luminaries such as Rafael de Corazon and Hardestadt cautioned temperance.

My great-grandsire — the wonderful, generous Julia — had fallen to torpor as a result of Anarch actions and has never awoken. I am sure she would have agreed with the Camarilla founders' assessments, for she was ever merciful. But now the Burning Times are returning, led by inquisitors armed with detection devices and flamethrowers and brought about by Anarch pride. Clearly, we should have eliminated our enemies while we had the chance.

There has NEVER been an Anarch movement that was not operated in the secret interests of one methuselah or another—pushed in the direction indicated by their suzerain, without any of them having the slightest suspicion of that fact. They are and always have been tuppeny pawns in the great eternal war between mighty immortal powers. They riot against the machinery of "tyranny" because they have been told to do so, and because they do not possess the mind, knowledge, or willpower to think for themselves. When they were embraced, instead of becoming reborn, they remained within the illusion that all mortals labor under, the illusion we have given them. Instead of becoming free, they became stubborn, wrathful slaves to a malevolent master. In rising up against us, they serve far worse monsters than we.

— Josefin Adelbrant, Sheriff (Brandvakt) of Stockholm

"The first panacea for an Anarch revolt is to upend all of the Traditions, the second is the rule of terror. Both bring temporary unity; but both also bring permanent ruin. Each is nothing but the refuge of the craven political opportunist."

-HARDESTADT THE YOUNGER

Why We Must Rid Ourselves of the Anarch Menace

By Karl Schrekt, Head of House Tremere and eldest of his bloodline

The clans of the Camarilla kept the Anarch activity at an appropriate level for many centuries after the Convention of Thorns, and we should take solace in that what all we suffered made the sect strong. In 2012, however, we finally parted ways with the last of our Anarch-friendly allies.

Many blame Gavrilo Princip for starting World War I when he assassinated Archduke Franz Ferdinand, drawing the Austro-Hungarian Empire into conflict with Serbia. But the Great War wasn't merely brought about by one man, and nor is our current situation. There were signs of a return of the Anarch-provoked Burning Times and the rise of a Second Inquisition long before the incident in Prague.

It was 2002, the mortal War on Terror was on, and the Inner Circle had decided to use it to their advantage against the Sabbat, finishing the war for America once

and for all to weaken their crazed Gehenna Crusade. At first the tactic was a triumph, and their cities fell to us one by one. But sometime around 2006 the Inquisition started targeting our own. How did this happen? Who gave them the information that lead them to Vienna? Clearly the Anarchs. It was then that the Justicars decided it was too late to turn back. They subtly added Anarch groups and domains to the kill-lists. It was a cold move, but they had it coming.

As the Anarchs grew wise to the plot, they began to voice their dissatisfaction. They did this by lopping the heads off of several notable Princes and mailing them to the Justicars. Alas, poor Voorhies of Amsterdam. I was with Justicar Carfax when we received his skull.

One might look at the series of events and say the Camarilla betrayed the Anarchs, but they had gone too far. They weren't content to attack us directly, they attacked the Masquerade itself, causing prominent — and I mean prominent, just look up the footage — breaches in Glasgow, Marrakech, Dallas, and New York, and bringing the Second Inquisition to our door. At that point we had to remove them from our sect.

Such a formality may seem inconsequential when compared to

other fates, but it was an important declaration. It meant that the Anarchs no longer would benefit from Camarilla protection or have access to our cities, herds, Elysia, or resources. They were left to their petty little domains, isolated, dilapidated lighthouses in a sea of night.

And this is their fate now. Finally left on their own to deal with the monsters they have awoken. Soon enough they will come back to us, whining for aid, but we shall refuse them. As the torch lights move in on them, we will look on from the shadows, many and strong, but motionless. We, who respect and protect it, deserve this gift of immortality, they do not.

How to Talk About Anarchs

After the Conclave of Prague and the recent unfortunate events in Berlin, the Anarch Movement has become a topic of discussion in Camarilla Elysiums across the world. This is a delicate historical moment, so it's important to talk about the Anarchs in a way that supports Camarilla principles; especially when your childer or other young Kindred ask about them.

1. Anarchs are incompetent, and this incompetence characterizes everything they do. Contrast Anarch youth with Camarilla experience. Even when they are not violent, the Anarchs are sloppy, fail to think things through, and take risks without considering the consequences.

2. Anarchs tear down. They never build. Anarchs are famous for destruction, rioting, and murder, but when it comes to establishing any kind of order of their own, they fail. This is why the Anarch Free States in California has never managed to establish a clear set of laws or a system of government.

3. Anarchs don't know what they want. Many Anarchs talk about change, but they have no coherent vision or clear demands. This makes it impossible to negotiate with them, as their ideology is too incoherent to produce a negotiating position. This is made worse by their perennial inability to produce leaders one could talk with.

4. Anarch are hypocrites. For all their talk of freedom and equality, they still use humans the same way as any other Kindred do. They preach the right of Kindred to live how they want, yet oppose the desire of Camarilla Kindred to live in the Camarilla.

5. Anarchs should be grateful, but instead they're motivated by envy. Without the Camarilla and its Traditions, mortals would have eradicated the Kindred a long time ago. Anarchs fail to understand this. Instead, they

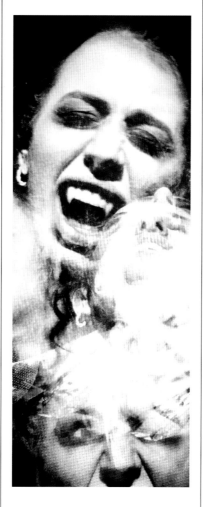

are envious of the power elder Camarilla Kindred have accumulated. They want that power for themselves, but they don't have the patience to work for it.

6. Anarch areas are not safe. The lack of a Prince or Sheriff means that Anarch cities are dangerous, violent places where Kindred can get killed for any reason, or no reason. Without laws and authority, Kindred society is ruled by the most powerful and the most brutal, who take from others what they want.

7. Anarchs endanger the Masquerade. Because they have rejected the Traditions, the Anarchs breed like rabbits. Every Anarch city is overpopulated with Kindred. This means that even if the Anarchs had the ability to maintain the Masquerade, breaches would happen.

8. Anarchs collaborate with the Second Inquisition. Many Anarchs have never developed a clear Kindred identity. They still see themselves as part of their mortal communities, and because of this, they collaborate with the Second Inquisition to attack all of our kind.

9. Last and most importantly, remember that everything the Anarchs want is always unrealistic. They don't understand how the world works, and their ideas are impractical. Sure, their ideas can sound beautiful and just, but they won't survive contact with reality. This is why the Camarilla is the best and only option.

CLAN GANGREL

A pretty useless clan, romantically speaking.

I know that some Toreador like to romanticize the Gangrel as authentic savages who are somehow more honest and real than the rest of us. But I don't buy it. There's nothing as fake as authenticity. The filthy, matted hair of a Savage is just another surface, their pretense at not caring about appearances merely a pose.

This is embarrassing to admit, but I fell for the whole Gangrel mystique once when I was much younger. I had just arrived in America for the first time. He was tall, rugged, handsome in a bestial way. He did not talk much, and I imagined his silence hid a rich inner life.

I even lived in a rural cabin with him for half a year, drinking the blood of animals. Can you imagine? Me, as a homesteader?

It took me a long time to understand that the fantasy I'd fallen in love with was my own creation. I had just projected an idea on to a man who was not much more than a beast.

Do you wish to know the silliest part? When I tried to leave him, he cried. He pleaded, and tried to stop me. I was terrified for a second because he had always seemed so much stronger than me. I thought he would kill me in his jealous weakness.

Even his strength was less than it seemed. I was faster than he expected and he met the sunrise with his own axe in his face. His Blood tasted good, though. I'll give him that.

As proclaimed by
Calebros, Formerly of New York City:

First among betrayers, the Gangrel silently declared for the Anarch Movement near two decades ago. They were an ill fit for the Camarilla, anyway. They made perfect Sheriffs and Archons, and wonderful scouts into hostile territory, but expecting one to take on a political role was as useful as putting a monkey in a suit. Yeah, yeah. I know, I was a Nosferatu Prince. Fuck off.

They joined the Camarilla when it was first founded. They understood our strength and so made uneasy allies. We appreciated them, they respected most of our rules. Good times were had by all.

It was in the late 20th century one of their chiefs, a vampire named Xaviar, melded with the earth (as they are able to do) and claims to have found himself occupying more than mere dirt. He swore he and his coterie were in a living entity that consumed

his friends and spat him out. He became convinced he'd had bodily experience with the Gangrel Antediluvian. He met with the Justicars and told them all this, and they, of course, did not believe him.

Whether they passed it around using cave paintings and smoke signals or text messages and frantic telephone calls, the Animals upped and left. Like the Brujah, many remained — regarded by their bloodline as tamed dogs.

…I suppose if Xaviar had actually

been in contact with a powerful ancient, he may have gained some previously unknown ability to commune through the Blood, but that is pure supposition on my part.

The Camarilla was incensed by the Gangrel departure. Yet, we took no action against the Animals. We felt it was best for our security to pretend they were still with us by never admitting they were not.

Unbeknownst to us, the more politically- and financially-minded Gangrel (they do exist) were channeling support to the An-

arch Movement this entire time. Despite their ostensible independence, these "Wolves of Wall Street" essentially took the Anarchs on as their union, forming a give-and-take agreement with the minor sect that essentially went "when we want to militarize you, we will." You choose the speaker and the addressee in that statement, because it could have gone either way, I've got to be honest.

When the Brujah went over to the Anarch Movement, we felt like they were fools for abandoning structure and alliance in favor of loose independence. Then,

the Gangrel spoke up. They were firmly on the side of their Rebel brethren, had been supporting the Anarchs all along, and would fight tooth and claw for the Anarch right to exist outside Camarilla interference.

Those bastards. After everything we did for their mongrel clan, they spat in our faces and laughed while they did it. If this was vengeance for concealing the truth of Antediluvians, then fine, we got what we deserved. I still feel they picked the wrong side.

CLAN BRUJAH

The Brujah like to see themselves as philosophers and revolutionaries, but personally I think their main utility comes in when you want a good hard, angry-at-the-establishment fuck. I mean, who would ever want to have a relationship with a Punk? A Rebel lover? The idea is ridiculous. They lose their temper at the slightest provocation, and the rest of the time they will surely be lecturing you on something terribly uninteresting.

Ideally, try to avoid talking to them at all.

Normally, I like a good, long seduction. I like it when someone exciting and new pursues me, and tries to win my favour. I also enjoy seducing so-called impossible targets, those others tell me will never be interested. It is a tantalizing game, and it makes the success so much more delicious.

None of that applies to the Punks. Here it is best to be direct, to be physical right from the first glance at one another. Lay your hands on their chest, let them feel how you tremble a little so close to them, and make sure to accidentally bare your neck or open your lips (depending on whether you want to lead or be led). Let nature do the rest. If your desired rebel still talks at this point, perhaps they are not worth it, after all.

The Conclave of Prague

As spoken by Damien, Childe of Critias, Hellene of Clan Brujah:

We Brujah were long a double-edged sword in the Camarilla's hands. The principle clan of the Anarchs, yet afforded the same rights and privileges as all others. Most of us were rabble but I pray you also remember our line as remarkable speakers, thinkers, and truly possessed of a passion remarkable for our kind. Few of the other clans trusted us, but few of them trusted each other, so no

big deal. They assumed — naively, perhaps — that my clan appreciated the security of the Camarilla and our limited flexibility within it. But once a rebel, always a rebel. It's the Brujah way, and probably they should have known better.

The Conclave of Prague saw representatives of all Camarilla clans meeting to discuss the coming century and the best way of handling what was at that time assumed to be a government-funded branch of the Society of Leopold. Almost ten years on, some refer to the event as "The Convention of Prague", mislabeling the conclave to put it on the same

level of importance as the Convention of Thorns. But the Convention written in Prague was not an accord signed in blood, it was a declaration of war underwritten with the spilt gore of one of our founders.

I am of the clan of the Philosopher-Kings — a proud Brujah — and I loathed Hardestadt, as does my sire. Still, what happened was betrayal.

The first part of the ceremony was recitation of the Traditions. Everyone spoke the words. Renewed their oaths. The second part was for each clan's spokesperson to descend to the central stage and kneel before their clan's representative of the

Inner Circle. The whole thing was planned to impress, to awe, held in an ultra-modern theatre, all chalk white and artfully lit. Refreshments were seated in the back rows. Silent witnesses, bound and gagged. Appropriately enough, the reps stood in a circle on the stage.

Theo Bell. Archon of the Camarilla. Born as slave and reborn as killer. For over a century he served the sect and did his clan — my clan — great honor through his loyalty, resolve, and willingness to do anything for the Ivory Tower. He was also a Brujah. When he knelt before Hardestadt, there was a ripple of consternation throughout the amphitheatre. Bell was a Brujah, Hardestadt was a Ventrue. I understand the Ventrue spokesperson — Jan Pieterzoon — was nonplussed to say the least. Bell had taken his spot! Makes me laugh even now to think of it.

Well, they didn't have time to debate ritual, ceremony, or kneeling positions. As Hardestadt looked down at Bell, Bell looked up at him, and from his jacket emerged the barrels of a sawed-off shotgun.

Hardestadt was ancient. His body must have been as granite. Yet Bell had loaded his gun with some kind of incendiary, detonating the Camarilla founder's skull. Before Pieterzoon could cry out, Bell rounded on him and blew

This isn't a title I take on lightly. You know what we think of monarchy where I'm from. Yet, it's got to be done, so I'll do it for all of you and for the Camarilla. I made my choice to stay true to our vision, and it's cost me every friend I ever had, everyone I ever called kin. I'm a Hellene of the line of Troile, and this, our Tower, is the cause I'll die for. The ideal I will kill for. I'll set laws for you to live by, I'll enforce them without mercy, and if you follow them, you'll flourish. If you break them, you'll be punished. Simple as that. Consider me a tyrant if you like, but I'm here for your benefit.

-Donal O'Connor, Brujah (Hellene) Prince of Dublin

him away. I understand Bell denies killing Jan, but I do know he didn't emerge from the theatre. Whether it was Bell or someone else, the Brujah in the building launched a coordinated all-out assault on the Ventrue present, with Tremere and Toreador getting caught in the chaos and conflagration as most attendees fled rather than fought.

I doubt Bell would have rebelled in a vacuum. That is to say, he was always trustworthy, and while he famously chafed under Justicars like Pascek and individuals such as Hardestadt, he knew the Camarilla stood for order. Bell appreciated order.

So why did he finally rebel in unlife as he did in life? I think he fell prey to that old weakness of ours. I think a Ventrue such as Hardestadt said something before the ceremony, or he'd heard of the Camarilla plans

to throw the Anarchs to the Inquisition to save our hides. He lost his temper, grabbed a weapon, and performed this murder on impulse. It wouldn't surprise me if Hardestadt called him "boy" as he took the knee. Maybe Bell was keeping his anger in check, until the Ventrue degraded him one last time.

So yes. We Brujah took a grand ceremony and used it to perform a flagrant assassination. Within nights word was across Europe, and after a week, the world knew. The Brujah had declared for the Anarch Movement. Cities lost swathes of protectors. Primogen Council's found their numbers reduced. Herds and retainers vanished with the clan as my kin migrated to Anarch strongholds such as L.A. and Berlin or attempted to overthrow weak Camarilla rule in cities like Portland and Stockholm.

Many Brujah — including myself and my sire — still remain loyal. We call ourselves Hellenes and speak more to the philosophical, scholarly branch of the clan than the fiery Prometheans of which Bell and his cohort are members. But now, in these nights, the Brujah are effectively seen as traitors. We are all Anarch, as far as the world knows. That makes existence very complicated for someone like me. All I can do is stand my ground and continue to prove my loyalty.

THE CAITIFF

By Fiorenza Savona

Some vampires are not welcome in the Camarilla, as they would weaken us from within. This goes doubly for those with no clan at all. Caitiff is what we call those who do not belong to any one bloodline and who do not manifest their natural clan bane or blessings.

Lineage is important. The Blood remembers, and so should we. This is why we Ventrue recite the deeds of our ancestors at court and call on them for wisdom when we struggle. A fledgling who does not have the good sense to be of decent Blood, or who refuses that which they have, has no potential of becoming a worthwile neonate, simply because they do not have a real identity.

If I don't know who Embraced you, I don't know if you are a liability. Most Caitiff are liabilities. Thrashing around, looking for a parental figure who won't be disgusted by their pointlessness. Such desperation never ends well. It brings disharmony to the structure of our society, interrupts the progress of our great history. The clanless are not like the rest of us. Even the Ravnos — Lilith bless their dozen or so souls — are defined by something. But the Caitiff have no past and thus no future. They do not fight for anything bigger than themselves, and so they are ruled only by momentary desires. Compared to most immortals, guided as we are by great destinies, they barely exist.

Caitiff were nominally permitted within the Camarilla with a sponsor, until recently. We can no longer afford to entertain the trope of the lost royal heir by playing saviors to these orphans. Cutting them off cost us two Princes, one of which revealed himself to be a member of the Ministry all along, but their places have already been filled by better Kindred of worthy lines. Still, the Camarilla respects those who are willing to bleed to uphold the Traditions, and even a Caitiff may prove themselves and gain rights in certain domains. It's all about understanding your position.

THE THIN-BLOODED

As described in an intercepted report by Talley the Hound, Noddist Praetorian, to Marcus Vitel of Washington D.C.

Until recently, I would not have described the thin-bloods as a real threat, let alone disloyal to the Camarilla. You always heard tell of mortals Embraced by weak-blooded individuals and somehow surviving, but those instances were commonly attributed to poor judgement or badly kept records of lineage. And it seemed the mistakes were easily enough fixed.

Not anymore. The thin-bloods have become many and danger travels with them. The Book of Nod foretold their coming. Depending on your translation and your priest, the awakening of the 14th, 15th, or 16th Generation is said to signal Gehenna. I do not know which is true, but I do know we experienced the end of the world just over a decade ago, and only the great sacrifice of one of the clans and a lot of Blood staved off the end.

The thin-bloods do not belong, but in the Camarilla, they can. At least that's the cruel lie they're being sold. Why, the Camarilla even dangles "true vampirism" before the thin-bloods as a reward for slavery, letting them jump and dance for the hope of sanctioned diablerie.

Until they do become true vampires, the Camarilla subjects them to old-fashioned branding by scarification. It's tradition, a rite of passage, the Camarillistes will tell the young one as they carve the crescent moon into their flesh and ink it with Tremere blood and the ash of traitors, making it impossible to remove until their blood has become thick enough to heal the mark.

What of the thin-bloods among the Anarchs? The Scourges of the Tower actively pursue leads on these omens of the end, purge them, and return to their Elysia. Not all of them deserve it. Few choose the Embrace. But these hunts satisfy the superstitious and the jealous. In times of crisis, having someone to blame calms the spirit.

Have you heard some thin-bloods can walk in daylight? Eat and drink and make love like the living? Some pass medical inspections with ease, while others change their gender through strange alchemies using their blood. Some, it's whispered, have been able to return to full life, taking all the knowledge of our world with them back into the daylight. All of this makes them uniquely suited to avoid detection by the new Inquisition, which is why the Camarilla wants them. It also makes them great threats to all true Cainites.

The thin-bloods and Caitiff make for a threatening alliance in the Anarch Movement. They symbolize a new way, punching up at the elders and Princes and sects, or even worse, ignoring us and getting on with their unlives, unbound and unconcerned by what they are. As their numbers grow, they look at the way of the clans as anachronistic. They spit on Tradition.

They are fundamental to the brewing War of Ages, and even if they are not signs of the end, they do signal another Anarch Revolt. It is simply in their nature, savage as it is. I respect the Camarilla's intents, but the thin-bloods cannot be trained, broken in, or bent to heel. They are too far removed from us. A scientist might call them a new breed of vampire, or an evolutionary step forward. But mark my word, this isn't progress, this is devolution, and it needs to be stopped before it spreads.

THE SABBAT

As you may have gathered from my writing, I treasure feeling and sensation above all things. New emotions and fresh experiences have filled me with a desire to meet the next night and the next, burning through more centuries than I care to admit in a flurry of passionate affairs and vendettas. I am made of jealousy, lust, greed, and hate. I exist in a state of constant desire. Even a wicked breed of love has played its part in making this dead heart beat for centuries. Predictable feelings in a Rose, yes? How about fear? Terror? Revulsion? For the most part unlife in the Camarilla holds no such thing for me. Even cold elders with nightmare stratagems play a game I recognize. They maintain human, if antiquated, facades as they ply their nightmare schemes. Polite monstrosity I can deal with. But there are dead things that scare me. Things that have scarred me. Things I never want to have to think about again. While this compendium concerns our order of the bedchamber, I must include a warning here.

You may seek the razor's edge to feel alive, this I can understand. Just never, ever deal with the Hand. When the Sabbat comes for you, you fight or you run. Do not make my mistake and try to humanize or understand them. There is nothing but hopeless emptiness waiting for you if you try.

Have you ever met someone about to be swallowed by the Beast? Looked into the dead eyes of a wight in the making. If you have, you have surely felt it. The revulsion rising from the realisation that this inhuman thing could be you if you just gave in to the hunger. We recoil from the edge, cling to memories of hot life to keep it at bay.

The Sabbat are frightening because they look back at us with these same inhuman eyes, but they do so with full cognition. Here are dead drones of the Beast, yet they are gifted with a collective intelligence disguised as faith and purpose.

Some think the Sabbat weaker or less dangerous now that they have (seemingly) given up on controlling the cities of America and flocked to the war zones of the world, supposedly to revel freely in their vampiric nature under the cover of systematic bombings, atrocities, and the chaos of human warfare. I'm sure they do, but that is not their purpose. These revenants, hardly Kindred at all, seek to transcend what it means to be human. They want to consume the eldest and wisest of us and infect all our species with their loss of self. This Gehenna war is not the end of them, it is another stage. It's a chrysalis. War is changing the Sabbat from the inside and out, and I dread what they will become, twisted and scarred by the fires of their victory. I hate to be serious now, but you should know, whatever official reports are saying about the Gehenna war, we are not winning it.

I feel an itch under my eye. There is still a dark spot there in the shape of a snake eating its own tail, barely visible, where my Sabbat lover touched me. I've made up my mind. That touch was the last. If ever another soulless blood-drone of the Black Hand reaches out to touch me again, I will rather end this eternity than let it. I suggest you take the same approach and steel yourself for what, in a few short years, will come crawling out of Jerusalem and back into our nights.

In most things, I believe knowledge is power. In the case of the Sabbat, I say the less you know about the nihilist Magisters and the flesh-melting Fiends of the Lasombra and the Tzimisce, the better. I will leave only fragments here. Use them to avoid the corrupted clans. Never think you can ally with, reason, or even parley with the Sabbat. You may think me emotional — some of them can seem quite reasonable. At first. But they are not just another sect or gathering of clans. They are infected by a virus, a sickness, a conscious disease. You won't find an essay about the clans of the Sabbat here, and now you know my reasons. Understanding brings danger. I don't love you, but I never want you to feel the fear I did during those endless hot nights in an Atlanta trainyard, reduced to screaming flesh in the claws of the Black Hand.

As remonstrated by Kalinda, Assamite Vizier and Primogen of Milan:

The Anarch Movement is problematic, but once upon a time they agreed with the Camarilla that a greater threat existed. That threat calls itself the Sabbat.

The Sabbat's origins and motives are lost to history, and we do not repeat much of their practices within Camarilla domains. [1] Sometimes, it is better to not know, than in knowing, fall to the Beast.

Tales tell of a mediaeval death cult that drew homicidal and sadistic vampires to it like flies to a swollen corpse. A sect that wanted to dominate humanity, like the vampire emperors of old. But this has not come about, and frightening as they may be in stories, I think it's safe to say the Sabbat have failed. Or at least that we do not understand their aims, except that they are always hungry. The peace they've left behind is eerie at the same time as it is a relief.

First, she believes we are winning the Gehenna War. This is a lie. It's the party line, yes, but still a lie. I have lived through week-long night wars in Donetsk, Aleppo and Ramallah (twice in the last case) and never seen our side come out on top. In Ukraine I fought alongside a militia group consisting of IT-programmers, teachers and a handful of highly suspect "nationalists" using cellphones with Google Maps and Facebook messenger to coordinate artillery strikes against the pro-Russian DPR forces. There were three of us. Me, an Armenian Haqimite called Narek, and our elder, a Greek force of nature who waded into battle in a grey business dress, armed with nothing but an impressive command of foul Russian language. Her enemies became her weapons as she spoke. By any measure we should have been unstoppable. We lasted less than an hour when we met the first pack. I wish I could tell you how they fought, but I can't. The night turned from translucent black to ink. There were screams and the elder's voice: "I see, that changes everything," she said in ancient Greek, her commanding voice cutting through the shelling and the screams. Then she was silent. It was over.

So the next time someone tells you we're winning, think again.

Most Sabbat domains are still out-of-bounds to the Camarilla, unless you are Fiorenza Savona of Clan Ventrue, who swiftly brought Mexico City under control. But most are empty or emptying as the Sabbat packs after, riddled with blood madness, gather by the greatest source of vitae in the world: the Middle East. My home, where methuselahs rise and destroy all these foolish Sabbat who run up to take a bite from them.

Do I diminish their actions? Possibly. The sect makes a frightening sight when one meets them, but give me a legion of armored, drilled, and loyal soldiers over a ravenous horde of Sabbat baboons any night. They terrorize, they butcher, they draw the Inquisition wherever they tread. But we stand tall.

Let the Sabbat consume itself in an orgy of violence. We have paid for the good seats.

Strip lights lining the corridor ceiling flickered to life as Big D hit the switch. "See, this place isn't so bad. We can host our rave here, no problems." She peered into one of the sealed off wards. "They've even got trolleys and what looks like medical equipment still stowed away in here. Were they thinking of coming back someday, do you think?"

Ark shook his head, only half-listening. The idea of hosting a party in an abandoned hospital was pretty predictable, but he couldn't deny the location's aesthetic appeal. Something didn't smell right, though. It was understandable that D, being so thin of blood, wouldn't pick up on it, but he was older and had certain gifts for this kind of thing. There was vitae and death here, and not that long ago.

"Hey, Ark! Look! Some of the wards down here don't have chains on them. Maybe we can-" the young one's voice was cut off as she stepped back from the door she was pushing open. "What in the ever living f-" she never finished her sentence as something not quite arms, legs, and fingers pushed through the swinging doors, disappearing as quickly with her thrashing form. Ark didn't waste time, but bounded backwards as fast as he could toward the staircase. He was stopped, as a long taloned hand grabbed his shoulder and teased bone through skin.

"Going somewhere, little Anarch? Come, come. If you must trespass, you should at least stay for dinner."

Ark and Big D were never seen again. Not the way people remembered them, anyhow ∎

CARMELITA NEILLSON

Desperate elders seeking ways of staving off Gehenna and the Beckoning increasingly seek out the Brazilian-Irish Toreador archaeologist Carmelita Neillson. She unearths the past and interviews Kindred, chronicling a vast array of vampire history and conversations with vampires as old as two millennia. The Camarilla forbids her from archiving any of her findings electronically, so she has established several "Neillson Libraries" in discreet locations.

Her friendly manner, natural curiosity, and abilities as a polyglot make her a natural choice to debrief a Methuselah just awakening from torpor, investigate a ruined temple, or interpret a captured Sabbat scripture. Believing that art need not be in a frame or museum to be admired, Carmelita strongly feels the greatest art, one ignored by Kindred for so long, is the storytelling of their own kind. A gifted storyteller and writer, Carmelita's skills appeal to many Toreador who wish to break the "pretty and talentless" stereotype.

  LORE

● **The Art of Story:** You and Carmelita share the belief that storytelling is one of the lost art forms. Whenever regaling other vampires with historic lore or tales of myth and legend, Toreador naturally gravitate to hear your words, regardless of your standing toward each other.

●● **The Art of Will:** A specific objet d'art or relic, entrusted to your safekeeping by Dr. Neillson, inspires and enthralls you. If you spend an hour meditating on this object (and make a Resolve + Academics test at Difficulty 5) before resting for the day, you awaken with one extra Willpower point. You can meditate in this way once per session.

●●● **Neillson Library:** Carmelita Neillson's small libraries dot the world in Camarilla domains, serving as hives of information used to prompt and support elder vampires' memories. You are the curator or warden for one of these libraries, which counts as a two-dot Haven (●●) with a two-dot Library (●●). Other vampires and Kindred historians meet there as well, which has both advantages and downsides.

●●●● **Interview With the Methuselah:** You have obtained a recording of Carmelita interviewing an impossibly old vampire who divulges secrets about one of the clans in your domain. Once per story, you can ask the Storyteller to provide you with such a

secret. Whether Carmelita knew of this recording and gave it to you or someone made the recording in secret, the information in the interview gives you an advantage over the vampire in the clip and the clan discussed. Interestingly, the voice following Carmelita's at the end of the tape mentions further recordings.

●●●●● **Ancestor's Tomb:** Carmelita has entrusted you to guard the supposed resting place of one of your ancestors. As long as you keep it safe, you can call upon her for a major boon once per story. Should you fail to keep it safe, there will likely be… other consequences.

FATIMA AL-FAQADI

Embraced in the 12th century C.E., Fatima al-Faqadi is ancient among tonight's active Kindred. Known within the Children of Haqim as the Hand of Vengeance, she is one of the most dangerous and skilled assassins who have ever been among the Kindred.

Fatima is a faithful Muslim and a sworn enemy of the blood cultists of Ur-Shulgi. She once worked for vitae, undertaking contracts for Blood funneled back physically or by sorcerous rituals to her clan's fortress, Alamut. But these nights, Alamut is under Ur-Shulgi's control, and Fatima is reported to be the leader of a charge of Banu Haqim fighting side by side with the Camarilla in the Gehenna war.

Evil tongues would have it she is in the fight only to find out what happened to her once-lover and rival, Lucita. For her part, Fatima silences such rumors with a stare almost as deadly as her knives.

LORE

● Weapons Locker: Your connection to Fatima or her network of Banu Haqim gives you access to a hidden weapons locker somewhere within your domain, or the domain you are visiting. You know from rumor or reliable sources where one of these lockers should be located. Once per chronicle you can use this knowledge to equip yourself with a hand-held weapon of your choice, subject to the Storyteller's approval.

● ● Extended Web: Fatima once held membership in the cult known as the Web of Knives. Though the Web remains loyal to the demonic Ur-Shulgi and the Alamut branch of the Banu Haqim, some cultists from the Web followed Fatima in making overtures to the Camarilla. You are either a member of the Extended Web, or have a close bond to those who are. You can take three dots allocated to Allies, Contacts, and Mentor and assign them to members of the Extended Web, who may assist you for a price, or school you in the art of killing. Note that unlike regular Backgrounds, use of these dots require payment, often severe.

● ● ● Missed Hit: You are one of the rare Kindred to survive an assassination attempt by the Hand of Vengeance. Whether or not you were the target or collateral damage, you have a reputation as someone Fatima couldn't bring down. As well as granting two dots in Status, this lore grants one bonus die to Social dice pools when your survival story can be used for good effect.

● ● ● ● Recognized Judge: The Banu Haqim are meant to be judges of other Kindred. Either you were taught the ways of judgement by Fatima, or the Web of Knives taught you Ur-Shulgi's dictates. In either case, in any non-Camarilla domain you may formally announce judgement and execute a Kindred without open retaliation from the ruling sect, as few wish to cross Banu Haqim law. Your judgement does not prevent other Kindred from subtly attempting reprisals.

● ● ● ● ● Open Contract: Your relationship with Fatima is such that she has agreed to eliminate any one opponent of your choice. She will not ask questions. Perhaps your relationship is one of trust or care, or perhaps Fatima owes you. Her success is not guaranteed, but is likely.

FIORENZA SAVONA

When the Lasombra reasserted control over their old religious power centers, the Ventrue responded by expanding their influence in the new nobility: government and multinational corporations. With global political pull, Fiorenza Savona keeps the clan relevant and dangerous – at the center of global power.

Hard-nosed and unafraid to tell another vampire to take a running jump, Fiorenza worked hard as a mortal and continues to do so as a Kindred to ensure that wealthy and powerful vampires remain in their positions.

Moving up through NGOs and the UN, she knows everyone worth controlling in the Davos elite. Her sire targeted her for her contacts list and discovered her Machiavellian political and business acumen.

A fresh power player in the Camarilla, many elders and ancillae consider her a mere "new money" Ventrue. Their wiser clanmates know her actions sway councils, corporations, and individual mortals possessing real power. Where her predecessors focused on vampire politics, Fiorenza believes the key to Kindred longevity lies in the manipulation of the living.

LORE

● **On Fiorenza's List:** Fiorenza knows who you are, which either means she thinks you're an asset to the clan or a problem. Consequently, she has assigned a Gifted mortal (p. 185) Retainer – bodyguard, driver, butler, etc. – to you, though they remain in her employ. They make no secret of spying on you and reporting back to Fiorenza, and they never drift far, even if dismissed. If the mortal is harmed or killed, Fiorenza makes a note that you're not to be trusted, but if your conduct is good, you move further into her good graces.

●● **Breakfast with Fiorenza:** Despite her high-profile role, once per story Fiorenza will make a space in her busy schedule to meet with you. Maybe you have dirt on her or perhaps you are close friends. A meeting with Fiorenza can be lucrative and informative, if you ask her the right questions.

●●● **Friendly Benefits:** You were close to Fiorenza before she became "the next big thing" in Clan Ventrue, and this friendship pays dividends: she can smooth over ruffled Ventrue, provide you with insider trading tips, loan a Gulfstream equipped with polarized windows and pre-cleared flight plans, etc. If you overuse or misuse this connection, the equivalent of a three-dot Mawla (●●●), she cuts you off without hesitation.

●●●● **The Directorate:** The shadowy Ventrue Directorate approached you. Concerned about Fiorenza's meteoric rise, they chose you to approach her, suborn her, and break her to their will. If you accept, you submit to a Blood Bond and have your memories of the Directorate's identities erased – but you receive six dots to select from among Contacts, Mawla, and Resources. Of course, you could approach Fiorenza and offer to work as her double agent.

●●●●● **Government Motion:** Fiorenza owes you a favor – once per chronicle, she agrees to influence a mortal political leader as you request. Her suggestions equal five dice to distribute as you like among any roll involving government action. If you create a major political disturbance or otherwise act to reinforce Fiorenza's "suggestions," the Storyteller may add other dice based on your plan and on how well you succeed at it.

PURE VENTRUE LINEAGE

(VENTRUE CHARACTER ONLY)

More than any other clan, the Ventrue obsess over lineage, reciting their ancestry many generations back. Some claim their ancestors convey abilities to the descendants, while others state reputation is power enough.

The Ventrue understand the importance of history and purity of vitae. When they speak, others listen. It is one thing to know your ancestry, it is quite another to speak it proudly in a court of peers or as a challenge to your enemies. At important occasions, whether a public function or the hours before going into battle, Ventrue expect each other to not only list the names of their ancestors, but to recite their deeds, accomplishments, failures, and — in some cases — dramatic deaths, to honor the past, lift the spirit, and best impress the audience, whether a rabble of Brujah or a jaded Prince.

LORE

● **Sire of Renown:** Your sire is a Ventrue notable for their nobility and adherence to clan values. To an extent, you can lean on your sire's name to curry favor with other Kindred mainly of Clan Ventrue. This lore enables you to gain one die in appropriate Social checks where naming your sire could have impact. If the sire still exists, they may come to resent you using them as a line of credit.

●● **A Lineage of Title:** You come from a line of Princes, Primogen, or possibly Barons. If you ever attempt to acquire title in a domain, Ventrue — even those you've never met — will automatically support your claim, unless they have sufficient reason to oppose you.

●●● **Recitation:** You can name your ancestors all the way to a methuselah of the Fourth Generation, impressing all Kindred within listening distance. Each Kindred of your line has a tale, and you know at least a shortened version of every single one. Reciting the whole thing (something that takes a good 30 minutes or more) gives you a one die bonus to all Social-based tests against other Kindred for the rest of the scene. This can be used once per story.

●●●● **Legendary Lineage (choose one):**

THE LINE OF ALEXANDER: A patron of the arts, passions, and beauty, Alexander of Paris appeared to many as more a Toreador than a Ventrue. Kindred who name their ancestor as Alexander of Paris gain two bonus dice on all Persuasion and Performance rolls made in a crowd of people, as Alexander's line love an audience. If someone interrupts your oration, you must make a fury frenzy check at Difficulty 3.

THE LINE OF ANTONIUS: Antonius was a strategic thinker, obsessive planner, and master architect of Clan Ventrue until his apparent destruction. If you descend from Antonius, you gain two bonus dice on all Academics and Leadership rolls made when planning the defense or building of a domain. If someone disrupts you while making a long-term plan of this nature, you must make a fury frenzy check at Difficulty 3.

THE LINE OF MITHRAS: Mithras exemplifies pride and power. Kindred of his cult claim he was impervious to flame, and somehow this fortitude ripples through to his descendants' willpower. Your Difficulty to resist fear frenzy from exposure to fire is reduced by two. You suffer a two dice penalty when attempting to withstand Dominate attempts by older vampires also of Mithras' line.

●●●●● **Name the Antediluvian:** The Ventrue Antediluvian went by many names, and each methuselah of his clan knows the ancient entity by a different epithet. You know one of these names or titles, and once per chronicle can announce yourself as the descendant of this creature to force all Ventrue in the vicinity to stop what they're doing, fall silent, and sometimes drop to their knees. The name vanishes from the minds of all who hear it, but they will stop anything — even combat — to hear you speak.

THE CULT OF MITHRAS

Some vampires claim the status of deities among both Kindred and kine. Next to Set, Mithras is likely the most infamous of the god-Cainites. A Ventrue of incredible age and power, and one of the longest standing Princes in Kindred history, Mithras formed a cult of faithful adherents to the Mithraic religion, incorporating trappings from the legitimate religion of old and ancient vampiric traditions.

Though Mithras was destroyed in the 20th century, and his diablerist in turn reportedly destroyed in the Second Inquisition's purge of London, his long-time seneschal and confidant Roger de Camden leads the Cult of Mithras in his absence. You may be a member of the cult, or even one of its leaders. Perhaps you believe the cult is the key to dominance in the Jyhad, taking Mithras' millennia of rule as inspiration.

  LORE

● **Neophyte:** Your service to Mithras is in its infancy, but you have learned how to manipulate the kine with talk of religion and grandeur. You can effectively lead a small mortal cult, granting you one bonus die to all Social rolls when interacting with your herd or retainers. This lore comes either from adherence to the cult or through study of its practices.

●● **Nymphus:** Mithraists award the title of Nymphus to new sires within the cult. This lore grants you knowledge of Ventrue lineage and customs of Embrace, along with the ceremonial status of a revered sire. You gain two bonus dice to all rolls in which Ventrue or Mithraic customs are discussed or studied, and the equivalent of two dots in the Status Background when among Ventrue.

●●● **Leo:** Among the most honored members of the Mithraic cult, those Kindred with the title of Leo are entrusted to deliver clandestine messages between Mithraists, and sometimes even outside the order. Mithraists will not hesitate to trust you with information and messages, and you gain one dice to all non-Discipline rolls in which you attempt to get other vampires to trust you. Of course, if your allegiances lay outside the cult, this lore grants you access to deeply dangerous intelligence.

●●●● **Perses:** The Cult of Mithras frequently indulges in ritual bloodletting and sacrifice, with the Perses as the master of such ceremonies. A vampire declared Perses of Mithras receives a short sword and authority to murder enemies of the cult, with the guarantee of full protection (alibis, secret havens, access to resources) should their identity as killer become known. This lore gifts you three Background dots to allocate in any domain in which the Cult of Mithras is present.

●●●●● **Unconquered:** You carry the spark of Mithras within you. Perhaps you took vitae from his diablerist Monty Coven, or maybe you once drank from Mithras himself as part of a Blood Bond. Now, Mithras lives in you. Occasionally the ancient vampire speaks to you in command or guidance, though he's not powerful enough to compel. When you please Mithras, you gain three additional dice in Dominate, Fortitude, or Presence tests (choose one) for the remainder of the night.

THE PYRAMID

TREMERE CHARACTER ONLY

It was not so long ago the Tremere were the strongest clan, or at least, one of the most organized. You know the Pyramid was a perfect structure for Kindred hierarchy, enforcing loyalty through bonds of Blood and oaths of loyalty to house and family, ensuring power rose to the top, with the rewards trickling down. Or perhaps you studied the Pyramid for the corrupt bastion it was, and celebrated its collapse.

You know the inner workings of the Tremere Pyramid. You could construct such an hierarchy again, or help to erode it.

 LORE

● **Apprentice:** Despite their recent destabilization, most sires of Clan Tremere still readily awards their fledglings the rank of apprentice. You are one such apprentice, or the master of one, awarding you with the equivalent of a one-dot Mawla.

●● **Savant:** Despite your new entry into the Pyramid, you have already drawn the attention of members greater than yourself for a successful experiment in which you courted danger, the creation of a new minor ritual, or the discovery of lore once lost to the clan. Once per chronicle, this lore enables you to ask a major boon of a Regent, and providing the boon is not insulting, remain on good terms with that Tremere thereafter.

●●● **Regent:** Every chantry has a Regent. The Regent is responsible for the tutelage of all other Tremere in the domain. While the Regent may not teach them personally, she must ensure all Tremere are being educated. The Regent's other duties extend to the clan's protection in the domain, and sometimes its representation on the Primogen Council. You are the Regent of a chantry. This gives you a dot in Tremere Status, as well as three dots in Haven, representing the chantry. Be aware that you are expected to oversee the safety of the chantry, as well as provide lodging and resources to other members of the clan.

●●●● **Pontifex:** Each Warlock on the Council of Seven has seven Pontifices reporting to him. These Pontifices will oversee a vast domain, though it is rarely geographically defined. Different Pontifices are appointed as clan representatives in the fields of art, economics, werewolf studies, and other such fields. You are seen as the clan's foremost expert in whichever domain you're made Pontifex, and your resources regarding that field are extensive. You gain a three dice bonus to any information-gathering test relating to your particular field, provided you have access to your library, as well as three dots in Tremere Status.

●●●●● **The New Council:** The new Tremere Council of Seven was assembled as an emergency measure following the Second Inquisition's successful attack in Vienna. The explosion was timed to coincide with a meeting between the Council's members, rendering all but a couple into ash, while the remainder entered torpor. You are considered one of the new potential members of the Council of Seven because you have something unique to offer the Tremere clan. What that is and how you wield your power is up to you and the Storyteller. You also have four dots in Tremere Status.

VICTORIA ASH

Victoria Ash stands as one of the most prominent and influential Kindred active tonight.

Embraced in the 17th century C.E. when she was still known as Victorine de Perpignan, she came from poverty, worked as a camp follower for the French army, and drew little regard but for her beauty and stunning singing voice. Her eventual sire, Maximillian, recognized her true talents of diplomacy, etiquette, and strategy, Embracing her for them and for the reasons the mortal soldiers adored her so.

Combined with the devotion Victoria draws from Kindred due to her charisma and apparently benevolent personality, she is remarkable for her steady success in rising the ladder of the Camarilla. Most recently, she was selected by the Justicars of the Camarilla to seal the Vermilion Wedding agreement with Tegyrius of the Ashirra.

The kine bend over backwards to serve her every whim, her clan adores her for natural talents and wit, and our sect points her out as everything other Kindred should aspire to be. One wonders if Tegyrius knows what is awaiting him.

 >> LORE <<

● **Ashen Kiss:** At some point you have danced, kissed, or even slept with Victoria Ash. This does not make you a rarity, but it does make you special. Victoria has a perfect memory for faces and intimate encounters going back centuries (some suspect it's how she clings to her humanity). Difficulties of Social rolls involving Victoria Ash or someone connected to her is reduced by 1.

●● **Vermilion Invitation:** Maybe you were a guest at the Vermilion Wedding or you just know one of the attendees well enough to describe what took place. This enables you to recognize those who attended the wedding, their function, and where they stood on the matter of union between the sects. Once per story you can use this information to blackmail, spin tale, or relate to other attendees of this tense meeting in a familiar way, gaining a three dice bonus to a Social test, provided you can come up with a plausible explanation.

●●● **What Makes Them Tick:** Victoria Ash is an expert at reading people. She knows how to get to your most sensitive secrets and exploit them and has taught you a few tricks. You gain two extra dice to Insight when scrutinizing a target for their vulnerabilities.

●●●● **Celebrity Affectations:** Emulating the stories of Victoria Ash, you too have access to a well-stocked tour bus to allow ease of transit between domains, and a small crew of roadies. Whether you masquerade as a singer, magician, actor, or any other form of entertainer, is up to you. This is equivalent to holding two dots in Haven (Mobile Home) and two dots in Herd or Retainers (Roadies).

●●●●● **Patron, Lover, Companion:** You occupy an important place in Victoria's heart. Once per chronicle she will move heaven and earth to protect you, potentially cashing in the good will she carries with the Camarilla to do so if your crimes are egregious. For an entire session she counts as a five-dot Mawla and provides you three dots of Status.

INSTITUTIONAL CONFLICT

Some vampires prefer to battle in the boardroom, not the street or even the ballroom. Secret masters and manipulators of the world, they use human institutions as weapon, as camouflage, and as armor at once.

Institutional conflict exists within the story either to transfer local power and control from one vampire or coterie to another, or to act as backdrop to a personal drama.

Getting the player characters into position to control an institution might require weeks or months of play and preparation involving lots of Influence (core book, p. 187) earned in story and bought with Experience or just a line on a Loresheet and Storyteller fiat. Whatever makes the chronicle work, the drama juicy, and the players interested is the right approach.

Storytellers should use the Three Rounds and Out model (simply counting up a "best of three" to determine the winner) or the One-Roll Conflict system (core book, p. 298) to depict battle between institutions. Three rolls can happen at the beginning, middle, and end of the story to allow player characters to alter the circumstances through action; roll a One-Roll Conflict at the climax of the story and then direct the drama to play out the consequences.

Whichever system used, the troupe and Storyteller should establish the stakes of the specific conflict to the ongoing chronicle. A rivalry between two countries or two multinational corporations, like that between two vampires, can go on for decades with only local and conditional shifts in power — enough to grant victory on that scale, but not enough to end the contest.

Institutional Scale

The first question to ask is: at what scale does the institution operate? For these purposes, institutions exist on one of three scales:

CIVIC: This institution can affect a city. It might be a major local employer or bank, or a city agency like the police department or zoning board. It might be the Catholic Archdiocese, the hometown news network or paper, or just a billionaire patron of society.

NATIONAL: This institution can affect a nation. Major corporations, main reserve banks, government branches or agencies, or media and activist groups with a truly national reach count as national institutions. This scale also covers groups with a global presence but without the resources to truly act globally (e.g., Greenpeace, al-Qaeda).

GLOBAL: This institution can affect the whole world. Immense multinational corporations, superpowers and other major nations, multinational groups (e.g., Interpol, the UN), or a very few non-governmental actors (e.g., the Catholic Church, the Camarilla).

Institutional Attributes

Institutions, like humans and vampires, have Attributes. For the sake of elegance, we only consider three Attributes here:

FORCE: The raw power of the institution; its ability to simply force change or enforce agreement. The equivalent of Strength.

PRESTIGE: The ability of the

institution to influence and affect the world behind the scenes, on a mental or moral level, or at a lower level of visibility. The equivalent of Dexterity.

DEPTH: The ability of the institution to withstand adversity, if only by simply outlasting it. The equivalent of Stamina. Most vampiric institutions have at least Depth 2.

Like character Attributes, institutional Attributes use a five-point spectrum. One point in an Attribute this scale equals five points in that Attribute on the lower scale: a Civic scale institution with Force 5 has Force 1 on the National scale.

A coterie of vampires who all agree and cooperate might (just barely) have one dot in one Attribute on the Civic scale. The exception: characters with the Influence Background theoretically can deploy organizations with Civic scale Prestige one lower than their dots in that Background. If such deployment makes tactical and dramatic sense — and if the character wants to risk losing their Influence in the backlash of a loss — they can take part in the conflict.

A city's full court unified behind their Prince or Baron (or who obeys that figure reliably, at least) might (just barely) have one dot in one Attribute on the National Scale, depending on the city and the nation involved. Sarrasine of Sydney is more likely to show up on the National Scale in Australia than whoever is the Prince of Hobart, for instance.

Institutional Conflict Pool

Begin the conflict by determining the Institutional Conflict pools involved. If a vampire directs an institution behind the scenes, the pool uses the institutional Attribute appropriate to the situation and one of the vampire's Skills. Finance and Politics may be the most immediately obvious choices, but a vampire could use Prestige + Investigation to turn a city's newspaper against its police department, or Force + Intimidation to use the gendarmerie to silence an inconvenient mosque, or Depth + Subterfuge to activate an entrenched radical group and lure a nation's army into an unwinnable guerilla war.

Institutional Conflict Modifiers

As with One-Roll Conflicts in general, a single vampire (or even a coterie) can seldom affect the outcome with a Discipline or other "normal" force multipliers such as Willpower. To gain an advantage in Institutional Conflict, the players should seek special knowledge of their enemies' weakness, possibly via Memoriam (core book, p. 311) or by suborning a specific SPC. In other words, they should gain advantage through story.

Multiple institutions allied in a conflict use the rules for Multiple Opponents (core book, p. 125).

Institutional Damage

Institutional conflict does damage just like regular conflict: based on the differential of successes between the winner and loser. Apply damage to the institution's Resilience, a tracker equal to its Depth +3.

Most institutional conflict, even open warfare, does only Superficial damage in the time span of a chronicle. To do Aggravated damage, the attack must be targeted precisely at the institution's weakness, almost always one discovered in play.

Once an institution's Resilience starts taking Aggravated damage, its forces and agents may lose dice from their pools, or simply find their actions constrained by the narrative facts on the ground. The Storyteller may set specific losses for each point of Aggravated damage taken by the institution ("At two points lost, the Archdiocese has to sell the hospital. At three points lost, they close down five churches, including the one in your domain.") or just abstract the effects of damage on the story.

Unless the Storyteller decides differently, institutions heal Superficial damage at the rate of one point per story, and Aggravated damage at the rate of one per chronicle. Other institutions may administer "first aid" (economic bailouts, deploying the National Guard, etc.) to speed up this process.

Dear Childe,

I hope you have found this collection of disparate perspectives into the Camarilla somewhat useful. This is a cold, impersonal way to enter the Camarilla, but I've come to think it's for the best. When I was Embraced a long time ago, my Sire told me beautiful things about eternal love, beauty, and immortality. He was a man who wanted very much to be adored by pretty young girls, and knowing no better, I adored him.

Nothing he told me was of any use in the Camarilla. He gave me the love story so many yearn for when they think about our kind, but the only thing that allowed me to navigate the dangers of the Elysium were my wits. I learn fast and you must learn too.

I say without exaggeration that my wedding will change the course of the Camarilla. This will affect you as well. The hopeful and the desperate will ask you for favors, imagining that you can help connect them with me. If you wish, you can use this to your advantage. If you use my name to play politics with enough style, I won't mind.

Still, I do not wish you to become a wastrel. I have spent a lot of time trying to avoid it, but the temptation is there. The identity of your Sire can make things seemingly easy for you, but that road will not take you very far. You can live among the other childer of Camarilla luminaries, wallowing in luxury, and in ten or twenty years you will die in some kind of an embarrassing, ridiculous incident.

Build your own empire. Use the resources I have left you. It will be a harder road, but it is the one you can walk for as long as you like. That's what immortality is.

Your loving Sire,

Victoria Ash

"If the Pope orders the elimination of someone in defense of the faith, this is carried out without question. He is God's voice and the Holy Alliance is his right hand."

CARDINAL PALUZZO PALUZZI, 1623-1698, HEAD OF THE HOLY ALLIANCE